THE ROAD TO ELEUSIS
A journey into mystery.

An investigation into the reality of the spirit world with reference to various published materials and the historical influence of the spirit-world within the European hermetic movement and secret societies.

Put on the full armour of God, so that you can take your stand against the devil's schemes. For our struggle is not against flesh and blood, but against the rulers, against the authorities, against the powers of this dark world and against the spiritual forces of evil in the heavenly realms. Ephesians 6.11

Table of Contents:

INTRODUCTION

This and a previous video are following a thread which was started three videos ago by a viewer asking for a little more analysis about gang-stalking. My previous video was a response to that and just a very small example of what I had experienced because we can tell stories all day but if we don't get down to analysis and hard-facts we don't make any progress. My previous video outlined my beliefs that Gang-Stalking is carried out by mentally ill individuals, at least, shall we say, what most people would consider mentally ill. They however exist within a different paradigm and their inner world is a realm we would never suspect exists.

My claim is that Gang Stalking has the potential to be a recruitment drive: harassing and stalking people and making them fearful and terrorized until they reach the Adrenochrome crisis which as outlined in the work of Dr Abraham Hoffer who discovered the connection between Adrenochrome and schizophrenia but also a potential permanent cure for this condition using nothing more exotic than vitamin B3.

Carl Jung was also a proponent of the idea that schizophrenia was a result of some kind of bio-chemical poisoning though it was Dr Hoffer who fully developed this thesis.

I explained this chemical process in the previous video and you can find a bit more detail in some of the articles on my Truthspoon.com website. Just do enter the relevant search query and you should find what you need.

It's my belief that the biggest secret of the Freemasons and Illuminati is their techniques of hypnosis, trance induction and transformation of consciousness by acting on the bio-chemical structure of the body.

But the question is, what is the origin of the Freemasons and what drives them?

HELLO OPERATORS

This work is inspired by a message I received from another viewer who found his comments strangely blocked from Youtube so he wrote his comment on my website. It was the recommendation of an extraordinary book called Operators and Things. A strangely unrevelatory title at first glance which one might think was some kind of glossary of telephone switchboard terminology but it was anything but mundane. It is one of those books which reading forces you to reconsider your whole perception of reality itself and the events of the story, which are in fact autobiographical and the kind of story that you could probably only make-up after a 3 day LSD and Domestos bender at Disneyland.

The book was written by Barbara O'Brien, a lady who apparently developed schizophrenia in the 1950's as a result of a long and stressful period at work during which she was forced to observe the behaviour of various psychopathic personality types using underhanded means to displace good people from their jobs, and step into shoes they were wholly unfit and unable to fill. She then observes how the psychopaths turn on each other and even manage to undermine the whole foundation of the company with their self-serving pursuit of power and their employment of malicious lies and deceptions to reach their power goals. The author at her place of work seems to be one of the few people to notice these nefarious shenanigans and she, knowing the true nature of some of the people around her starts to live every moment in fear of them, what they can do, what they represent and perhaps how utterly unsuspecting and defenceless the company and other employees are when it comes up against such malign intelligence. But this is not a story about psychopaths, it is a story about a schizophrenic, and one morning after the mounting fear and terror of the psychopaths at work comes to some kind of head, Barbara awakes to find three ghostly forms at her bedside telling her that she is now part of a special secret experiment. The nature of the experiment is to reveal the secret 'world of the Operators' to one of the 'Things' and to see what happens.

A 'Thing' is the operator's term for a human being and the Operators themselves are an organized non corporeal collective intelligence which apparently 'buy' operating rights or charters for human beings, and then they control them by directly dictating their thoughts and supposedly guide them through life. The aim of this is apparently to feed themselves as they seem to gain energy by causing reactions and emotional feelings in the 'Things' or humans they control and possibly they benefit human development in general, indeed one of the discarnate voices of the Operators speaking to Barbara makes the claim:

"If it weren't for Operators, Things would still be wandering in and out of caves."

A similar line of thought appears referenced in a Masonic compendium book from 1847 entitled The Golden Remains of Early Masonic Writers compiled by George Oliver:

"In the history of man, there is nothing more remarkable than that Masonry and civilisation, like twin sisters, have gone hand in hand. The Orders of Architecture mark their growth and progress. Dark, dreary, and comfortless were those days when Masonry had not laid her line, or extended her compass. The race of mankind, in full possession of wild and savage liberty, mutually afraid of, and offending each other, hid themselves in thickets of the wood, or in dens and caverns of the earth. In those poor recesses and gloomy solitudes, Masonry found them, and the Grand Geometrician of the Universe, pitying their forlorn situation, instructed them to build houses for their case, defence, and comfort. It is easy to conceive that in the early state of society, genius had expanded but little. The first efforts were small, and the structure simple and rude; no more than a number of trees leaning together at the top, in the form of a cone, interwoven with twigs, and plastered with mud to exclude the air and complete the work."

For much of the story this is what Barbara believes and is told, and she is repeatedly told that a rival gang of Operators are trying to drain her energy, or otherwise involve her in detailed and ultimately pointless delusions about her own imminent death; or that her life is under threat by members of the Operators guild who are apparently not happy that she has been made aware of the existence of the Operators and that the information she has learned could endanger all their operations. This leads her to travel apparently pointlessly across the country, while some kind of convoluted astral legal drama plays out in the background, with the voices telling her of court hearings, legal writs being sought on her behalf and various motions filed in order to protect her while her mind remains in the realm of the Operators.

She travels the country on Greyhound buses which are apparently full of 'Flies' or Operators who do not belong to the committee and apparently spend their time playing a game where the winner is the one who can put a thought into the head of the person and elicit the strongest emotional reaction.

At one point she rents a cabin in the mountains thinking it will put her out of reach of the Operators who have told her they are actually humans who were born with psychic ability who can project their consciousness into the minds of others, and that they have a limited field of operation, and that travelling beyond that range would leave them powerless to act. So she finds herself a cabin in the mountains but finds that the voices have followed her there, but when she spots other cabins nearby she rationalizes that they must also have rented out one of the cabins in order to maintain psychic contact with her. She falls ill with various maladies as one might expect in her nervous and destressed condition and ends up finally seeing an analyst in California where miraculously the voices finally disappear.

One thing that is eye-opening about the book is how after reading about the inner world of the schizophrenic, the term 'hearing voices' which we have always been told is the classic symptom of schizo-affective disorder doesn't fully explain how convincing in their way the delusions can be. It is not merely hearing voices, but it is the insinuation and the 'reasoned' if that is the correct word to use here, acquiescence to the 'logic' of the voices. They are telling you things no-one else knows, but they are real, they are trying to help you; the Greyhound bus-driver secretly works as an Operator cop which means he has the power to protect a Thing from other Operators as long as the owner Operator of the 'Thing' posts their charter with him.

And as Barbara says herself:

"It forces me to live in a double world. It's like having a magic mirror through which I'm observing what's happening on the moon while I'm going about the business of living on the earth."

One of the strange things about schizophrenics is that they are extremely sensitive to human emotions: at the beginning of part one Barbara tells the reader how she 'read' psychoanalyst, Dr Donner, "Uneasiness hung around the room like a thick mist. He's walking up and down, I thought, spraying worry around. The room is filled with worry."

Throughout the interview with her analyst she seems perfectly able, despite her apparent mental illness, to be fully able to read the emotions and even the thoughts of her analyst whom it seems has personal moral scruples about referring his patient Barbara to the hospital for shock treatment, and the personal wrestling with his own feelings on the matter conflicting with the then perceived medical wisdom of the efficacy of shock therapy.

In this first chapter Barbara is able to perceive that something is troubling the analysist and she writes that she 'leaned forwards to study his face' however this action was not entirely her own as we are then told that one of the Operators, Hinton, was apparently studying the analyst through her eyes. Hinton, as a classic 'voice in her head' then gives her instructions on what she should say to best get out of being forced to undergo shock treatment.

This theme of the schizophrenic seeming to be extra-sensitive to emotions and people's thoughts is something which is later revealed to even more interesting and thought-provoking degrees as it is suggested that the schizophrenic, through whatever new sub-conscious faculties are brought to light as a result of their illness, apparently develop the ability to read people's deepest thoughts and motivations. Barbara states:

"Many psychiatrists had noted, among the patients who did talk, an odd ability to throw the doctor off balance by a feat which might have been called mind reading except that the psychiatrists described it as 'the schizophrenics uncanny sensitivity to unverbalized and only partially conscious feelings in the psychiatrist.'"

Barbara's belief is that some innate power of the unconscious mind which she calls 'Something' and this faculty, which during the early phases of her recovery from schizophrenia, performs astounding feats which defy reason and logic. One time the 'Something' urges her to go to Las Vegas; she only has five dollars but the 'Something' urges her to go to a specific roulette wheel and then that 'Something' tells her which numbers to put her money on:

"Something kept me rooted at one wheel and Something urged me violently to play a certain number at a certain time. I played a dollar chip and won. I waited, rooted, got another strong urge, played, won again. I played six times, won six times, and found myself with a purse full of money. Something stopped giving me numbers. I stopped playing and came home."

Another time the Something helped her to find a job, specifically directing her to be in the right place at the right time:

"As my money was running low, I decided that I would try to find a job whose chores were not too demanding. As I started out, Something urged me to walk in the opposite direction from the bus line, toward a large building a few blocks away. Something urged me so violently to enter the building that it would have been impossible, almost, not to have gone in. I went to the building's personnel department and found the employment manager not at all surprised to see me. She had phoned an agency that morning for a receptionist. She hired me."

According to Barbara, the 'mind reading' ability which some psychiatrists have apparently observed in schizophrenics is part of the Something of the unconscious mind.

"Something can extend into the unconscious minds of others. Nevertheless, it was nice to know that other schizophrenics had demonstrated a similar talent. It made the business more normal, at least for us schizophrenics. Anyway, it wasn't witchcraft."

This is something for which I have long sought an explanation as during my travels around the world and the continued attempts to recruit me into what, for convenience' sake I will call 'the Illuminati' despite that name evoking an automatic response of derision. The people I had contact with were Freemasons, but to say they attempted to recruit me into Freemasonry seems to fall short of the truth, since these people were of an elite branch of Freemasonry, it might therefore be more accurate to describe them as Illuminated Freemasonry. My personal conception of what these people represent is something I would call 'The Family' since there seems to be a genetic component connecting all of these people and this is what has been generally referred to by such researchers as Fritz Springmeier as The Illuminati Bloodline.

I have had to observe the terrible sounding truth that there are people out there who are able to read people's mind. It is a terrible truth because for many, one's private thoughts are considered an inviolable personal sanctuary and represent the ultimate idea of personal privacy.

If one were to be exposed to people who demonstrated to you that they could read your mind then it is likely that a great fear might grow in you, perhaps you would wonder whether these people were really human, since they exhibited abilities long considered beyond humanity.

Fortunately, there are not many of them and most of them seem to acquire this ability as part of their initiations and training with the secret societies, and if some of the rumours about secret societies which have reached us over the years are correct, then part of the attraction of belonging to an occult secret society, and there really is no other kind, is the development of psychic powers and abilities.

In his book Freemasonry for Beginners, Freemason Robert Lomas writes:

"Your new skills may appear miraculous and uncanny to others. but it is a fact of our Masonic Science that new consciousness gives rise to new faculties."

According to the website:

https://spiritwiki.lightningpath.org/index.php/Freemasonry.

"The psychic-powers are awakened as part of a continuous initiatory process of progress through various levels, degrees and 'kingdoms' of which there are apparently five." From Robert Lomas' book:

"...every kingdom is self-contained. It is shut off, as though by closed bulkheads, and no leap from a lower to a higher kingdom is possible save on one condition - a previous death to the kingdom below."

And an elucidatory description on the website:

"The process ostensibly involves uncompromising repression of one's 'human' faculties. The process, which masons call the Secret Science of Initiation or Secret Science of Mystical Death is symbolized as death and resurrection, i.e. death of the human level/kingdom and the emergence of the trans-human."

I can give three immediate personal examples of experiencing people reading my mind, and there are actually others however these three are the clearest and most evident.

The first one was in Tokyo when I had apparently signed up to the Devil's Bargain to become a famous writer with a skeletal ghoul like figure from Yorkshire who ran what appeared to be a small language school in Tokyo.

The strange recruitment system of the Illuminati Freemasons meant that I was never solicited directly to join the Freemasons, just hints and allusions in a constant stream. For example, the man, whom I call the Demon King of DK for short, would roll up the trouser on his left leg frequently for no apparent reason and ask me if I knew who I was. He would have these strange imaginary phone-calls in the classroom next to mine which I could hear quite clearly, where he would be talking to someone, rather strangely, about me. He would never explicitly talk about me but he would allude to things he must have somehow found out about me, but then de-contextualise them so it would appear random and more startling. In these phone calls he would loudly refer to himself as 'Mr Mason'.

The odd thing about these Masonic people who have reached a certain level of initiation is that they seem able somehow to read minds or at least use some highly accurate system based on uncanny synchronicity. For example, in my mind I would wonder 'what did he just say?' and strangely in the next room he would repeat it. I found that if he said something which I didn't catch he would repeat himself in his imaginary conversation next door.

This was the first time I noticed this and on subsequent occasions have observed that some people are very definitely capable of reading minds, but this is not strictly accurate, it would be more accurate to say that they are 'told' what you are thinking. This is one of the results of serving what Manly P Hall the Masonic philosopher termed: the 'arcanum arcanorum', the secret mystery. An invisible and all-encompassing awareness that knows all and communicates to its servants in Freemasonry and other walks of life.

One speaks and acts without understanding, but is fed information and instructions from this mysterious source, so that other people involved understand the words and actions and their significance. When one serves these 'invisible masters' one is little more than a marionette, acting for unknown purposes and without any concern for the consequences of their actions; service to the unknown 'force' is the 'be all and end all' to these advanced Freemasons. This force is what people generally know as spirits or demons.

The second occasion came in Egypt when I met a Nile delta farmer who provided tomatoes and various salad vegetables to Sainsbury's supermarkets. He seemed very well off and wore a suit; to say he was a farmer is probably over-stretching his role in the whole affair of growing vegetables but the fact is he was the smooth faced affluent and fluent English speaker who made all the deals and got all the money. He owned the farms and since he said he was providing for Sainsbury's his network must have been rather a large one. Without remembering the specifics about the particular conversation, I came to the startling discovery as we chatted that he always seemed to say exactly what I was thinking; it was unusual because our backgrounds had been vastly different: different countries and cultures, yet somehow, he would say exactly what was in my mind only a couple of seconds after I had thought it.

When I stilled my thoughts and literally had nothing going on inside my head, he suddenly fell quiet. Until this point, he had been carrying on a machine gun fire of conversation lifted directly from my thoughts, suddenly he was still. He kind of looked at me as if beaten and shrugged. He said nothing more and left shortly afterwards.

It seemed there had been no information in my mind to feed on and as such he had no instructions to follow. It was as if this was how he talked to people, by lifting ideas and thoughts from their own minds and when he encountered someone like me who can enter the Zen state and stop their thoughts at will, he had no material to work with. It seemed to me at that point that the man was wholly possessed by the 'arcanum arcanorum' his every thought and action being a mere series of 'suggestions' from this force; always a reaction to the thoughts of the person he was speaking to, he simply had nothing of himself in any of his conversation because he no longer existed as an individual, he had become nothing more than a human interface with the hidden power.

A third example is highly instructive as to what kind of condition these people who can read minds might be dealing with. Far from being able to read people's minds making you a superman or some kind of God amongst men it is much more likely to have the opposite effect and reflects something which has gone very wrong with natural human brain-chemistry.

I was working as a teacher at a Pupil Referral Unit in West London which is where the kids who get excluded or suspended from school end up. In almost all of these cases these students exhibit a range of various psychological issues and it is often the use of violence and a lack of self-control which has resulted with them being removed from the schooling system and sent, as a temporary measure, to a Pupil Referral Unit, while their return to school is being negotiated.

One student, a young black boy of perhaps fourteen years old was throwing a tantrum and running around refusing to enter the classroom. I thought to myself how the boy seemed demon possessed.

He then reported there and then that I had called him demon possessed. Obviously, I had not spoken those words but I had thought them, yet somehow, he had heard me. I was already at that stage, used to the possibility that some people might be able to read minds or somehow 'hear' what is being thought but for the first time I observed this phenomenon in someone who was clearly psychologically damaged and most likely schizophrenic.

By the end of the book, Barbara has rationalised away the existence of the 'Operators' as being part of her unconscious mind which had been brought in as an emergency remedy to help heal her mind. It is not entirely clear to me at least how the symptoms of mental illness can form part of its cure and I am not entirely convinced that these Operators were merely something conjured up by her own mind.

If for instance Barbara can admit that 'Something' guided her on the winning numbers for the Las Vegas roulette wheel; how upon deciding that she needed to find a job, how that same 'Something' led her to the precise street and building where an opportunity had just arisen, and furthermore, in one passage how one of the 'Operators' apparently advised her before leaving her mountain cabin to take a flashlight with her, it being early in the day Barbara herself could not understand the logic of the Operator's demands but she took a flashlight with her all the same. It was only when she arrived in town to find that the bus-service she had intended to use to return to the cabin had been discontinued and that she had a three hour wait for a different service, by which time when she finally returned home it was not only dark, but she was apparently being tracked by a mountain lion, which with judicious application of the flashlight, she managed to scare off. There is no way Barbara herself could have foreseen any of these events and one is left with the conclusion that it must be some kind of all-seeing all-knowing force which exists beyond the human realm.

The great rivening and striking point here which splits and sends people to man their trenches and rally to their standards and fight with all their might is whatever they would give in answer to the ultimate question: Does God exist? Those who answer no, consider belief in God unscientific and wishful thinking; the belief in spirits and demons as delusion and superstition, and possibly consider those that do as intellectually challenged. For them, schizophrenia is solely a disease of the individual's own mind and the delusions and the cast of voices show the astonishing power of the human brain.

Those that do however, see God as being present in the elements and experiences of life which science cannot answer. They consider spirits and demons as a possibility; the human body is only a vessel which the spirit temporarily occupies so could it not be that since consciousness continues after death in the spirit then it must logically follow, that spirits can exist independent of a physical form, without human bodies, or physical bodies at all. All religion and folk traditions have some commentary to make on the existence of these discarnate beings, and according to many of the descriptions of these creatures in many of the ancient holy books of the world's religions the creatures which alternately persecuted and apparently aided Barbara, seem like a combination of the angels, demons and Djinns of the ancient faiths.

A very peculiar comment is made by the Operators about God which evokes something almost Biblical about the fall of man and the fallen state of the world:

"Operators, very early in the history of civilization, had surrounded the earth with an airfield of steel rays so powerful that even God couldn't get through."

An airfield of steel-rays is clearly just a metaphor for some other form of power and it reminds me of the work of CS Lewis whose remarkable science fiction trilogy, ending with That Hideous Strength, evokes this idea, less that God is banished from Earth but more that an evil principal known as Oyarsa: the bent one, has taken ownership of Earth, leading to a kind of spiritual quarantine of our planet by the spiritual forces of the solar system. The condition of this quarantine is that Earth's Oyarsa cannot travel beyond the Moon's orbit but nor are the other spiritual powers or Oyeresu allowed to come to Earth to intervene.

Another thing which makes me wonder whether the Operators might be a real phenomenon and that Barbara wasn't hallucinating their existence but that due to the adrenochrome toxin in her blood, was able to perceive things which our consciousnesses usually filters out of our reality as being perhaps too strange and disturbing, is one of the dangers of being targeted by malicious Operators.

"At least, buy some nails and a hammer nail down the windows. Because that's the way you're going to go. Wait until you have twenty Operators from the council in here, working on your mind, telling you to jump. Believe me, you'll jump. So far as the council is concerned, you're a monstrosity and a source of danger, something that has to be put out of the way."

When one notices the same trends in different people's experiences then one has to assume there might be some commonality at the root of those experiences. It is very common for those suffering from schizophrenia and hearing voices, to be driven to suicide by those voices. If these voices were part of our own subconscious mind, then why would it have any desire or interest in killing itself? It makes no sense, considering the natural imperative for survival which is supposedly one of the strongest instincts in man. This seems to go against nature and it would seem to make sense that only a maliciously inclined outside force which takes pleasure in human misfortunes would have any desire to drive a person to suicide.

In the book The Siren Call of the Hungry Ghosts, which deserves a full investigation all of its own and Youtuber 'Zap Oracle' has actually published an excellent two hour video which explains anything I could go into here; suffice it to say that it is an investigation into the world of channelling, ghosts and mediums which Joe Fisher, who at 22 set a record as England's youngest ever editor in chief at the Staffordshire Advertiser and later went on to become one of Canada's leading investigative reporters, becomes personally embroiled in discovering whether there is any truth to the existence of ghosts and spirits. His last words to his editor-in-chief at Paraview Books Patrick Huyghe shortly before he threw himself to his death from a limestone gorge at Elora Gorge in Ontario Canada, were that the spirits were still after him for having written his last book which was The Siren Call of Hungry Ghosts.

My fundamental question here is do these ghosts, demons, spirits, djins actually exist in some real spirit form which can interact with the human world to a limited extent and are there certain people in certain circumstances who find themselves in full contact with these beings?

If the answer is yes then it forces us to reconsider a great deal about what we think we know about the nature of humanity, its origins, the problems we face and in truth, it answers a lot of questions I think we all have and many of the mysteries which have plagued us for millennia can be solved by incorporating this shadowy world as a fundamental causative agent over much of the history of human activity. Perhaps even, a causative agent over some of our very thoughts.

Cross-referencing the 'Operators' of this book with the demons from CS Lewis' Screwtape Letters and Evelyn Waugh's The Ordeal of Gilbert Penfold convinces me that there is some objective reality to these ghostly Operators since the same characters using the same kind of programme can be discovered in other people's experiences.

The Screwtape Letters is a series of correspondences between a junior devil or 'tempter' Wormwood, and his 'uncle' Screwtape, where uncle Screwtape advises his nephew on how best to lead the human, described as 'the patient' he is tempting astray from God and the road to salvation and towards a petty-minded self-concerned cynical intellectual materialism, which CS Lewis satirically alludes suits the devil so well.

It's not necessary for the temptee to do anything particularly evil to find himself drawn into the devil's party, merely when the thought of eternity, heaven and salvation may come in the way, be distracted into forgetting all about them by thoughts of lunch, or the passage of the number five bus and the front page of the newspaper.

As Screwtape later says:

"The safest road to hell is the gradual one-the gentle slope, soft underfoot, without sudden turnings, milestones, without signposts." Conversely the road to heaven and the glimpse of the transcendental can be achieved in the most mundane of actions as Screwtape admonishes Wormwood and accuses him of allowing the patient to slip through his fingers when he allows him to read a book he really enjoyed, then compounded this by letting the man walk down to the old mill (a walk through country he really likes) and have tea there, alone. By allowing the patient two real pleasures his soul edges closer to God and out of the grip of hell.

Screwtape wants to eradicate any pleasure that is not actually a sin, such as a fondness for country cricket or collecting stamps or drinking cocoa because "there is a sort of innocence and humility and self-forgetfulness about them".

CS Lewis' demonic tempters bear a similarity to the Operators except that they have not revealed themselves to the 'patient' but exist, just as the Operators were said to exist to normal people, as a voice which most people assume to be the voice of their own thoughts and ideas. It is only at the end of the book when the 'patient' is killed during the war by a falling bomb that he finally glimpses these spirits which have guided him through life for better or worse:

"There was a sudden clearing of the eyes and he saw you for the first time, and recognised the part you had had in him and knew that you had it no longer. Just think (and let it be the beginning of your agony) what he felt at that moment; as if a scab had fallen from an old sore…"

For Lewis, death is where we glimpse these opposing factions continuously trying to direct and gently nudge the soul either to heaven or hell and the patient, finally breaking free from Wormwood and seeing his part in influencing his thoughts while alive, it is as if "he shuffled off for good and all, a defiled, wet clinging garment."

From Lewis' vision and the classical orthodoxy of demonic beings it is generally understood that they exist apart from the kingdom of God and are antagonistic to both it, and mankind which is an emanation of this kingdom since it is also generally considered within all of the literature of the world's religions and metaphysics, that man has some divine spark, some small portion of the creator within himself. I always find this passage intensely moving and Lewis' astonishing description of what might happen at the moment of death and passing to the next life seems itself to be so radiantly full of light and understanding that I am humbled by his eloquence and the beauty of his vision:

"As he saw you, he also saw Them. I know how it was. You reeled back dizzy and blinded, more hurt by them than he had ever been by bombs. The degradation of it!— that this thing of earth and slime could stand upright and converse with spirits before whom you, a spirit, could only cower. Perhaps you had hoped that the awe and strangeness of it would dash his joy. But that is the cursed thing; the gods are strange to mortal eyes, and yet they are not strange. He had no faintest conception till that very hour of how they would look, and even doubted their existence. But when he saw them, he knew that he had always known them and realised what part each one of them had played at many an hour in his life when he had supposed himself alone, so that now he could say to them, one by one, not 'Who are you?' but 'So it was you all the time'. All that they were and said at this meeting woke memories. The dim consciousness of friends about him which had haunted his solitudes from infancy was now at last explained; that central music in every pure experience which had always just evaded memory was now at last recovered. Recognition made him free of their company almost before the limbs of his corpse became quiet. Only you were left outside."

According to writer and devotee of the occult Alan Moore:
"Aleister Crowley once stated that the most important grimoire, or book of magical instruction, that anyone could ever conceivably own would be an etymological dictionary."

An etymological dictionary is a book which gives the precise origin and construction of words, it tells the story of the development and meaning of words which we may have forgotten. The word 'Genius' for instance is a case in point where looking into the etymology of the word reveals something about the secret history and development of the human race. The Latin origin of the word means "attendant spirit, present at one's birth". Some scholars contend that the word genius is related to the word djinn but the relationship, and as to which word came first is unclear.

The word 'spirit' has its origins with the Latin word 'spirare' and we see this connection in the word 'respiration'. This idea that the 'breath' is the soul which animates the body is the reason why the ancient Semitic languages of Hebrew and Arabic do not depict the vowels in writing, only the consonants is because the vowels are produced from the breath and have something of divinity in them, which because of the innate iconoclasm of these cultures, cannot be physically represented.

Similarly looking at the word 'demon' in an etymological dictionary, we are informed that the word comes from the Greek word 'daimon', and has a similar meaning to the Latin word 'genius' in that it means a 'personal guiding spirit' or 'divine power' and has none of the negative connotations which emerged in the Renaissance during the interest in Jewish magic. The word is derived from Proto-Indo-European 'daimon': provider, divider (of fortunes or destinies), from the root da: to divide. Daimons were possibly seen as the souls of men of the golden age acting as tutelary deities, according to entry δαίμων at Liddell & Scott's Greek English Lexicon.

The 'His Dark Materials' trilogy by Philip Pullman features an alternative Earth where people all have a personally embodied spirit creature called a Daemon which although distinct from the human individual has a kind of intensely symbiotic relationship: their relationship being essential to their continued mutual existence. The Daemon represent the strength and protection of the person and in the story in order to dominate or subjugate another individual it is only necessary for one's own Daemon to dominate another's. I believe this is probably something of the conception of the daemon of the ancient world, that it was seen as a protecting agent which guided and strengthened the individual and was inseparable from it.

In the Hellenistic ruler cult that began with Alexander the Great, it was not the ruler, but his guiding daemon that was venerated. Quoting from Bengt Ankarloo and Stuart Clark's Witchcraft and Magic in Europe: Ancient Greece and Rome:

"Xenocrates ... explicitly understood daemones as ranged along a scale from good to bad. ... [Plutarch] speaks of 'great and strong beings in the atmosphere, malevolent and morose, who rejoice in [unlucky days, religious festivals involving violence against the self, etc.], and after gaining them as their lot, they turn to nothing worse.'"

"Much the same thought as [Plato's] is to be found in an explicitly Pythagorean context of probably late Hellenistic composition, the Pythagorean Commentaries, which evidently draws on older popular representations: 'The whole air is full of souls. We call them daemones and heroes, and it is they who send dreams, signs and illnesses to men....'"

More than two thousand years later we find this idea that dreams are sent to us or created by discarnate psychic beings, indistinguishable from demons known as Operators is repeated by Barbara O'Brien who says that the Operators provide us with dreams they call 'black out movies' which apparently can serve specific psychological functions:

"Sharp and Hinton were arguing. Curiously, both were in favor of erasing all information about Operators from my mind. Hinton believed that the blotting out process could best be achieved by black-out movies. Sharp agreed with this. He was in favor of my staying in the hospital to have the movies administered."

"I had strange dreams which the Operators called Black-Out movies. In the movies, an unseen artist painted a portrait of Burt with horns. It was a child's picture painted with a child's malice. It was a personal, malicious picture and I remember thinking at the time that Hinton must have been the unseen artist. It was obvious even to the dry beach that to a Hinton, a Burt would be a villain. The portrait painting in the Black-Out movies is interesting when compared with the apparitions of the Operators that moved before my eyes every day. The apparitions were impersonal, sharply symbolic figures drawn by a more objective hand."

Is it possible then that some of these spirits are always present with us, perhaps helping us at times in ways we can't even imagine? What is easily demonstrable is these beings' capacity to cause chaos and destruction all around them.

Barry Miles biography of William Burroughs, 'Call Me Burroughs: A Life' gives us an honest insight into the activity of one of these demonic entities and what it can lead you to do:

"William Burroughs believed in spirits, in the occult, in demons, curses, and magic. 'I do believe in the magical universe, where nothing happens unless one wills it to happen, and what we see is not one god but many gods in power and in conflict.' He felt himself possessed, and had spent much of his life trying to isolate and exorcise this demon.

Throughout his life Burroughs felt engaged in this struggle against the Ugly Spirit. Burroughs had first identified the Ugly Spirit very early on, back in St. Louis: 'When I was a young child, a feeling of attack and danger. I remember when I was five years old, I was sitting with my brother in the house that we had on Pershing, and I got such a feeling of hopelessness that I began crying. And my brother said, 'What's the matter with you?' and I couldn't tell him. It was just a feeling of being completely at a hopeless disadvantage. It was a ghost of some sort, a spirit. A spirit that was inimical, completely inimical.'

Burroughs believed the Ugly Spirit was responsible for the key act that had determined his life since September 6, 1951. That day he had been walking in the street in Mexico City when he found that his face was wet. Tears were streaming from his eyes for no logical reason. He felt a deep-seated depression and when he got home, he began throwing down drinks very quickly. It was then, later that day, that Bill killed his wife, Joan Vollmer, fatally wounding her while attempting to shoot a glass from her head in a game of William Tell at a drinks party. Burroughs never really understood what happened that day, except to recognize that what he did was madness.

Near the end of his life he said, 'My accidental shooting of my wife in 1951 has been a heavy, painful burden to me for 41 years. It was a horrible thing and it still hurts to realise that some people think it was somehow deliberate. I've been honest about the circumstances—we were both very drunk and reckless, she dared me to shoot a glass off her head, and for God knows what reason, I took the dare. All my life I have regretted that day.' It was not until 1959 that the malevolent entity was given a name. Burroughs and his friend Brion Gysin were conducting psychic experiments at the Beat Hotel in Paris when Gysin, in a semitrance state, wrote on a piece of paper, 'Ugly Spirit killed Joan because...'"

Burroughs explained how writing became his main weapon against possession by the evil spirit:

"I live with the constant threat of possession, and a constant need to escape from possession, from Control. So the death of Joan brought me in contact with the invader, the Ugly Spirit, and maneuvered me into a lifelong struggle, in which I have had no choice except to write my way out."

So, are there really spirits which are continually present in human affairs, but whose existence by most people at least, providing they do not engage too deeply in metaphysics or mental illness, is completely unsuspected?

Wormwood from The Screwtape Letters, as a tempter, is charged with ensnaring the soul of the patient by making him caught up in the values of the world and forgetting God. The devils, if that's what they are, in Evelyn Waugh's The Ordeal of Gilbert Pinfold, seem to have a different, but no less malicious purpose.

Evelyn Waugh's extraordinarily entertaining psychotic drug episode entitled The Ordeal of Gilbert Pinfold, which Waugh assures us is a 100 percent autobiographical experiences and like Operators and Things, it would have to be because there are some things that just cannot be made up.

Here an overstressed, overweight, slightly self-critical and over-drugged Evelyn Waugh experiences an extraordinary episode of psychosis in which he becomes mentally embroiled in a series of convoluted intrigues from a cast of characters while on what was supposed to be a recuperative cruise.

He spends the time somnolently lying in his bunk, hardly knowing whether it's night or day, furtively venturing out of his room on occasion to the bar to drink, unable to eat and when he attempts it he is reduced to 'gazing sadly at his curry' and effectively taking a such a copiously potentially fatal combination of strong sedatives and booze over the course of his ordeal that it could fuel a large outdoor music festival.

It begins when he returns to his cabin after a fairly unremarkable saunt around deck where he meets his neighbour, to hear the sound of a jazz band and a dog's footfalls in the cabin next door. He assumes therefore that his neighbour had a gramophone and an illicit dog. This seems to be the opening of the door to the dimension of strangeness as from apparently accepting the presence of a gramophone playing jazz next door and a snuffling dog pattering around, he seems to open the door to something which does not hesitate in accepting the invitation.

He then hears a religious sermon which soon becomes a deeply personal conversation between someone called 'Billy' and the clergyman during which he overhears a confession of perceived sins of a sexual nature. Pinfold then shocked and embarrassed at being an interloper to a personal conversation of this kind, takes his walking stick and beats it against the floor to hopefully give some indication that someone is able to overhear such a private conversation, but the knocking of his stick is integrated into the conversation

"Did you hear anything then, Billy? A knocking. That is God knocking at the door of your soul. He can't come and help you unless you are pure, like me."

He goes out to investigate only to find upon inquiry that there is no chaplain on board the ship, but he rationalises that one of the officers must be a lay preacher of some kind. Upon later going to the bar, he asks his neighbour how his dog is, his neighbour is confused and confesses he has no dog, nor indeed a gramophone.

The jazz music continues to come from next-door at full volume despite his neighbour not having a gramophone. Later after a great deal of alcohol, and some paranoia over dinner he returns to his cabin to find that a jazz band is rehearsing directly under his own cabin, and can also make out conversations between the various band members and it is here that we are reminded of the maliciously playful behaviour of the Operators as they discuss whether to play a song in a three-eight Pocoputa Indian rhythm, which the band leader states the Gestapo used to play over extended lengths of time to drive their prisoners insane. They go on to play the rhythm and Pinfold is forced to empty his bottle of sleeping drugs in order to escape.

He awakes to the sound of something like a mutiny on deck and some kind of terrible accident involving a quantity of copper in which a man has been crushed and pulverised but is apparently still alive. Surveying the ceiling of his cabin he sees a thick nest of wires and cables and imagines that somehow they are transporting voices from all around the ship's various rooms into his own. Slowly a kind of conspiracy against him starts to be overheard, which gradually becomes more and more threatening until he hears actual threats of violence against him and people whom he terms 'the hooligans' apparently planning to swarm into his room and attack him. Pinfold prepares himself as best he can with his heavy walking stick, but the attack never materialises… the assailants fume outside his door claiming his unlocked door is locked against them, but the threats continue, culminating in a conspiracy involving a hostile Spanish vessel ostensibly acting on the orders of General Franco to assert Spanish sovereignty over Gibraltar but secretly on a mission to abduct a British secret agent working on a matter of national security. The voice impersonating the captain of the cruise ship announces a plan to waylay Pinfold and stuff his pockets with forged papers passing him off as the secret agent and allowing him to be taken by the Spanish vessel. However, when he finally emerges from his cabin, resolving to nobly offer himself to be substituted for the secret agent on his own terms: for the good of the country and as an act of national service and supreme self-sacrifice, he finds the deck deserted with no sign of the conspirators or any Spanish vessel.

It is then that Pinfold becomes afraid that he might be going mad and imagining the whole thing, until the voice of Margaret is heard telling him that he is hearing their voices not because of the wires in his cabin but because of wireless technology. This seems to make sense to Pinfold and his delusions continue, and with wonderfully irony, he is supremely relieved that he is not going mad after all.

It's quite possible and perhaps even likely that we are all at home to these spirits one way or another, but they are so well integrated into our consciousness that we think they are us. This reminds me of the powerful scene from the Guy Ritchie movie Revolver where Jake is seemingly enrolled on a path of self-discovery by two mysterious men who want him to break free from his greatest enemy and they do this by repeatedly robbing him and manipulating him to the extent that he is forced to abandon everything he holds dear including his ego, after which he discovers that this is not his authentic self but a parasite which only has its own protection and nourishment in mind, pun not intended. This is what is known throughout the story as Sam Gold: a mysterious enemy which is feared by everyone but has never been seen and in the words of one of the mysterious men from the film who seem able to read Jake's mind:

"You've heard that voice for so long you believe it to be you; you believe it to be your best friend."

He then asks:

"Where's the best place an opponent should hide?"

"In the very last place you would ever look."

"He's all up here pretending to be you, you're in a game Jake: you're in THE game; everyone's in his game and nobody knows it. And all of this, this is his world. He owns it. He controls it. He tells you what to and when to do it."

"He's behind all the pain there ever was, behind every crime ever committed. And right now, he's telling you he doesn't even exist."

"We just put you to war with the only enemy that ever existed and you think he's your best friend."

More ominously, if we remember the fate of Joe Fisher "No one lives and displeases Gold." Many have interpreted the character of Sam Gold to represent the ego, and within the context of the story this explanation fits, but could it not also be that Sam Gold represents one of the Operators, or one of the Tempters surreptitiously influencing us? The movie shows us that Sam Gold is not the authentic self so then what is the ego? Could it not be a convenient place for the discarnate entities to hide? As Avi, one of the two mysterious men from the film says:

"Where's the best place an opponent should hide? In the very last place you'd ever look, he's hiding behind your pain Jake, you're protecting him with your pain embrace your pain and you will win this game."

"If you change the rules of what controls you, you will change the rules on what you can control."

This is why the voices harassed Evelyn Waugh, playing on his insecurities: in his youth Waugh had homosexual experiences and much of his novel Brideshead Revisited seems based on the life he had at Oxford and frequenting a circle of members of the elite and aristocracy and this is one of the things the voices taunt him with. Once he seems to have ostensibly defeated the voices by failing to be cowed by them and not even being afraid of the bizarre prospect of being captured by the Spanish and drawing a virtue of noble self-sacrifice from the prospect and finally by abandoning the nonsense of Margaret's phantasmagorical teasing and going to sleep, he emerges from his cabin to find that the voices have left the confines of his cabin and now appear to be amongst his fellow passengers:

"That's Gilbert Pinfold, the writer."

"That common little man? It can't be."

"Have you read his books? He has a very peculiar sense of humour, you know."

"He is very peculiar altogether. His hair is very long."

"He's wearing lipstick."

"He's painted up to the eyes."

"But he's so shabby. I thought people like that were always smart."

"There are different types of homosexual, you know. What are called "poufs" and "nancies"—that is the dressy kind. Then there are the others they call "butch". I read a book about it. Pinfold is a "butch"."

"Oh, Pinfold lives in great style I can tell you. Footmen in livery."

"I can guess what he does with the footmen."

"Not any more. He's been impotent for years, you know. That's why he's always thinking of death."

"Is he always thinking of death?"

"Yes. He'll commit suicide one of these days, you'll see."

"I thought he was a Catholic. They aren't allowed to commit suicide, are they?"

"That wouldn't stop Pinfold. He doesn't really believe in his religion, you know. He just pretends

to because he thinks it aristocratic. It goes with being Lord of the Manor."

"...There he is, drunk again."

"He looks ghastly."

"A dying man, if ever I saw one."

"Why doesn't he kill himself?"

"Give him time. He's doing his best. Drink and drugs. He daren't go to a doctor, of course, for fear he'd be put in a home."

"Best place for him, I should have thought."

Once the experience is over and he is safely returned to England he consults with Dr. Drake who tells him:

"Lots of people hear voices from time to time—nearly always offensive."

If such a thing were the construction of one's own consciousness, why would they generally be offensive? From a psychological perspective such a thing would make no sense. It would seem much more logical that these voices are NOT part of the psyche and are inimical to it and somehow, they benefit from attacking the person in question.

People as diverse as Philip K Dick, Mahatma Ghandi, Winston Churchill, Anthony Hopkins and Brian Wilson had all reportedly heard voices. Some relentlessly critical and offensive and some, ostensibly seeming to be helpful, but in the case of Ghandi before the end of his life a voice apparently told him:

"You are on the right track, move neither to your left, nor right, but keep to the straight and narrow."

It might have been more useful if the voice had told him some crackpot was going to assassinate him. Ghandi also said, of the voice which he attributed to God itself:

"Charitable critics impute no fraud to me, but suggest that I am highly likely to be acting under some hallucination. The result for me, even then, will not be far different from what it would be if I was laying a false claim. A humble seeker that I claim to be has need to be most cautious and, to preserve the balance of mind, he has to reduce himself to zero before God will guide him. Let me not labour this point."

"The hearing of the Voice was preceded by a terrific struggle within me. Suddenly the Voice came upon me. I listened, made certain it was the Voice, and the struggle ceased. I was calm. The determination was made accordingly, the date and the hour of the fast were fixed..."

There are two things which ought to stand out in Ghandi's account, the fact that the hearing of the voice was 'preceded by a terrific struggle within' which we can perhaps assume was a kind of hormonal crisis, the kind we have seen with the story of Barbara O'Brien, we can therefore assume that Ghandi may have experienced a similar condition to Barbara O'Brien, namely Adrenochrome toxicity but also this seems to be a factor not only of secret occult groups but also UFO groups as is referenced in Jacques Vallee's book Messengers of Deception:

"For every individual who is openly identified as a contactee, how many more have received what they regard as a 'secret illumination'? It is apparent that the transformation they undergo can strike at any place and at any age. Is it purely random, then, or do the UFOs select their 'victims'? Does it spread like an epidemic, or does it develop like a psychosis?"

Anthony Hopkins went on record in a 1993 News of the World interview:

"I've always had a little voice in my head, particularly when I was younger and less assured…While onstage, during classical theatre the voice would suddenly say, 'Oh, you think you can do Shakespeare, do you?' Recently, I was being interviewed on television and the voice inside my head said to me, 'Who the hell do you think you are. You're just an actor, what the hell do you know about anything'".

Brian Wilson is one of the most high-profile people to go on record about hearing voices, his voice was typically threatening:

"Well, a voice is saying: 'I'm going to hurt you, I'm going to kill you.' And I'd say: 'Please don't kill me.'"

Like the Evelyn Waugh voices but seemingly more menacing, I wonder if the tenor of the voice changes depending on how you react to them; as we saw with Evelyn Waugh, he refused to be intimidated by the voices, even though he was under the delusion they were actual physical agents, it was only when he thought he was going mad that his defences seemed to crumble, but Waugh despite his somewhat dissolute student life and obese drugged form in later life, served in the Royal Marines and was given a position of command; he was prepared to fight or even if all odds were against him surrender, but on his own, noble terms. I suspect the voices see what they can get away with and if their victim proves to be made of stronger stuff then they adapt their tactics, though it would still appear that their final goal is either the destruction or complete possession of their victim. Furthermore, in his conversation with the doctor who has told him that they were part of his own subconscious Pinfold/Waugh is puzzled:

"What I can't understand is this…if I wanted to draw up an indictment of myself, I could make a far blacker and more plausible case than they did. I can't understand."

Mr. Pinfold/Evelyn Waugh never understood this; nor has anyone been able to suggest a satisfactory explanation. I have an explanation. What Pinfold means is that although the voices were insulting to him, if the attacks were from his own mind, then he would have been able to draw up a far stronger line of personal attack on himself. The attacks were very general: attacking his excessive use of drugs and alcohol and his previous homosexuality, but nothing very specific or damning about him as a person and his decisions, just somewhat general comments about his lifestyle choices. The reason might be that possibly the 'voices' can only hear your thoughts in the present moment but do not have a deeper access to your memories and your past deeds. Since they do not have that level of access to information one might assume that they do not come from the self but are interlopers and opportunists which exist in a kind of mental astral realm and can pick up on people's thoughts and in exceptional circumstances such as Waugh's experiences with his unique combination of drugs and personal stress, can in turn be heard themselves, at which point presumably, knowing that they can be heard, they start to mentally abuse and torture that person for their own demonic pleasure.

While shaving he hears the family of voices conversing about him which develops from the lines that he drinks too much and to his own suicide. The voices make no pretence at this stage that he is not a party to their dialogue and they directly address him:

"'I know you can hear me Gilbert, why don't you kill yourself' Then Goneril's steely voice cut in: 'I can tell you what he was doing on deck. He was screwing up his courage to jump overboard. He longs to kill himself, don't you, Gilbert. All right, I know you're listening down there. You can hear me, can't you, Gilbert? You wish you were dead, don't you, Gilbert? And a very good idea, too. Why don't you do it, Gilbert? Why not? Perfectly easy. It would save us all—you too, Gilbert—a great deal of trouble.'"

He emerges from his cabin, believing the voices are a product of some old war-time inter-ship communication system which hasn't been decommissioned properly, and emerges onto the boat deck to find everyone talking about him in an incessant dialogue.

They encouraged him to commit suicide but Waugh being a Catholic and a fairly successful man, wealthy and probably in his own way, quite pleased with himself, such an effort wouldn't lead to their desired results so instead they settle for continual abuse, except one of them, a character called Margaret.

It seems that what the voices want from Gilbert is his attention and when the threat of violence fails to cow him and he reveals that he is prepared to physically fight, even in his infirm and bloated condition, then the voices try a different approach.

This leads to the development of the character: Margaret who reveals that she is impressed by how Gilbert bravely confronted the prospect of hooligans which he faced down outside his door and how he nobly chooses to offer himself as a sacrifice to preserve the security and safety of the secret agent which the Spanish authorities were trying to capture. She declares herself in love with him and ready to yield herself to him. This story becomes increasingly bizarre until at one point Margaret is all ready to enter Pinfold's nocturnal bed chamber and yield herself to him utterly. Naturally she never materialises.

The voices of Margaret's family are overheard coaching her and preparing her for her nuptials and things take a grossly comic turn:

"That's my beauty. Go and take what's coming to you. Listen, my Peg, you know what you're in for, don't you?"

"Yes, Father, I think so."

"It's always a surprise. You may think you know it all on paper, but like everything else in life it's never quite what you expect when it comes to action. There's no going back now. Come and see me when it's all over. I'll be waiting up to hear the report. In you go, bless you."

Pinfold then awaits her in the darkness, in his delirium, expecting a girl he'd never met before whom he can hear speaking with her family in her cabin and who can read his mind which is all somehow connected to some kind of radio technology left over from the war, to come into his cabin and have sex with him. There is some hesitancy however on her part in showing herself and her father the General is surprised that things have not developed to their natural conclusion.

"What the hell's going on? You ought to be in position by now. Haven't had a Sitrep. Isn't the girl over the Start Line?"

It would seem that although Margaret and the hooligans' approach is radically different, the hooligans attempt to instil fear in Pinfold while Margaret tries to instil love, in a manner of speaking they are both doing the same thing, that is getting 'attention' and in that way drawing a kind of energy from Pinfold.

Although Pinfold is unwell and heavily drugged it seems something in his mind is able to perfectly well articulate a highly complicated and serpentine plot, almost Dickensian in its colourful cast of characters and their high levels of melodrama, but the one common thread which runs through the whole experience is that of abuse, abuse and denigration of himself. Since the experience and the organisation and colourful characterisation of the voices are so similar to the voices which haunted Barbara O'Brien then we can collate these experiences within the same category.

So, we might therefore draw the conclusion that Barbara O'Brien's analysis that the voices were from her own consciousness and were there to help her become sane again, was incorrect since nothing of this nature can be drawn from Evelyn Waugh's similar experience.

So, if we can allow ourselves the belief that such a thing as God exists, then logically there must be an invisible world of the spirit which accommodates a varied flora and fauna of disembodied entities. Not all of these entities have our best interests at heart and perhaps for some unknown reason, they are directly opposed to us.

I wrote an article about the modern phenomenon of Electronic Harassment which is the belief that some shadowy government or military organisation is using advanced wireless technology, also known as psychotronic weapons, to directly beam thoughts and voices into people's heads. This is a very dangerous delusion since it makes an enemy and source of terror of common place things like internet routers and mobile phone masts. I am not going to argue whether 5G technology is dangerous, it might be: I just don't know, but I am fairly certain that it is not being used to beam voices into people's heads because people have been hearing voices for thousands of years and calling them demons, angels, Gods and lately, aliens. It is understandable that people, like Pinfold in our story, might seek to find a half-way rational explanation for what they are experiencing rather than face the stigma of the realisation that they are perhaps suffering from a psychotic episode and losing their mind.

Believing you are being targeted by unknown agencies by microwave or psychotronic weapons leaves you utterly defenceless against an invisible enemy, at least if the enemies are perceived as demonic then there is the remedy of spiritual empowerment through Jesus Christ which has historically proved highly efficacious at repelling demonic attacks and even, surprisingly, attempts at alien abduction as well. The fact that it has been reported that people undergoing an alien-abduction have called upon the name of Jesus and suddenly found the ordeal ended, ought to inform us perhaps that alien phenomenon may have more to do with the supernatural than the extra-terrestrial, and creatures which are presently masquerading as 'grey aliens' and such may just be a modern-make-over for a much more ancient enemy which has plagued mankind the whole length of its history.

The book Messengers of Deception written by UFO expert Jacques Vallee presents an ambiguous view that the alien phenomenon is real, but it is not what it seems to be. Jacques Vallee's research concludes that something is behind the aliens phenomenon but is deliberately manufacturing an extravagant hoax using a combination of unknown technology and psychological manipulation, in order to further a strange agenda of world transformation using the aliens and UFO phenomenon as the catalyst. This intelligence has abilities which far exceed those understood by modern science and seems to exist outside the physical and mental limits of human experience but whose activities also have a lot in common with the activities of the occult and para-psychology.

Vallee's book has some reservations about the existence of physical UFO's from outer-space and instead describes witnesses seeing 'the image' and 'perception' of

UFO's and the unavoidable presence of psychophysiological effects in the witnesses of UFO and aliens phenomenon such as distortions of perception and post hypnotic symptoms such as visions and hallucinations suggest that the truth of UFO's is even stranger and more mysterious than merely being space travellers from a distant solar system.

"I propose: that the UFO we see is, among other things, a device which creates a distortion of the witness's reality; that it does so for a purpose, which is to project images or fabricated scenes designed to change our belief systems; and that the technology we observe is only the incidental support for a worldwide enterprise of 'subliminal seduction'."

Could it not be that the Operators experienced by Barbara O'Brien which she eventually rationalises as belonging to her own unconscious mind; the spirits which drove Joe Fisher to suicide and the tormentors which plagued Evelyn Waugh during what was supposed to be a recuperative cruise, are all part of this same phenomenon.

Quoting from Jacques Vallee's book again:

"In the sixties, according to conversations I had in the Soviet Union, a leading plasma physicist was pushed under a Moscow subway train by an 'indirect contactee' who had been instructed by a 'voice from space' to kill that particular man. In 1975, a French contactee was arrested by the police as he was entering the headquarters of the French television network, carrying a carbine and fifty shells: a similar voice from space had instructed him to kill a newsman who had written several books on UFOs."

Furthermore:

"In 1968 a man named Sirhan killed Robert Kennedy in Los Angeles. Sirhan was a member of AMORC Ancient Mystical Order Rosae Crucis. He had used the Order's technique for self-hypnosis while preparing his role in this tragedy."

While on the subject of unsavoury members of the Rosicrucians not quite living up to their reputation of an enlightened and advanced brotherhood, expert on all things Hermetic Mark Stavish writes on his website how:

"'Baby Doc Duvalier,' former dictator of Haiti, has been photographed sporting an AMORC ring, said to have been given to him by Bernard the elder."

As well as:

"Several central African heads of state are also on the list of well-known associates – and from a different line, Manuel Noriega, former head of military intelligence and eventual de facto ruler of Panama from 1983-1989 whose desk sported an array of AMORC paraphernalia after his capture by United States forces."

Vallee mentions the case of Gregory in order to clarify the point that people with an interest in this domain are not necessarily rudderless-crackpots but can be highly intelligent young professionals. Gregory was a systems programmer and is described as working for one of France's leading Think Tanks.

"He quit his job to form a psychic center. He is now publishing a newsletter devoted to his experiences with higher entities; he believes that, in so doing, he follows the telepathic instructions of a superior force."

The psychic communication he received was of the following tenor:

"On the eastern shore of the Peaceful Sea, God brought forth the American Republic ... For the purpose of assembling the high consciousness required to conceive and establish this new Union, God sent His son Melchizedek, one time Lord of Salem, unto Christopher Columbus..."

Tied to the alien contact groups are various occult groups, one in particular The Order of Melchizedek attracts Vallee's particular interest and he even finds himself strangely drawn into a disconcerting web of synchronicity when, after investigating and actually being made an offer to become a member, he returns to New-York and hailing a taxi cab, discovers that the driver's name is Melchizedek. This leads him to hypothesise an interesting new approach to the nature of reality itself.

The leader of another saucer group told Vallee:

"The Earth is the property of one group of saucers that controls this end of the universe, and they call themselves the Brothers, and they are the ones who brought the Christ on Earth 2000 years ago ... If we get a little out of control, and maybe Russia would start to throw some missiles at us, from Cuba ... well, they might step in, if it got too bad, and help us out. They told us they would."

In contrast to this, the order of Melchizedek seems to have a distinctly Jewish flavour in the Messianic expectation of UFO visits and Vallee reports that Zalman Shachter was involved in an organisation called the California Institute of Transpersonal Psychology and initiated eleven students into the Order of Melchizedek in a hot-tub. In 1947 Zalman was ordained a Rabbi within the Chabad Lubavitch Hassidic community and was a well-known Kabbalist who throughout his life advocated for and fully supported the LGBT movement and feminism. If the UFO cult is an agent of change, then Zalman and his work represent one of its greatest foot-soldiers. In 1974 he ran a month-long Kabbalah workshop in Berkeley California and, based on the writings of Rabbi Leiner who lived in the early to mid-19th century, taught that anything, even what others consider sin and heresy, could be God's will."

In a way, is it possible that the present LGBT movement and all the other agitators who rewrite the accepted social conventions are just an expression of Jewish currents going back to Rabbinical movements of the 19th Century and before. The idea that there is 'no such thing as sin' or that sin can somehow be beneficial, is a key belief of the

Kabbalah and it is said that it is even essential to engage in sin, in order to receive a better repentance and draw closer to God. Personally, if I may speak personally in what I am hoping is a fairly rigorously annotated, evidence-based work, I consider such thing to be the very doctrine of the devil.

Vallee comes upon the term 'The Manipulators' to describe unknown agents whom he suspects have an agenda of their own, which he seems to think is one of mass social-change and societal transformation.

Fairly recently, in December 2020 an article in the Jerusalem Post appeared in which former Israel 'space security chief' named Haim Eshed is quoted in an article with the splash-line: "aliens exist, humanity not ready" and declares that the "Galactic Federation" has "been in contact with Israel and the US for years".

"Speaking in an interview to Yediot Aharonot, Eshed – who served as the head of Israel's space security program for nearly 30 years and is a three-time recipient of the Israel Security Award – explained that Israel and the US have both been dealing with aliens for years."

But Eshed insists that Trump is aware of them, and that he was "on the verge" of disclosing their existence. However, the Galactic Federation reportedly stopped him from doing so, saying they wished to prevent mass hysteria since they felt humanity needed to "evolve and reach a stage where we will... understand what space and spaceships are."

This sounds like a rehash of the old kooky UFO cults which Vallee investigated in the 60's and found little of substance except the strange evocation and hints at some kind of Jewish connection behind everything. Vallee reached the conclusion that something else was going on behind the mysterious façade of UFO's and aliens but something even more mysterious deliberately generating this illusion and using it for their own manipulative purposes:

"The Manipulators... I have given this name to the hypothetical agents who might cause the UFO contacts and engineer their effects. Everything now centers on their role, their identity, their designs. Who could they be? Alien beings coming from the end of the galaxy? Psychic entities from the 'other side'?...But perhaps we are looking far away for something which is right under our nose: could they simply be human? Could they be masters of deception so skilful that they plan to counterfeit an invasion from space? Beyond the attention of academic science, below the dignity of official history, there are groups, cults, and sects that serve as 'leading indicators' of mass movements."

Vallee met an enigmatic and mysterious man whom he calls Major Murphy and appears to have been a high-level insider of military intelligence during World War 2.

"'In 1943,' he said, as we sat in his study, 'we already had evidence that several countries were working on circular aircraft that they hoped to develop into secret weapons. The Germans were also doing advanced research on controlled electrical discharges and 'controlled lightning,' and tried to combine these things together.

When we invaded Germany, a lot of hardware fell into our hands, but the Russians had gotten most of the good stuff. Then people started seeing the modern UFOs in Sweden in 1946....General James Doolittle was sent to Sweden by the United States in 1946, apparently under cover of the Shell Corporation. In fact, he was to investigate the 'ghost rockets' with the Swedish authorities. Whatever came of that?'

Ghost rockets was the name given to some two thousand reports of rocket shaped UFO's appearing in the skies of Sweden between May and December 1946. Radar tracked some of the objects as they fell to Earth and fragments were discovered where they had impacted the ground. It seems likely that the sightings were the result of Soviet testing of rockets taken from the Nazi V2 construction base at Peenemunde.

However, some of the sightings apparently reported objects which moved without leaving any exhaust trail while others moved horizontally and a hissing sound was sometimes heard accompanying the moving object.

Major Murphy believes that the UFO's might be 'psychotronic devices' and goes on to say:

'Research had already been done in great secrecy by 1946 concerned mind control and the effects of electromagnetic radiation (what we now call ELF, or Extremely Low Frequency) on the human body... suppose somebody had obtained a device by the end of the war, which perhaps wasn't a very effective weapon. Perhaps it couldn't fly very effectively, couldn't carry guns and bombs, but had other properties. For instance, it could emit radiation that caused paralysis and hallucinations as it flew over an area, so that witnesses exposed to it would think they saw the phantasms of their own imagination. Did somebody test that kind of a device in Sweden in 1946, and in the States in 1947, and find it to be ineffective as a flying machine, but very useful as a means of propaganda? Has such a group already understood what UFOs were, and are they confusing the issue by simulating UFO waves? Or is the entire phenomenon under their control?'

'I can only tell you that silent, disk-shaped flying machines can be built. If they are equipped with the right devices, they can create astonishing effects and be reported as flying saucers. I wish I still had my files on the German experiments.'

'You have V2s in 1944, and you have the Atlas rocket in the '60s. You have foo-fighters in '43, and the green fireballs of New Mexico nine years later. A lot of people got involved. Industrial concerns. Laboratories engaged in psychotronic research. The

Nazi research on microwaves was child's play compared to the sophistication of modern experiments. If someone is using this technology, we can assume they have also mastered pharmacology, the use of drugs to distort the memories of witnesses, the use of mind control to suggest stories, to plant fake observations. Don't you think people should try to get some information about that before believing in friendly space visitors?'

'It's hard to believe that these techniques would already be applied on this kind of scale,' I said.

'Don't you read the newspapers? Don't you follow publications on mind control? The military has been using this kind of technique for years.'

He pulled out of a file a series of New York Times clippings beginning in 1977. It described part of a U.S. project which spanned 35 years and involved hypnosis, narcoanalysis, electronic brain stimulation, and the behavioral effects of every physical vibration known to science, from ultrasound to microwaves. He showed me a book entitled Operation Mind Control, in which W.H. Bowart describes his meeting with a young man who had just returned from a tour of duty with the Air Force. He suffered from amnesia. Like many UFO contactees, he remembered vaguely that he had had a good time, but couldn't describe in detail where he had been.

After many therapy sessions, he began to recall part of his activities. He had served, it seemed, on a military committee in Vietnam. He had dreams in which he was standing at a long table on a beach, with Communist officers on one side and Americans on the other. Although the discussion was heated, nothing was written down. His assignment was to remember everything that was said. He had been trained for total recall..then his entire memory of these assignments was erased like a magnetic cassette. 'I am not suggesting that secret agents are going around the world giving these thousands of people individual suggestions to see UFOs. As we found out when we began developing the science of propaganda during the last war, you don't need to do all that. A few well-placed stories, a well-planned program publicizing sensational incidents, will do marvels. The contactees are being manipulated. And I think we should not look in outer space for the Manipulators.'"

Hans Kammler was an SS Obergrupperfuhrer responsible for Nazi engineering projects such as massive underground bunkers and construction plants and was director of its secret weapons programme being responsible for the V2 rocket programme and was in charge of weapons projects at Peenemuende and Nordhausen. He disappeared in mysterious circumstances in May 1945 at the end of the war. He was said to have committed suicide in Prague attempting to defend against 500 Czech resistance fighters in order not to be taken alive.

The US Occupation forces opened a file for Kimmler stating that he had been seen in Munich shortly before the arrival of US troops. His wife reported that she had seen him for the final time on 7th May 1945, one day before the German surrender. She said that the Americans were after him and had made him offers which he had apparently refused.

A report written in 1949 by special investigator Oskar Packe stated that he had been arrested by US forces in the Bavarian Alps but that he had escaped. Detailed information held by the Counter-Intelligence Corps and accessed by the Denazification Office in Hesse about his arrest and subsequent escape made Packe discount the rumours of his suicide in Prague. Shortly before his death, Donald W. Richardson, former OSS agent, a precursor to the CIA, told his sons that he had brought Kimmler to the USA as part of Operation Paperclip and had personally supervised him until 1947 and at some point Kimmler apparently hanged himself.

It is no longer a secret that the Americans sequestered many of Nazi Germany's elite scientists including Werner Von Braum and over a hundred others who contributed their rocket expertise to the American space programme. In total there were said to be 1,600 Nazi scientists brought to America between 1945 and 1959. The infamous post war mind-control project entitled Monarch supposedly has its origins with German Nazi scientists and many of the Nazis made a deal with the United States: scientists such as Kurt Blome, director of the Nazi's biological warfare programme who conducted lethal tests of bacterial and chemical agents on the inmates of Mauthausen concentration camp. Some secret Nazi technology also became a basis for top secret military prototypes such as those based on the swept delta-wing design of the near supersonic Horten Ho 229 stealth bomber, built and tested as a prototype in 1943. It is likely that the US Air Force's testing of their F117 Nighthawk stealth prototype was responsible for the sightings of triangular UFO's such as the delta-wing craft seen in the Carson Sink UFO incident of 1952 during which three unusual delta-wing aircraft were seen flying in formation.

If we can make a broad connection between the testing of post-war secret Nazi technology being classed as UFO's by a public ignorant of developments taking place within secret military projects and also by a government keen to keep their technological secrets during the cold war (meanwhile the media and Hollywood covering for them by fuelling the UFO mania) then why should any sightings taking place in the present day be any different?

On May 18th 1946 a solitary hiker Gosta Karlsson was enjoying a peaceful night walk through the heavily wooded shore of Angelholm Sweden in the Kronoskogen forest.

Climbing a small hill, he noticed bright lights streaking up from the forest floor. He was surprised to encounter such lights because it was not expected to encounter any fellows at this time of night, this deep in the forest. He might have wondered whether he had stumbled upon some kind of group of Swedish pagans celebrating their strange rites late into the night. Or maybe wondered whether this might have something do with test-flights being carried out by the Swedish Air-Force which had their main headquarters nearby: having been there since late 1945 and hardly more than a mere three miles from his present location.

He descended into the strangely illuminated clearing and found in the centre, a brightly lit object resembling what would later become known as the classic 'flying saucer'; the description comes from an interview with Swedish UFO investigator Klas Svan:

"It was shaped like a disk and stood on two telescopic supports. In the lower part, there was a lowering hatch with a ladder, like on ships, at a height of one and a half meters. I saw the light coming from the cockpit and tried to look there, but the view was too narrow and I saw only light. At the top of the object was an oval cabin about eight meters in diameter, with oval windows at 1-meter intervals and approximately 30 cm high. While I was looking at this structure, I thought that someone was trying to mess with me, but then I thought that maybe this facility was built by German pilots and they were trying to escape from the POW camp on it. But deep down, I believed that there was something else.

On top of the cockpit, there was something thick, like a periscope four meters high. It had that bright purple light source that caught my attention. Light along a strange curved trajectory softly enveloped the entire object and pulsed slightly like water in a fountain.

The air smelled strongly of ozone. There were no joints or rivets visible anywhere on the hull, the cockpit and hull seemed to be created as a whole."

What conclusions do we the reader in the year of writing this 2021 reach upon examining this report? Well despite this being what is classically considered to be a flying saucer and potentially a highly advanced spacecraft from another planet we cannot help but notice that apart from flashing lights, it doesn't seem especially high-tech compared to the kind of technology which is available today. Telescopic supports don't sound especially alien, nor do hatches and ladders; that's not to say I'm suggesting it was an old window-cleaner's ladder or anything quite so rudimentary but from the modern suggestions and stories of alien-abductions we have been given to understand that aliens don't need ladders: that they can materialise and dematerialise people, their ships and themselves at will, so reading an account of what must be one of the earliest modern-sightings of what is supposedly an alien spacecraft but with a technology which is still within human understanding, of aliens having to climb ladders and pass through hatches, it is certainly an interesting historical example.

Admittedly the lack of joints or rivets is the kind of thing we might expect from an advanced civilisation but not necessarily beyond the ability of advanced post war engineers and we can't help but feel that what he saw might be the kind of spaceship which would look 'alien' and futuristic for 1946, but one wonders whether someone from 2021 seeing this craft might not think it was an escaped prop from a 1950's science fiction B movie.

Even more interesting is the fact that Gosta Karlsson met the alien inhabitants at close-quarters and rather than quickly seizing the opportunity to pull off his trousers and soundly probe him or abduct him for any of the strange sexual experiments which have become part of the aliens UFO lore, and the reason might be because this hadn't quite been written into the lore yet; they actually seemed somewhat inconvenienced by his presence. Neither eager to experiment on him by messing about with his bottom, nor apparently keen to teach him the wonders of the universe, instead they behaved as you do when someone comes round to your house when you're about to have dinner and you're just too polite to send them away. So you kind of just put up with them while you think about your dinner going cold. This is the description Gosta Karlson gives about the 'alien' visitors, bear in mind this sighting occurred in Sweden:

"They all had blond hair and looked like a typical Swedish or Norwegians. I saw three men near the windows of the ship, they were busy with some work inside. Then three girls appeared in front of me, all equally dressed in one-piece white suits with the same boots and belts. Each of them had a transparent hood pulled back around their neck. It was strange to see how they all looked at me as if I were an uninvited guest. I felt like a wild animal in a circle of light, a technique used by safari hunters in Africa. Then a dark-haired girl came down the stairs from the ship. She had a bag in her hand, and then she began to distribute cups to all other men and women. They began to quit all work and began to drink from these cups. When I wanted to get closer to them, one of the men, who seemed to be acting as a guard, blocked my path, raising his hand as a stop sign. Everyone around me was looking at me with serious faces. Then I stepped back and everyone went back to their work and no one was looking at me. I felt a little depressed."

What is remarkable is how honest this account is, all the way down to feeling 'a little depressed' that these advanced aliens weren't interested in him in the least. What is also interesting is that the myth of blonde-haired blue-eyed Nordic 'aliens' has become part of the lore: some UFO commentators even going so far as to be able to pinpoint their origin in the Pleaides star cluster. Perhaps the Nordic 'aliens' in fact come from the Nordic countries, Sweden and perhaps more pertinently Germany.

Then as he walked away, he saw the ship depart:

"Slowly and majestically, the heavy object was rising up and now I clearly saw that it was a flying ship. It made a sound like a vacuum cleaner motor. it is in a crown of red light, and at an altitude of 400-500 meters, it slowed down and began to sway."

The description of the saucer making a sound like a vacuum cleaner motor is quite an unusual description and again, although a flying machine being powered by some kind of advanced vacuum engine would have been alien and unfamiliar in 1946 we know that this kind of technology was just beginning to be developed: the jet engine. The swaying motion of the vessel too indicates a technology which has not yet been mastered. Several of these key elements from Gosta Karlsson we will find to be key elements of the Nazi secret weapons development programme, many aspects of which are matters of public record.

An eye-witness account of a Ukrainian prisoner known only as 'X' mentioned in Henry Stevens' book Hitler's Flying Saucers, who was interred at a work-camp near Peermunde makes a similar description of a flying saucer he saw late one night:

".. four workers appeared from a hangar and rolled out a strange looking craft onto the concrete landing strip nearby. It was round, had a teardrop-shaped cockpit in the center and was rolled out on small inflatable wheels, like an "upside down wash basin". After a signal was given, this silvery metal craft began making a hissing sound and took off, hovering at an altitude of about five meters directly over the landing strip. As it hovered, the device rocked back and forth. Then the edges began to blur. Suddenly the flying craft's edges seem to blur as it jumped up sharply and gained altitude in a snakelike trajectory. X concludes that because rocking was still exhibited, the craft was advancing erratically."

Something which isn't part of the public record however is the life and experience of a former member of the Illuminati known as Mauri. These days with the mass censorship of the internet a great deal of knowledge is being lost since website such as hers no longer appear to be indexed in Google searches. In fact, it is not only conspiracy websites which no longer appear in Google searches but any website or forum which is not part of the mainstream media. The result is that anything you tend to search for now usually elicits a page full of mainstream sources quoting an identical chunk of text, usually farmed from Wikipedia. It goes without saying that this is Orwellian in the extreme but this is the natural result of media and big-tech companies working hand-in-hand with government agendas.

The mainstream media were dying: print sales and television viewing on decline, meanwhile governments have their nefarious agendas and the internet was previously a venue where the internet's vox populi could lead the debate and challenge government lies and misinformation, forcing deep-state operatives like Hilary Clinton to repeatedly make shrill noises about conspiracy theories and declare 'we are losing the info-war'. Well they were, and they were good times, but it is a war which through sheer muscle of money and perhaps too many newly arrived bovine internetizens who care more about make-up tutorials and Amazon's Prime-Day sales, than sharing information, cheering a sheepish approval at denying free-speech and internet hosting services being denied to certain tactically positioned agent provocateurs like Andrew Anglin, then we are now refugees and guerrillas trying to find somewhere to hide from the conquering army of relentless censorship. Andrew Anglin, or Andre as he used to be known on the old David Icke forum, was a left-winger living in the far-east deploring 'white people' for all the problems of the world and extolling a mixing of the races. This information has long gone but it certainly ought to make us suspicious of Andrew Anglin's 180 degree political heel-turn and if we consider perhaps that without his website and its deliberately and needlessly provocative articles cynically engineered to be as offensive as possible, then we might wonder whether he was the necessary 'problem reaction solution' agent required to instigate the avalanche of relentless internet censorship of which his de-platforming seemed to be the signal governments and the tech agencies had been waiting for.

So websites like reflectionsinthedark.com linger like virtual phantoms, the only way to find them is by knowing they are there in the first place. Google these days certainly has no intention of taking you to them, even if you were to fill in exactly the relevant search terms you would still find yourself being directed to a mainstream news website or else a website specifically debunking and attacking what you had just typed in. So for instance typing the search terms 'Illuminati, Nazi, UFO's' which in the past would have served up Mauri's website on the first page or at worst the second page now gives you results from Amazon.com, Popular Mechanics, Ebay, the BBC, Wikipedia, NBC news, the Washington Post and even the CIA. Basically all of the media and information control outlets with the most money to field your query and refute it without you ever having had the chance to glimpse an honest response as used to be the case. The kind of responses we used to have for such a query might be a page from a discussion forum specifically dedicated to investigating the subject, or a website dedicated to researching the topic or an individual's personal account of something similar or connected to the broad themes. Clearly this was a much better way to get to the bottom of subject, rather than to be presented a politically motivated and corporate sponsored refutation of the query terms. These kind of websites were always top in the search results over the mainstream media because the mainstream media were losing ground to the expert analysis which easy communication between interested parties and experts had made possible, as a result these websites and forums grew until they had thousands of members online and millions of views.

Mauri hasn't published anything for eight years and I have twice attempted to contact her without success, asking for clarification about her experiences as a 'grey alien' which she goes into as being part of her duties as a member of a multi-generational Illuminati family.

"The grey alien is a creation of Nazi innovation. An alien being was needed to accompany the secret advanced flying machines made during WWII in Germany, which after the war developed into the Nazi UFO hoax in America. What was their secret formula in creating the grey aliens? Let's start with the stocking mask. It turns out the nylon stocking was useful for more than just a gift to the ladies. The stocking contorts the face down to the bones and removes a person's individual facial features. The ears become just two holes and the nose (on a child) becomes two nostrils instead. The mouth becomes a nonfunctional slit. And the eyes disappear altogether. Why it makes you look almost alien; except for the eyes. One could add a nice pair of WWII army surplus goggles to hide the lack of eyes. Oh wait; if one hides the elastic on the goggles, each lens (which is almond shaped) becomes an eye. Cool! If the stocking is wrapped around the head, covering the hair, the head becomes bigger and bald. Add a little white bath powder to blend it all together. And, oh did I mention that the Nazis liked to use children, specifically little girls. The Nazis were not only innovative; they were cheap. The little grey alien doesn't even get clothes, but has to run around in the cold night air naked. Berrrrr.

The grey aliens were a part of a larger program of mind control, especially of cult-connected members (victims.) No one comes back from an abduction with anything good to say about grey aliens because they were a substitute in what used to be "Satan" programming, as in Satan is watching you, only now it's the greys and they are inserting implants and watching you. Same difference. Both Satan and grey aliens also like animal mutilations, not to mention both are involved in the sexual creation of hybrids, Satan-human and alien-human. Who would like an alien that mimics Satan? Actually I consider that view unfair. When I was a grey alien I just stood there, cold and scared, ready to piss in my pants, if I had been allowed to wear them.

With the Earth going to hell as we speak, the Nazis have supplied us with an otherworld salvation, about which we have a choice. We can all form a One World Government to fight the alien invasion, or we can all form a One World Government to follow our alien overlords, it's up to you."

It is your prerogative whether you believe Mauri or not, but I think the people who listen to these stories of ritual Satanic Illuminati abuse and mind-control and quickly dismiss them are certainly at a disadvantage in this present age of endless deception. I also think that many of the former Illuminati insiders such as her and Svali, believed the Illuminati were a far-right Nazi organisation and that it controlled the world, but it has become obvious in recent years that Nazis, white people and the far-right have no role in world control and probably never did: the real operators have become exceedingly clear and it is only the wilfully deluded, apathetically ignorant and cowardly souls who do not wish to accept this reality.

It is likely that 'The Illuminati', like the Freemasons, is a sub-group which is used to control those non-Jews whose cooperation and servitude is essential for the continually unfolding of the Jewish agenda of world domination which is just about reaching its apotheosis. The amount of anti-white hatred which the media and politicians are willingly engaged in is only the first step of what I fear will eventually become acts of mass violence against white people. Such things are already taking place in the United States and we have seen how white-children are being sexually groomed and trafficked by Pakistani gangs, with a blind-eye being turned by the police and even the arrests of white girls who report their abuse to the police.

It has already reached the point in the United States and to a lesser extent in the UK, where the media are inciting minorities against white people and when crimes are perpetrated against white people the police and courts will tend to side against them. There are so many examples but I don't want to sully this book by getting into these most unpleasant events, suffice it to say, this is just the beginning of something which if it reaches its logical conclusion can only end in some kind of mass genocide or ethnic civil-war, or else some kind of sustained oppression of white people as permanent second-class citizens in education, employment and cultural and political representation. In many ways we have already reached this point in the United Kingdom and as to whether this obvious oppression can be sustained by the media, criminal justice system and politicians, remains to be seen.

Becoming better informed and having an open mind to conspiracies is now a matter of survival as many of those unfortunates who trustingly took the various Covid 19 'vaccines' on offer might be discovering to their cost as they deal with a variety of long-term side-effects or even the death of their loved ones, but here again the media is in full control of the message, and will not tell you anything about these instances unless you already know where to look. I would say these big-tech censors and their ubiquitous agents along with those working for the mainstream media have blood on their hands and perhaps within their lifetimes they will have their complicity revealed to the world and will have to live with the consequences of 'just following orders' which apparently wasn't a valid excuse during the Nuremberg trials and shouldn't be now.

Henry Stevens' highly informative book Hitler's Flying Saucers: A Guide to German Flying Discs of the Second World War, is a thorough and systematic documentation of various Nazi secret aeronautical projects of the final stages of the Second World War. However, there are some parts of the book which deal with some of the more 'hypothetical' elements of the possible propulsion systems for some of these saucers and while some theories are quite plausible and convincing, others such as the 'free energy' Schappeller Device, are probably stretching credulity and it would have been better perhaps in this instance to have stuck to what is demonstrably known and documented rather than delving into more arcane and fringe areas of so called pseudo-science; if only to put Hitler's flying saucer programme on a more historically sound and documented basis and remove it from the classification of 'conspiracy theories' which it seems relegated to, to this day.

In his book he refers to several documented newspaper reports marking the first reference in the press to the term: 'flying saucers'. The first report referring to 'flying saucers' appeared in 1947 in the November 9th edition of the Denver Post, some months after several documented UFO sighting across America.

The article is entitled 'Spies Bid for Franco's Weapons' with a subtitle which reads 'Agents Ascribe 'Flying Saucers' the New Rocket' and reports a potentially fascinating story about an unnamed 'European spy organisation' successfully smuggling blueprints for advanced weapons out of Spain which had been designed by three unnamed German scientists. One of the weapons is described as 'an electromagnetic rocket' which, it is claimed, is "responsible for the 'flying saucers' seen over the North American continent last summer.."

Another article he refers to is an edition of the Los Angeles newspaper The Mirror dated March 24 1950 quoting Italian engineer, Professor Guiseppe Belluzzo who makes a matter-of-fact report about the development of flying discs. Belluzzo who was formerly Minister of National Economy and later, Education Minister in Mussolini's government was quoted after a spate of sightings in the continental United States:

"There is nothing supernatural or Martian about flying discs…but they are simply rational application of recent technique."

He also said:

"Some great power is launching discs to study them."

At this time there was growing curiosity following the Roswell and Aztec retrievals of crashed saucers and the release in 1950 of the first American feature film to feature flying saucers. What is interesting is that film does not try to make out that the saucers come from space but that the saucer is an invention of an American scientist. The plot revolves around a race against the Russians to be able to gain this technology while a communist turn-coat attempts to sell the saucer to the Soviets.

It is interesting that at the earliest stage in the UFO controversy there were independent attempts to get the truth out, however one can assume that, as the arms-race against the Russians heated up it became necessary to be more guarded about the nature of the development of American aeronautical technology and for this reason the cover of 'aliens from space' what created by various sponsored science fiction writers and Hollywood producers who were deployed in this propaganda effort to sell the possibility of visitors from space to the American public.

The article, apparently quoting Belluzo from an article from Italy's Giornale d'Italia, whom the article credits with the building of the first steam turbine in Italy in 1905, states quite plainly:

"..types of flying discs were designed and studied in Germany and Italy as early as 1942."

He was also interviewed for the March 30 edition of Der Spiegel in 1950 where he said that in the early 1940's, flying saucers were produced in the BMW factory Prague where scientists such as Klaus Habermohl, himself and Walter Miete, who was also part of the V2 project, worked on flying disc projects following Schriever's work.

"... Rudolph Schriever, who says engineers throughout the world experimented in the early 1940s with flying saucers, is willing to build one for the United States in six to nine months. The 40-year-old Prague University graduate said he made blueprints for such a machine, which he calls a flying top, before Germany's collapse and that the blueprints were stolen from his laboratory. He says the machine would be capable of 2,600mph with a radius of 4,000 miles, Schriever is a US Army driver at Bremerhaven."

According to the Henry Steven's book the earliest designs for flying saucers in World War 2 are by aeronautical engineer Rudolf Schriever who was mentioned in the 1950 Der Speigel article, and these designs were dated to 1941 and first flown and tested in 1942. Schriever developed a flying saucer which used a jet-engine, a technology which had been in existence since Frank Whittle built the first jet-engine in England in April 1937. Two years later in Germany Erich Warstiz piloted the world's first jet aircraft the Heinkel He 178, which was limited to speeds of 372 miles per hour, somewhat slower than the Messerschmitt 109, and had a combat time of little more than 10 minutes. For these reasons it was not a success, however in 1944 the Germans built the Messerschmitt Me 262 which was effectively the world's first jet-fighter.

A few years later, on page 148 of an edition of Popular Science magazine from October 1955 in an article entitled: "Giant Pie Cooked Up by Frenchman is Latest Flying

Saucer" French aircraft engineer Rene Couzinet is shown standing aside the Couzinet RC-360: a flying saucer shaped aircraft 27 feet in diameter, resting on three landing struts. The article describes him as 'making a bid for the flying saucer trade' which is an interesting thing to say and seems to infer that there might be a commercial interest in designing saucers, presumably for secret government and covert military programmes.

The article quotes Couzinet on the method of propulsion: "The engines will spin the upper and lower discs in opposite directions and whirl the craft on its way." Perhaps it was a secret which he was supposed to have kept because tragically, on 16th December 1956, he and his wife Gilberte apparently committed suicide in Paris barely a year later.

What is noteworthy here, apart from the fact that Couzinet was apparently trying to break into the potentially lucrative 'saucer business' as inferred in the article, or the suspicious double suicide not long after the publication of this article, is the spinning element of the flying saucer Couzinet designed. This is something which had been observed and reported in many UFO phenomena subsequently.

1955 was a busy year for flying saucer engineers by all accounts. According to Henry Stevens in his book:

"Almost ten years after the war, on March 28, 1955, Heinrich Fleissner filed a patent application with the United States Patent Office for a flying saucer (Patent Number 2,939,648). Fleissner's saucer was unlike Schriever's, Habermohl's, or Miethe's. The engine employed by Fleissner rotated around the cabin on the outside of the saucer disc itself. It was set in motion by starter rockets as with Schriever and Habermohl. The difference is that this engine was really a form of ram-jet engine. It featured slots running around the periphery of the saucer into which air was scooped..... The cabin itself was held stationary or turned in the desired direction of flight using a system of electromagnets and servo-motors coupled with a gyroscope."

This patent seems very similar in principle to the Couzinet design, except for the method of propulsion but the key elements of spinning wings and fixed cockpit are familiar themes.

According the Stevens, the spinning wing is an element engineered to negate drag and air resistance and could allow this saucer design to move very fast without creating any sonic boom since the boundary layer of air which causes a sonic boom would not get a chance to form because the air is sucked in by slot air intakes and blown out by the jets. The saucer would have also been able to fly at high altitude, perhaps putting this more in the realm of the kind of UFO technology which more recent sightings have testified to rather than the wobbly B movie props of the past.

Stevens quotes the May 1980 issue of Neue Press magazine and an article about Heinrich Fleissner:

"Fleissner reports that the saucer with which he was involved would have been capable of speeds up to 3,000 kilometers per hour within the earth's atmosphere and up to 10,000 kilometers outside the earth's atmosphere. He states that the brains of the developmental people were found in Peenemuende under the tightest of secrecy."

An enduring mystery to this day which has entered the cultural consciousness and also the name of a rock band, is the so called 'Foo Fighters'. These appeared late in World War 2 and would apparently appear as mysterious balls of light or energy and would harass allied aircraft but without causing any actual damage. This mystery is also explained in Stevens' book:

"A German researcher, Friedrich Georg, recognized a valuable entry in a microfilm roll, titled a 1944 U.S. Strategic Air Forces in Europe summary titled An Evaluation Of German Capabilities In 1945, which, somehow, had eluded the censors. In that summary report German devices called by American Intelligence 'Phoo Bombs' are discussed. Sources for this summary were reports of pilots and testimony of prisoners of war. Phoo bombs were described as 'radio-controlled, jet-propelled, still-nosed, short-range, high performance ramming weapons for use against bombing formations'. Speed was estimated at 525 miles per hour."

So now we have a possible arsenal of the identifiable features of human designed saucers and delta-wing type aircraft such as the whirring of a vacuum jet engine, spinning mid sections, slightly wobbly motion and people testing these crafts. What we have not yet investigated is the other aspect which first became associated with UFO's on the night of 19th September 1961 through to the morning of the next day. Barney and Betty Hilly claim to have been the victims of an alien abduction, subsequent to the sighting of a UFO, but examining the details of the experience, which for me, the whole incident has so much which will explain the incident but not quite within the context which Betty Hill herself believes.

Betty spent much the rest of her long life publicising the event and has put Zeta-Reticuli on the map as a major system of origin for alien visitors to our planet, and many of the frankly fraudulent or wilfully self-deluded have jumped onto this particular band-wagon and are riding it hard to this day, suckering-in the somewhat weak minded, those lacking discernment or simply those who would rather escape reality altogether and devote their minds to fantasies about aliens. Perhaps the only benefit of the massive sweeping tide of relentless Internet censorship has been the blessed washing away of the presence of Nancy Lieder and her Zeta Talk online presence along with Eric Dubay, despite myself actually having a couple of articles which he chose to post on his Atlantean Conspiracy website.

No doubt belief in aliens has a strong appeal to many people in this day and age: their intervention offers a possible explanation to the mysteries of the past which many people either do not have the time or inclination to properly investigate and 'it was aliens' can provide an easy to digest skeleton key which unlocks the mysteries of history and bypasses all the hard work of historical research and intellectual deduction: 'solving' mysteries as diverse as the construction of the Ancient Pyramids, who made Adam and Eve and the identity of 'God' itself. It's all aliens. Easy. No thought required.

Betty and Barney were driving back from Niagara Falls when Betty saw a bright moving point of light which initially she thought must be a shooting star, until it started moving upwards. It became bigger and brighter and they stopped their car to take a closer look and also to walk their dog. After a moment spent trying to decide what it was that they were seeing, the object started moving towards them, this caused them to get back into their car and attempt to find a better vantage point to see what it was. This led them up a narrow mountain road.

Betty said it was 40 feet or 12 metres long and appeared to be rapidly spinning and 'moved erratically and bounced back and forth in the night sky', a description which accords perfectly with the size and design of the Couzinet and Fleissner saucers and the flying behaviour mentioned in the Angelholme account.

At one point the vessel hovered some 30 metres above their vehicle and Barney advanced on the saucer with a pistol and binoculars; looking through the binoculars Barney saw nearly a dozen or so humanoid figures through the vessel's windows, and one in particular came to the front and communicated a message to him, though it isn't known whether this was spoken or communicated by other means. Barney says the voice said: "stay where you are and keep looking." It was at this point that Barney was overcome with fear, perhaps justifiably, and ran back into his car and sped off at high speed. The vessel then moved to a position directly above the vehicle, apparently matching the car's velocity, but stranger was yet to come.

This critically interesting revelation takes us to the next element of UFO phenomena of which the Betty and Barney Hill example represents the pattern of many subsequent reports. Whatever it was that was in the saucer communicated with him psychically and instructed him to 'keep looking'. The following is from the now defunct National Investigations Committee on Aerial Phenomena (NICAP) a non-governmental group formed to respond to the surging tide of UFO sightings at the time:

"As he watched the leader through the binoculars, the leader's large eyes burned hypnotically into his mind and a 'voice' within instructed him to keep coming closer, keep the binoculars to his eyes, and no harm would come to him. The witness said his hands seemed frozen to the binoculars, and he couldn't put them down. He kept walking toward the craft while the mind-voice directed him to 'just keep looking' and reassured him that no harm would come to him."

Hill said that the occupants of the saucer wore shiny black uniforms with a black peaked caps along with a possible allusion to Nazis:

"The figures reminded the observer of the cold precision of German officers; they moved smoothly and efficiently and showed no emotion except for one fellow operating a lever who, Mr Hill claimed, looked over his shoulder and smiled".

Could this saucer have been under the control of former Nazi officers for some reason still following their military regimen and training? This would certainly accord with Mauri's account along with the documented proofs of German Nazi saucer development during the war.

Initially, according to the report, Barney Hill encountered a mental block at this point and it was only under hypnosis that much of what subsequently happened could be recalled. This later involved an actual abduction of both him and his wife into the saucer, after the car they were driving was hit with a strange kind of beam of energy. Interestingly Dr Simon, the hypnotherapist who interviewed them, had his own conclusions about the nature of the craft and entertained the possibility, as do I, that it was a: "classified type rather than an extra-terrestrial aircraft".

Barney's description under hypnosis; his experience of one the craft's occupants: the possible leader, seeming to enter his mind and since he seemed able to project words into his brain it is possible that the leader was either, as many believe, an extra-terrestrial with uncanny non-human psychic abilities, or that he was a human being just like us, but one who as we have seen previously, had learned various occult psychic abilities generally held to be the domain of the occult and secret societies:

"Oh, those eyes. They're there in my brain...I was told to close my eyes because I saw two eyes coming close to mine, and I felt like the eyes had pushed into my eyes...All I see are these eyes.... I'm not even afraid that they're not connected to a body. They're just there. They're just up close to me, pressing against my eyes."

For the sake of reference, the presence of disembodied eyes is something which has been featured in victim narratives of satanic occult ritual abuse including sketches of eyes appearing in darkness and also of course the reference to the 'all seeing eye' in Freemasonry is well known, additionally schizophrenics report hallucinations of disembodied eyes.

They drove off at high speed, and were followed by the UFO hovering above their car:

".. Almost immediately, the Hills heard a rhythmic series of beeping or buzzing sounds, which they said seemed to bounce off the trunk of their vehicle. The car vibrated and a tingling sensation passed through the Hills' bodies. The Hills said that then they experienced the onset of an altered state of consciousness that left their minds dulled. A second series of beeping or buzzing sounds returned the couple to full consciousness. They found that they had traveled nearly 35 miles (56 km) south, but had only vague, spotty memories of this section of road. They recalled making a sudden, sharp unplanned turn, encountering a roadblock, and observing a fiery orb in the road."

In the midst of all this we must again return to our friend Evelyn Waugh in his alter-ego as Gilbert Pinfold. His book was published in 1957 and was based on his experiences some three years prior. Part of Pinfold's delusions about the existence of what the Russians termed psychotronic weapons were fed by one of their neighbours 'a bee keeping old bachelor' called Reginald Graves Upton. They had nicknamed him 'the bruiser' 'basher' and 'old fisticuffs' as a sobriquet derived from 'boxer' since he was in possession of 'a box', and according to Waugh/Pinfold, such a box was similar to one of the many boxes apparently being used in the country at that time.

"According to the Bruiser and other devotees The Box exercised diagnostic and therapeutic powers. Some part of a sick man or animal—a hair, a drop of blood preferably—was brought to The Box, whose guardian would then 'tune in' to the 'life-waves' of the patient, discern the origin of the malady and prescribe treatment."

Pinfold himself was sceptical and considers the thing to be some kind of sorcery and fears that his wife is harvesting his hairs for use with the box in order to cure him of his many ailments. Later, when Pinfold is at sea and in the midst of his inadvertent drug-intoxication, and as moved on from the delusion that it is some kind of war-time apparatus which is enabling the transmission of voices around the ship, and that it is some form of 'wireless technology' as suggested by Margaret, he uses the recollection of 'the box' along with his fraught experience with BBC engineers and an interviewer at his home to construct the edifice of his delusion:

"You might inquire. These B.B.C. people have made themselves a great nuisance to me on board. They have got a lot of apparatus with them, most of it new and experimental. They have something which is really a glorified form of Reggie Upton's Box. I shall never laugh at the poor Bruiser again. There is a great deal in it. More in fact than he imagines. Angel's Box is able to speak and to hear. In fact I spend most of my days and nights carrying on conversations with people I never see. They are trying to psycho-analyze me. I know this sounds absurd."

"The Germans at the end of the war were developing this Box for the examination of prisoners. The Russians have perfected it. They don't need any of the old physical means of persuasion. They can see into the minds of the most obdurate. The Existentialists in Paris first started using it for psycho-analyzing people who would not voluntarily submit to treatment. They first break the patient's nerve by acting all sorts of violent scenes which he thinks are really happening. They confuse him until he doesn't distinguish between natural sounds and those they induce. They make all kinds of preposterous accusations against him. Then when they get him in a receptive mood they start on their psycho-analysis."

The problem with delusions, particularly the one experienced by Evelyn Waugh, is that many elements of the scaffolding which support the delusion are actually well constructed and broadly based on things previously known or experienced. There can't have been many people in the mid 1950's who knew about the Soviet psychotronic weapons development programme and it is by no means common knowledge now and it may be somewhat due to the fact that Captain Evelyn Waugh had been an intelligence officer of the Special Service Brigade which went on to become the British Commandoes. Waugh was even seconded to Randolph Churchill to infiltrate into Yugoslavia and support Marshall Tito and the partisans' resistance but their plane crashed and they had to make their way back to Italy. So, it is clear that Waugh was very much an insider and not only part of the establishment but one of key men, albeit a not particularly successful one judging by his war record.

In general, the only people who seem to be informed about the development and existence of psychotronic weapons are those with an academic interest and/or some personal experience, like mine; those who may have been part of some insider-track and heard such knowledge on some military grapevine and also those, like Pinfold, who find themselves experiencing psychotic symptoms and seek a way to rationalise the experience without accepting that they may be losing their mind. This is very common from conversations with people who experience psychosis but seek to create an ongoing delusion that they are under attack from such weapons. That is not to say such weapons do not exist, but they are incapable of the wide range of experiences which they have been reported to elicit, whereas schizophrenia has a long and documented history throughout the ages and is more than capable of accounting for all of the symptoms reported by those claiming to be under attack by psychotronic weapons.

It is after receiving the message from Pinfold that he is a victim of some kind of technological psychic harassment that his wife instantly and correctly understands that he has become psychotic and he receives a curt telegram from her imploring him to return home immediately.

When first reading the Ordeal of Gilbert Pinfold I had assumed that 'the box' was entirely a fanciful invention of Waugh's or something which might have, at the limit, been used by a select and elect quasi occult minded group of the idly wealthy, it seems however that with a little investigation which this book had incited me to do and with the discovery of the work of Robert Beck, in particular his interviews with legendary radio host Bill Jenkins and his proto-parapsychology radio show of the 80's for Los Angeles' KABC radio, that there was indeed, an extensive interest throughout England and Europe in a period throughout much of the 20th Century, though fading by the time of the late 1950's in what might be called the science of Radionics.

The technology Waugh is referring to is Radionics, developed by Albert Abrams and involved the application of electro-magnetic energy to the body. He and his technology have since been discredited and relegated to 'quack-science' though I suspect this probably coincides with the US and Russian militaries' development of secret mind-control technology using similar principles.

Reports indicate that American soldiers captured during the Korean war were subjected to a peculiar type of brainwashing with the use of a small electronic box. A 1984 BBC documentary 'Opening Pandora's Box' explains the operation of a Soviet psychotronic device called Lida which was developed in the 1940's. Ostensibly it was designed to treat Soviet psychiatric patients by projecting a beam of sound, light and a 40 MHz radio signal at pulse-rates of specific brain-wave frequencies to induce certain states of consciousness to relax and put them to sleep without physical contact, but it seems that it could also be used as a kind of truth drug by inducing a kind of hypnotic trance-state.

The CIA acquired one of these boxes from the Russians using a Canadian front company and it was used, presumably for therapeutic purposes, at Pettis Memorial Veterans Hospital where it was operated by Dr Ross Adey.

While the machine was being tested, a member of the staff was alarmed and asked where he had got the North Korean brain washing machine. He explained that it was the same device which had been used on POW's and recounted how they had used it on him while asking him a series of questions and how the device had made him enter a dreamy trance like-state during which he had had no control over the answers he gave.

In the 1960's Dr Adey worked on the Defense Advanced Research Projects Agency's (DARPA) Pandora project which was a response to the discovery that the Russians had developed psychotronic technology after investigating the development of psychological symptoms of staff working at the American embassies in Moscow and Cuba. It was discovered that the Soviets had been bombarding the embassy with microwaves, which had been dubbed 'the Moscow signal'.

The Los Angeles based talk radio show Open Minds featured a series of interviews with Dr Robert Beck who went into fascinating detail concerning the possibilities of using bio-feedback machines and focussed electromagnetic energy and magnetic fields to induce particular states of being in a targeted person or persons. If a signal of a particular brainwave frequency is directed at a target, then that person's brainwave will modulate that frequency to create a change in state.

The version of what could be said to be a more advanced and scientific version of the quasi-quakery of Radionic black magic boxes, was developed in 1965 by Dr Joseph Kamiya of the University of Chicago who monitored brainwaves using an electroencephalograph and used encouragement and reward to induce specific brainwave states ranging from Alpha waves, the 'meditative' state of consciousness, Beta waves, the brainwaves of normal human operation and Theta waves, the brainwaves associated with extra-sensory perception and the subliminal state of consciousness at the border between waking and sleeping.

Dr Beck stated that this technology was already being applied in the commercial sector at the time of the broadcast and says that a certain fast-food restaurant chain was using magnetic-fields to induce states of mild anxiety and a 'fight or flight' response to encourage people to eat more quickly and therefore make them clear their table more quickly thus making room for more customers. He also stated that the military had expressed a strong interest in developing this technology and that it might be used to incapacitate terrorists and rescue hostages, but Dr Beck also expressed reservations and concerns that the government might also seek to use this technology for mass crowd control.

Jose Delgado is perhaps best remembered now as the man who made a spectacle of the practical application of mind-control technology by implanting a bull with an electrical receiver and pressing a button stopping the bull at full charge, but Dr Beck claimed that his researches at New Mexico had reached the point where he could do the same thing remotely without the need for implanted electrodes.

In the early 1950's at the Hospital for Mental Diseases in Howard, Rhode Island, Delgado had something of a free hand to engage in invasive brain surgeries and fitting electrodes to the brains of patients suffering from a variety of mental and psychological impairments. It is such horror stories which sometimes form the material for our Hollywood entertainment: for instance the movie Shutter Island dramatizes several different aspects of invasive research on defenceless patients as well as alluding to Project Paperclip.

In his book Physical Control of the Mind: Toward a Psychocivilised Society, Delgado alludes to results obtained with surgical interventions of the brain and the use of electrodes and radio signals to inhibit human thinking; inhibit speech and movement and also to induce pleasure, friendliness, laughter and evoke memories. In the book Delgado takes a great deal of time to try to demonstrate in his way that mankind is a kind of mechanical creature with no innate sense of soul or reality which cannot be induced and created. His vision of the human mind is like that of Galvani's severed frog's leg that twitches and moves when an electric current is applied to the muscle. It is probably unscientific to call Delgado evil, but he has that very specific outlook of the evil man, that is: the desire to break something to see how it works but also something of the man with no soul, the man with the damaged conscience with the terrible inner emptiness and haunting horrors from which he is eternally fleeing into the outside world, to fill that with more reality than the inner world and to reduce mankind and nature to toys which can be controlled by pressing buttons on a remote control.

70 years later one has to wonder how far Jose Delgado's initial experiments have been developed, perhaps to the level of astonishing horrors we can hardly conceive. Suffice it to say that Delgado had a particular interest in trying to reach the brain by by-passing the senses, sending visual impression and images directly. This is the stuff of the best tradition of dystopian science-fiction films like the Matrix, I would strongly suspect that such a thing, even in its nascent state, is presently being performed on unwilling and unwitting human guinea pigs somewhere in the world. Delgado himself foresaw a future where men could control other people via computers attached to stimoceivers implanted in individuals' brains which he imagines will also be able to control people's minds and create a robotlike humanity. I have to say that I suspect some kind of psychopathy in Delgado, that only a robotised psychopath would envision such a future for humanity, but it is often the case that evil men continually seek to externalise that evil to the world at large. It is hard to know what drives them, perhaps a malicious desire to break and corrupt which they may dress up as scientific progress but fundamentally the impulse is to create an externalisation of their own inner hell. Obviously if Delgado's world of transhumanism does come to fruition, it would be the

ultimate playground for all the forces of evil on planet Earth to come together and rule forever by reducing the vast majority of the population to human robots, devoid of free-thought, emotions or memories of their own except that which the controllers wish them to experience. There is no conceivably 'good outcome' for such a world. I only hope that Jose Delgado is presently a resident of Monkey Hell being eternally tormented by the legions of monkeys which he so cruelly tormented with his experiments which after all were only a stepping stone to doing the same to mankind.

The hugely popular radio talk show Open Mind with Bill Jenkins was something of an America cultural institution all through the 80's and had such an extensive and eclectic listening audience that even self-confessed long-time listener Deforest Kelly, better known Bones, the ship's doctor from Star Trek, once called-in to share his experience of seeing a UFO.

One particularly interesting caller on the show, featuring Leonard Stringfield, public relations manager for NICAP and writer of several books on the alleged retrieval of UFO's and alien bodies, talking about crashed UFO's, and while most of the guests on this show seemed a little too inclined to believe that UFO's were coming from a distant solar system a couple of callers joined the show and somewhat upset the apple-cart.

I frankly, consider Leonard Stringfield to be one of 'the Manipulators' an agent deliberately working to perpetuate myths about UFO's and ascribe their existence to 'little green (or grey) men'. The twofold reasons for the creation of the fake alien agenda are as we have previously seen with the research and investigations of Jacques Vallee: to promote destruction of the old order of society for a secret group with an agenda of social-transformation and simultaneously provide cover for the development of secret military technology. It is particularly remarkable that during one of their interviews a caller called David tells the story of how, very early in the morning of 10th December 1964, he saw a UFO when he was on duty, guarding the motor pool, at Camp Forsythe military base in Kansas.

While on guard he was relieved by a soldier in a truck, but instead of going back to the barracks where the guards slept, they drove away from the camp. Coming to a stop he saw two other enlisted men, from a specialist force class and a number of officers. The first thing that struck him as strange was that the men were usually given only three rounds of ammunition, but now each was given a full clip from the back of a truck. He was told that a secret aircraft from Offutt Air Force base Nebraska had become disabled and come down somewhere near the camp. They hiked three or four hills, taking about thirty-five to forty-five minutes, it was quite dark, when all of a sudden, he heard a thrashing sound: it was a Huey helicopter with a bright beam scanning the ground which then scanned then and all of a sudden it moved over the ground ahead and dramatically lit up a large round disc shaped object, some hundred and fifty feet away.

"My god it looks like a flying saucer" he remembers saying jokingly.

It looked like hamburger bun, and he noticed something like a fan or a large round port opening like a large exhaust port. He moved closer to the object, and at about a foot from the object he noticed warm air coming from the saucer.

Then they were told to leave as they were no longer needed. They were told never to reveal or repeat what they had seen because it was a secret object from Offutt air-force base, and as he wondered to himself later, why if that thing was paid in 1964 with taxpayer dollars why hasn't it been revealed now?

Despite hearing such an amazing first-hand account Leonard Stringfield and Bill Jenkins seemed almost underwhelmed, and Stringfield in particular continued to drone on about the things his sources had told him about seeing the bodies of aliens and spent a long seemingly interminable while just trying to waste airtime by going on in general terms about his sources and how he can't name them because of what might happen to them, meanwhile David several times tried to get a word in, but was rebuffed and ignored by the host and Stringfield. It seemed clear that his story didn't 'fit' with what they were trying to achieve, indeed, in a subsequent episode Bill Jenkins and Leonard Stringfield both agreed that anyone saying the UFO's are part of a secret military programme and not alien technology are part of a deliberate disinformation campaign.

It was only by sheer good fortune that another caller, Louie, called in after an interminable delay during which Stringfield played for time and seemed determined to try to block David and show no interest or even refer to his story.

Louis was serving with the National Guard at Wichita Kansas and recounts how they were taken to Camp Ripley in Minnesota during June 1964. They were part of some kind of night-time war-games simulation and had been trained on how to use special night vision scopes, and were told that a special assault group was going to attack them and they were not to move from their positions under any circumstances. However, after midnight he got tired of sitting in the same foxhole and went for a walk to stretch his legs, he heard something so he hid himself so he wouldn't get in any trouble for disobeying instructions.

He saw a soldier with a different kind of uniform and a different kind of helmet, and he had some kind of special night sighting device which looked more advanced than his and also his weapon looked different, like a submachine gun but smaller. He followed him for a while and the man seemed to suspect that he was being followed but every time he turned around the Louis managed to hide himself. Then suddenly Louis could no longer see the man and following his footprints he saw that they ended suddenly. He wondered where he had gone, and saw a tree and cursed himself because it must be that he had climbed the tree and had got the best of him. Then the air was strangely warm and there was a down-draft and he noticed that strangely there were no stars in the sky, he looked and saw that above him was a large black circular object blocking out the night sky. He heard a metal door slide away and heard electronic sounds and something like the sound of hydraulic equipment. There was a kind of gentle warm air current beneath the saucer, and he thought that this was connected to the form of propulsion. There was no motor noise, just a whine of electronic equipment; he was so startled he fell backwards on the ground. There were red black-out lights inside the open square door and he could hear voices talking inside about 40 feet above him.

He now felt that he was in way over his head and that he had violated orders. The next day the officers were so furious that someone had left their position that they had the whole unit standing out in the sun for three hours and they were screaming at them to find out who had disobeyed orders and left their post to follow the guy, he was so frightened that he didn't mention it to his best buddies for four years.

He added that on different occasions he also saw vertical take-off planes, they usually took off on a moonless night, from the Lockheed buildings and took off almost without noise, but with a kind of hydraulic whine similar to the sound of the UFO. He, like the other caller, suspected that they were something in the inventory of the US military.

Louis had called in to the radio show because it seemed to be the same kind of UFO which David had been guarding, complete with the feeling of warm air and the black colour. He then recounted how years later he had seen a copy of Mechanix Illustrated and a story about super soldiers and experimental military gear which had not been adopted for general use and he immediately recognised the same radio-helmet with an antenna in the top, he had seen the soldier wearing along with the new night vision scope, which the guy had been carrying.

In order to test the likelihood of these accounts we should look for common themes recurring in disparate and separate accounts. We have observed that UFO's with spinning sections and telescopic legs were a commonality between several different sightings. In this account from Stevens' book Hitler's Flying Saucers we find mention of a distinctive 'whine' which was mentioned in the phone-in caller Louis' account:

"The time of the sighting was in 1944, the place was Gut Alt Golssen, approximately 30 miles east of Berlin. The informant, whose name has been deleted, states that while he was a prisoner of war working for the Germans, a flying object arose nearby from behind an enclosure hidden from view by a 50-foot-high tarpaulin type wall. It rose about 500 feet then moved away horizontally. The only noise the object made was a high-pitched whine. The object was described as being 75 to 100 feet in diameter and 14 feet high. It was composed of a dark grey stationary top and bottom sections five to six feet high with a rapidly moving center section producing only a blur and extending the circumference of the vehicle. Notably, the engine of their farm tractor stalled during this event and the SS guards told the driver not to attempt a restart until the whine could no longer be heard."

What is it that can cause failure of car engines at distance? Ionized air, which accords with the reported smell of burning or ozone which is often associated with UFO's. It is likely that the Foo fighters of World War 2 were electromagnetic weapons and the intention was to interfere with the engines or allied aircraft and cause them to stall. The principle behind this is that by ionizing the atmosphere the engine is no longer insulated from the spark required to ignite the fuel, and the atmosphere because an electrical conductor so the voltage leaks out from the battery contacts and cannot form a spark to ignite the fuel and instead forms a static charge in the atmosphere which then grounds itself. As long as the atmosphere around is ionized with free electrons this will continue and the engine will only restart once the ionizing presence of the UFO's engines had departed and the atmosphere is no longer charged to form a flowing current which dissipates the voltage away from the spark plug.

The NICAP website speculates that microwave radiation is the source of this ionization; this would also account for the warmth or heating effects associated with UFO's not to mention peculiarities such as temporary spots of discolouration which were reported on the paintwork of the Hill's motorcar.

However, it is likely that there is not just one type of secret government UFO or one particular means of propulsion. From the following account it seems that during the 80's there were experiments using nuclear powered UFO's, and this might seem like a recipe for total disaster and so it proved to be. If there are any doubts that this craft was not man-made then how could it have travelled the countless billions of miles through the vacuum of space only to get to Earth and discover that the technologically advanced alien super beings somehow forgot how to fly their aircraft and promptly crashed it.

Another Betty and another UFO mystery: Betty Cash, her work colleague and friend Vicki Landrum along with her young grandson Colby Landrum were on the way back to Dayton Texas after dining out. On a lonely two-lane road in deep nigh-time woods they suddenly saw bright lights in the sky above the trees. They continued on their way and saw the lights again but suddenly they loomed closer and the alarming and unexpected sight of large UFO shaped like a diamond, but flat at the top and expelling roaring fire bellow.

The thing seemed to be out of control and the fire and heat was so oppressive that they stopped the car. The burning flame bellow seemed to be the only thing stopping the object from crashing completely and the flame burst out periodically, just about keeping the strange diamond shaped vehicle bobbing above the road. In a moment a fresh burst of flame sent the vehicle rising above the trees.

Then suddenly they heard the more familiar sound of helicopters, counting as many as 23 including some Boeing Chinook twin bladed military choppers, in a tight formation as if escorting the strange floundering burning vessel.

The UFO and helicopters went about their business and went off into the night but upon returning home all three of them started experiencing a range of symptoms including vomiting and diarrhoea, burning of the eyes and generalised weakness.

Betty Cash however got the worst of it. Painful blisters broke-out on her body and later she could not walk and started losing large patches of skin and clumps of hair; later developing breast cancer. Jerome Clarke in The UFO Encyclopaedia quotes a radiologist "we have strong evidence that these patients have suffered secondary damage due to ionizing radiation." This story was documented in a 1985 HBO documentary "UFO's What's Going on?"

Another example of an UFO phenomenon being associated with high levels of radiation occurred in December 1980 just outside RAF Woodbridge near Rendlesham Forest Suffolk in England and has become known, somewhat ambitiously, as 'the British Roswell'.

The following is taken from an article on the website for the East Anglian Times:

"Tim Acheson, measured the levels of radiation at locations around the site to see if they varied from other areas of the forest. He found that there were a number of radiation 'hot spots' at locations linked to the extra-terrestrial sightings back in December 1980.

In the original Ministry of Defence investigation, the Defence Intelligence Staff assessed the levels of radioactivity documented in Lieutenant Colonel Halt's official report as being "significantly higher than the average background.

This is a highly impressive and significant piece of work. The levels of radioactivity in Rendlesham Forest are an important piece of physical evidence, and a better understanding of this aspect of the story may prove critical when it comes to resolving the question of what took place back in 1980."

https://www.eadt.co.uk/news/could-radiation-data-help-rendlesham-ufo-case-2452390

The US Air Force had previously experimented with using nuclear power as a form of propulsion. Known as Project Pluto the idea was to apply heat from nuclear reactors to ramjet engines. A feasibility study was carried out in 1957 between the US Atomic Energy Commission and the Lawrence Radiation Laboratory. The vessel would take the form of a supersonic flying missile which would fly at low altitudes. In 1961 two test engines were successfully operated, mounted on a railroad car the first nuclear ramjet engine burst into life on July 1, 1964, but seven years later the project was apparently cancelled.

The ramjet engine would be fed by what was effectively a compact nuclear reactor which had been made to go critical. The missile was to permanently cruise the skies carrying a payload of nuclear weapons, ready to strike targets in the then Soviet Union.

Another atomic-powered flying vehicle in development in the United States was the Lenticular Re-entry Vehicle. Lenticular is highly suggestive of being saucer shaped and was described in an edition of Popular Mechanics from November 2000 as 'America's nuclear flying saucer'. The project was classified in 1962 but cleared for public release in 1999. In 1975 in Australia at Jean Fraser's farm south of Brisbane not far from a secret base where the British and Americans tested new projects, distinctive honey-comb type debris was discovered from a craft which was said to have crashed and been mostly recuperated in 1966. The idea of crashing saucers powered by critical nuclear reactors might be the stuff of the most pessimistic type of 70's science fiction thriller but from what we have seen regarding crashing saucers they were probably a fairly common occurrence.

Sometimes, in fact surprisingly often on this small lonely planet of ours, fact and fiction meet in a most disconcerting manner. Take for example the popular and long-running TV show Star Trek. Gene Rodenberry was the randy genius behind this remarkable programme which seemed to seamlessly combine the prophecy of technological advances of a distant future, while always highlighting themes prevalent on the Earth of the present day along with characters from our history and the same endless moral conundrums which have plagued our greatest thinkers but with one crucial difference: the humans of the future always get it right. They are humble yet wise with human sagacity: often the crew of the Enterprise seem to foil even the demi-gods they meet; it is clear that this is a utopian vision of the future, but something about it is not entirely based on fiction for Gene Rodenberry had a very interesting life and found himself eager to help humanity to live out the fictional reality he had created.

He became involved in a strange cult known as the 'Council of 9', what appeared to be a race of aliens using human beings of great power such as Uri Geller (who later dismissed them as a 'civilisation of clowns') to announce their imminent return to Earth in a fleet of flying saucers. What it actually appeared to be, after a series of suspicious deaths, was nothing more than an extraordinarily devious, complex and extremely unusual CIA mind control programme which seemed to harness elements of the supernatural and strange human psychic abilities.

Some of the odd characters involved in this odd mixture of the occult and the secret services are still active in the alternative media today: people like Richard Hoagland and his fake 'Face on Mars' scam, along with Palden Jenkins (crop circle guru who advises his followers to allow themselves to be possessed by aliens when they enter a crop circle) who admitted to me in his pride that during an informal chat after one of his talks in a London pub that he was presently advising the Bilderbergers. Even global-warming hot-airbag Al Gore was said to be influenced by 'The Nine'. This occult CIA mind-control is still very much active it seems, despite the noble efforts of one of its past protégées: Uri Geller, to help expose it as a fraud, albeit a very occluded and mysterious one and Jacques Vallee says it best when he states:

"...if you take the trouble to join me in the analysis of the modern UFO myth, you will see human beings under the control of a strange force that is bending them in absurd ways, forcing them to play a role in a bizarre game of deception....Are the manipulators, in the final analysis, nothing more than a group of humans who have mastered a very advanced form of power?"

There seem to be two distinct elements of the UFO and aliens phenomenon; it is these two distinct and seemingly conflicting and contrasting elements which have rendered the whole UFO investigation scene so confusing and leaves anyone who looks into it so confused that they are tempted, in the logic gap which appears in the UFO world, to believe that because the whole thing seems so inexplicable and mysterious that they might as well believe it all. They are unable to rationalise it since as soon as it appears that UFO's might be a material phenomenon of technology and physical aliens from outer space, then the UFO exhibits non-physical behaviour and starts to do impossible things which defy our laws of physics, for example this account from an eye-witness cited in Messengers of Deception:

"Following a UFO observation, a woman was awakened by a feeling of intense cold and saw a being with a bald head near the house. She called other witnesses, and all saw the apparition shrink and vanish on the spot 'like a TV image when the set is turned-off.'"

According to Vallee many of these UFO sightings do not behave as tangible physical phenomena:

"It is the behaviour of an image, or a holographic projection."

"A prominent doctor saw two large disk-shaped objects merge into one, and the single object send a beam of light in his direction. It vanished with a sort of explosion, leaving a cloud that dissipated slowly."

Conversely some of the early accounts of UFO show something reassuringly banal which has a hand in the aliens-phenomena - other humans:

"I do know this was made in America, I am sure. It had a plain old G.I. in it, I know that much. I would know the man if I saw him in Chicago tomorrow."

"Most witnesses are not primarily reporting an object or a craft; they are reporting a light, a massive, multicolored, intense, pulsating light, a playful, fascinating, impressive, hypnotic light, which is accompanied by strange sounds."

Vallee, an expert on UFO's with more than 50 years' experience, believes there is genuinely something at work in the UFO phenomenon which involves a form of non-human consciousness that can manipulate time and space. He says that this same force has been active throughout human history and appears in different forms to different cultures. One can therefore consider the possibility that the same mysterious diabolical creatures that were said to commune with witches during the middle-ages and the same voices, encouraging people in dangerous futile delusions all the way to pushing them all the way to suicide, are all part of the same phenomenon.

"Rather than a form of transportation invented by the denizens of some far-away world, the UFOs could be a stratagem devised by a human group to promote its own goals."

There does seem to be some conflict in Vallee's mind whether the UFO phenomenon is controlled by humans or, some kind of advanced non-human intelligence, although 'advanced' is even debatable since he observes, like Uri Geller with his 'civilisation of clowns' that "just because a message comes from heaven doesn't mean it's not stupid" adding that:

"Many of the contactees have fallen victim to a peculiar effect on their minds: they have lost their critical faculties."

Vallee sees two distinct elements of the UFO phenomenon, one of them involving some kind of technology which is able to produce the effects of saucers: flashing lights, and some physical form of a saucer to implant the suggestion that what the contactee is seeing is an actual visitation from space. The second element is strictly non-physical, what might be called a spiritual experience taking place on a different level of reality and having more in common with 'astral projection' and out of body experiences. He believes that these experiences can be triggered by hypnosis and even drugs, and the fact that strangely flashing lights always seem to the prelude to any UFO experience is deeply suggestive of this.

It is possible to use flashing lights to put someone in an altered suggestible hypnotic-state, in which the 'contactee' can be made to believe any suggestion which is made to them is wholly real and they are actually seeing it with their own eyes; or they may be able to be directly accessed and influenced by the 'non-human intelligence' which Vallee postulates exists, and shown any number of what we call 'dreams' which due to the contactee's unfamiliarity with the hypnotic state or even having been hypnotised, will be unable to differentiate from reality. This also explains why contactees often experience 'missing-time' or find themselves regaining awareness at a location some distance from their original location.

TV hypnotist Darren Brown put someone into a catatonic state using flashing lights integrated into a video arcade game. He then took them while in a hypnotised state into a specially prepared room with actors wearing zombie make-up where he was in a physical recreation of the video-game and there seemed to be no cognitive dissonance in the man, between the fact that one minute he was playing a video game and now was apparently shooting zombies for real.

Vallee makes the connection between the UFO phenomenon and occult groups, specifically the Rosicrucians. The Rosicrucians are a secret society who boast of their ability to master psychic techniques and even award their degrees psychically. While living and working in Morocco and teaching at a large language centre in Casablanca which was funded and sponsored by the US Department of State I taught a student who wore a Masonic ring. I am weary of the Freemasons as I have personally found them to be strange people involved in many nefarious activities and they have tried to recruit me several times. I found the distinct humming of something evil the closer I became drawn into their world and the suspicion of the worst kind of immoral criminal activities which were only being slightly hidden from me and I suspect that were I to join them then the curtain would open on all sorts of human degradations and the threat of death to anyone who speaks out on what they see and the activities of their so-called brothers.

The gentleman with the Masonic ring told me he had the ability to enter people's minds when they were asleep; this might seem unbelievable, certainly to a materialist, but if there are other states of consciousness and the human soul is not always strictly fixed to the body, especially during moments of so called 'un-consciousness', then might there not be techniques to enhance 'conscious' awareness during sleep: a technique commonly called lucid-dreaming?

If I tell you that a couple of nights later, while dreaming, I actually saw this man in my dreams and that he was directly communicating with me. also that when I lived in Tokyo I lived in a house with several Filipino witches who were able to project themselves into my mind, and like the Moroccan Freemason, could only be removed by an act of mental exertion or force of will, then you are welcome to disbelieve me, but consider some of the events we have encountered in this book, all real accounts of unusual mental phenomenon and consider that there might be more on heaven and earth than we are being told by the media system and mainstream science.

To demonstrate how these organisations can operate both openly and hidden at the same time I will refer to the following excerpt which comes from a young man who was enrolled in what he called Illuminati High School and goes into great detail to explain how at the University Laboratory High School there seems to exist an Illuminati continuum involving sex and mind control which he was involved with. His comments about trance induction even recall what happened to me in France at a government sponsored residential training course I attended, which was also a cover for shadowy secret society recruitment attempts:

"Before I can explain mind control, I should mention the existence of psychological trance. It's possible to put a person into a state of psychological trance in which the person seems sort of zombified, or sleeping while awake, passive, under the control of an outside voice. I suspect that psychological trance is actually used by the US government broadly on American middle school children, but I shall explain this later.

The gist of trance is something like this: there are certain combinations of words, sounds, and pictures, that will put an exposed person into a trance state.

There are audios that, if you put headphones on a person, and make them listen to a two-minute (roughly) trance-coded audio, then the person will go into a trance state and will become open to being controlled by another person. As an interesting aside, there are actually criminals who use trance in order to put victims into a trance state then command the victims to hand over financial information, I know this because I luckily (or synchronistically) met such a criminal, who told me about her scheme, and also told me that there's a secret law code dealing with crimes of magic (as trance induction is considered a form of magic) that deals an automatic death penalty to any criminal using magic. I was also told that there's a secret US Department of Magic that deals with trance and magic and so on. And yes, I know I'm into strange territory, but I'm just reporting what I've been told. Three different unrelated people have told me that there's a US Department of Magic."

Whether you believe there might be a US Department of Magic doesn't matter so much as the fact there are young people being inducted into secret society mind control programmes within specially set-up so called 'University high-schools' in the United States, who are told that this exists.

Ultimately, we are dealing with the power of suggestion and mind-control and although there is a great quest to find some kind of method of mass-technological mind-control, the Illuminati's ultimate secret is the use of various techniques to induce a permanent change in consciousness.

This is the purpose of many kinds of corporate and government training courses which operate both in the open and covertly: one such organisation which came to light some years ago is Common Purpose, and trainees undergoing Common Purpose training have been reported by their loved ones to have been somehow 'altered' becoming colder, more aggressive and generally undergoing a radical change in their behaviour; however organisations like Common Purpose don't just change behaviour, they alter the very mental chemistry of their trainees, or victims itself.

Following the advice of a mysterious man whom he names Major Murphy, a retired member of the US Intelligence service who used to intercept German spies and submarines on their way to the United States, Vallee goes on the hunt for 'The Manipulators' who are behind a deliberate campaign of disinformation for their own political ends:

"According to Major Murphy, the confusion in the UFO mystery may have been put there deliberately to achieve certain results. One of these results has been to keep scientists away. The other is to create the conditions for a new form of social-control, a change in Man's perception of his place in the universe."

Leaving Jacques Vallee to ask the question which would clear up the whole mystery:

"Everything now centers on their role, their identity, their designs. Who could they be? Alien beings coming from the end of the galaxy? Psychic entities from the "other side"? Automata controlled by some nonhuman consciousness? Holographic nightmares? But perhaps we are looking far away for something which is right under our nose: could they simply be human? Could they be masters of deception so skillful that they plan to counterfeit an invasion from space? ..Beyond the attention of academic science, below the dignity of official history, there are groups, cults, and sects that serve as "leading indicators" of mass movements."

Vallee discovers a book written by a Frenchman called Raymond Bernard. Bernard was Grand Master of the Rosicrucians, the Templar Order and The Martinists, and during his life had carried out extensive work to spread the beliefs and tenets of the Rosicrucian order throughout all parts of the world, particularly in French speaking parts of Africa which most probably would have been focussed on places like Morocco and Tunisia, as the countries with the strongest liberal current, not to mention a strong tradition of the occult.

The order claims to teach and preserve a genuine esoteric tradition, which is another word for pagan witchcraft and such occult practices which throughout the world usually involve the communication with and the possession by spirits. Vallee writes:

"True adepts of the Rosy Cross, it is said, are not of this Earth. They have transcended the bonds of time and space. They reach this exalted state, however, by a series of initiations that organizations such as AMORC claim to preserve as a body of 'sacred knowledge.' AMORC teaches it throughout the world, mailing its educational material from its lavish headquarters in San Jose, California."

"…some techniques used by occult groups have indeed been preserved from the most ancient times. They include excellent operating knowledge of hypnosis, suggestion, the laws of forms, and their use for ritual and behavior control."

According to Vallee, Raymond Bernard, using the initiatory techniques of transformation, had apparently made contact with a 'superior being' known as Maha who had the power to completely control him and communicate with him solely using his eyes. Their first meeting seemingly took place in the somewhat prosaic venue of the Carlton Hotel in Amsterdam, and one hopes that the hotel's conference facilities were up to the task of accommodating superior beings with psychic powers. In Jacques Vallee's analysis, this 'being' is one of the 'manipulators' behind the UFO program and people like the Grand Master of the Rosicrucians are merely their servants.

The being goes on to state that the hotel is not a suitable place for their meeting and instead they made for a park full of flowers, so my suspicions that the conferencing facilities perhaps might be a disappointment were well-founded. Maha revealed he was a member of something called The High Council, also known as 'A' and perhaps this is a reference to the Arcanum Arcanorum.

His speech to Bernard was full of the typical new-age tropes that we all know by now, usually full of woolly, high-sounding nonsense but with a few 'seeds' thrown in, almost hidden amongst the generalities, perhaps all the better to hide the noxious things that might eventually grow from them. This is a form of subliminal neuro-linguistic-programming, say a lot of things that on the face of it, are completely reasonable, then on the tail of this cavalcade hide the real purpose of the programme like a furtive and fearful third world despot hides the car chauffeuring him amongst a dozen dummies.

The furtive president hiding himself from the public gaze in this case was: "the abolition of borders, and the death of nationalism," without all of the New-Age embroidery presenting this, the message seems stark, radical and dangerous, and we are now living in the midst of this 'dream' and some of us are realising that it is a nightmare and what is more we have figured out 'qui bono'. Which nations have to submit themselves to open borders and 'the death of national identity' and which nation does not? Which nation, or state, has been given a special dispensation to build walls and preserve its ethnic and religious identity at the barrel of a gun, while other nations have to obediently lay down the red carpet to welcome those who will dispossess them of their own lands?

What is interesting however is that Raymond Bernard, Grand Master and universal 'Primo inter pares' of the Rosicrucians seems to be only a small confused player in a much bigger game. In his book he relates how he went to Vienna in 1967 where he met a man with a car with the licence plates of the Diplomatic Corps who drove him to an isolated house near a forest:

"There was no outward sign of activity, but as they knocked on the door, it opened onto a circular room with a floor of black and white marble triangles, where twelve men were standing, dressed in white robes.

There, Bernard witnessed a ritual with several striking peculiarities. First, he suddenly failed to hear the words of the celebrants, although he saw their lips moving. Then he heard a mounting vibration - not quite the om sound used by Eastern meditators. He lost consciousness and was later puzzled by the whole experience. Reflecting upon it, Bernard came to the conclusion that he had been subjected to an examination. In fact, he has no proof that he had not been given posthypnotic suggestions or reinforcements of earlier suggestions, whose existence may be indicated by the frequent perceptual phenomena he experienced."

Vallee observes that he does not question the experience nor appear suspicious that he apparently has no memory of what happened at the mysterious house during the ritual. One might fear the worst: that he was possessed by demons and even possibly took part in terrible acts of satanic worship. Who knows, but one would be right to be at least curious if not slightly fearful.

"After Bernard toured the entire house and was told its role in the function of the Order, the 'master' spoke a single word of two syllables: upon hearing this keyword, Bernard again lost consciousness. He assumed once more that he was reaching a level of cosmic ecstasy induced by the high meditative state of his hosts."

Vallee observes rightly that the man is clearly under hypnotic control and his loss of consciousness indicates that he had been hypnotised.

"Is there really such an organization as the 'High Council'? Probably not. The name may have been picked for Bernard's purpose. Could the owners of the houses he describes be found? That, indeed, would be most interesting..."

It seems clear then that the secret societies and even their apparent leaders, Grand Masters, and super dupers, are only serving some other, much more mysterious organisation which has mastered the art of hypnotic suggestion and has an agenda dedicated to open-borders and an end to national identity. According to Bernard these conditions will be necessary before the 'celestial knights of the macrocosm' can come down to Earth. It seems like a strange agenda for aliens to be so interested in open-borders doesn't it?

The Martinist Order is an advanced 'psychic' society within the framework of Rosicrucianism. A great deal of material from the so called Traditional Martinist Order, based in San Jose California presumably part of AMORC, was leaked onto the internet some years ago. Interestingly the symbol for the Martinist organisation is two triangles, one black and one white, interlocked to form a what is commonly called the Seal of Solomon or Star of David.

The following extract from this leaked material is from Associate Discourse number 14 and is interesting in that it shows that they acknowledge the changes in brain chemistry which higher initiates undergo and one must try to resist being drawn-in by the colourful new-age language employed to make some of the changes undergone seem generally beneficial and positive. For instance, the phrase 'astral images' can be translated as 'hallucinations': seeing things which are not there, and a common symptom of advanced psychosis and schizoaffective disorders:

"A very interesting point worth mentioning at this time is that the circulation of the nervous force within man puts him in communication with the universe. In highly evolved mystics, there occurs what in occultism is sometimes called the circulation of astral images. These astral images generally appear to be coming from the back of the head. This is not altogether exact, but it will give an idea as to the nature of this phenomenon….This will be important when we study the actions of the invisible world so important to every Martinist."

Similarly, the phrase 'being put in communication with the universe' sounds wonderfully exciting and like some jolly intergalactic adventure, but what it really implies is the hearing of voices and seeing beings which are not visible to other people: no different to the three ghostly forms at Barbara O'Brien's bedside telling her she was now part of a secret experiment.

This psychic transformation is something which appears to be part of the UFO agenda: Vallee discover a group in Palo Alto California operating from the campus of Stanford University, which appeared to be a cross between new-age spirituality and UFO cult:

"They were seeking real truth. The text was signed by flying-saucer believers who called themselves H.I.M. or Human Individual Metamorphosis. The announcement continued: '…are attempting to completely rise above their human nature under the direction of individuals who are members of a kingdom above human who have come in at close range to the Earth to help.' They compare this period of overcoming their human nature to the metamorphic process of a caterpillar becoming a butterfly."

Vallee attends a talk by the group and a bearded man speaks in terms of personal psychic transformation much like the Rosicrucian groups and possibly the kind of 'transformations' undergone by Evelyn Waugh and Barbara O'Brien:

"They are now just finishing completing their own physical metamorphosis. Their bodies have almost completely changed over physically, chemically, biologically. They look just like you and I on the surface. Within a few months there will be a demonstration. When we have changed our bodies over through this process, we no longer have to endure disease or decay or death."

Vallee reports that one person who joined the group in 1975 left the group after two months having some concerns:

"These two people are dangerous. It is not hypnosis. It is thought transplant."'

And when during one of the talks someone from the audience asked:

"How do you know that you're not being deceived by demonic forces?"

The unconvincing response which Vallee reports may lead one to rightly ask whether this is the reality behind much of the UFO phenomenon which cannot be explained by secret American post war technology.

Vallee asks one of his friends who had attended a meeting of the Order of Melchizedek some questions about the order and its aims. His friend reported on someone called Dr Grace from the Order of Melchizedek who delivered lectures:

"I asked her if she had ever seen a UFO. She had. She described to me what she had seen once in the eastern part of the United States, with her husband. It was a craft, only fifty feet or so away, and she felt that the beings on board were communicating directly to her, into her brain."

If Dr Grace was telling the truth, then it would appear that the people who were leading the UFO and New-Age cults of the 1970's were doing so under the instructions of voices in their heads. We have seen how Barbara O'Brien's voices and hallucinations managed to create an extremely cogent continuum of reality, and at times there were even things which the voices told her which she herself could not possibly have known and which potentially helped save her from danger on several occasions.

Returning to O'Brien's account she is told by the Operators that some humans are actually almost fully possessed by the Operators. These were known as 'Dummies' a Dummy had apparently lost its personality and personal volition and was fully under the control of the Operators:

"I was horrified. Why would an Operator want to make a dummy out of a Thing? "Well, Operators use dummys as hatracks," Nicky explained. "Most of the great comic entertainers are dummys. Bob Hope, for instance. When an entertainer like Hope is performing, he's merely giving out what some Operator is stimulating him to do. There's no latticework to interfere with the receiving of the stimuli. In certain situations, a dummy can be quite an asset to a clever Operator. It's something like having a puppet on a string."

Interestingly MRI scans have been conducted on the brains of those with psychopathic personality disorder. Many psychopathic murderers have historically attributed their sprees to some other agent operating through them, though of course their testimonies have been rejected as the ravings of madmen. But what if there were something to it? The research conducted by the University of Wisconsin-Madison shows that the brain-scans of psychopaths show extremely diminished activity in the prefrontal cortex area of the brain. The prefrontal cortex is the area which is linked to a person's personality, the will to live, personal volition and decision making. This really is the area which is the focal point of most people's lives and is in essence the part of the brain which makes them who they are: the decisions they make, the plans they have and how they act in social interactions.

Since the pre-frontal cortex is the decision making, will and personal focus area of the brain, then what we may be observing in the psychopathic personality is the person who is lacking a will and the ability to make their own decisions. So, who or what is making those decisions for them?

Perhaps these people have acquiesced their will to the hidden masters, or 'extra-terrestrial' beings which those leading the UFO cults claimed to be in contact with. What are these beings? Extra-terrestrial? Extra-dimensional beings? Demons? Most people live their lives mentally driving through life in the front seat of their car but the psychopath appears to be sat in the front seat, but is not the one driving. Something else is directing the course.

This may give an insight into the strange mystery that many of the people who had left the H.I.M. group:

"The people who left their group would just go home and, for several weeks, simply stare at the walls."

Some very powerful people have gone on record that they speak to spirits of the dead. Retired British army Colonel Richard Kemp, is a high-profile Zionist and British advocate for Israel and chairman of the Friends of Israel. In an article by investigative journalist Asa Winstanley from May 2015 he reports on Kemp's attendance at the Towards a New Law of War conference in Jerusalem organised by Mossad front-group Shurat HaDin, where he was described as "one of the Jewish state's greatest allies" and Kemp opined that the UK and Israel should be allowed to kill more civilians within the context of military engagement.

https://electronicintifada.net/blogs/asa-winstanley/allow-israel-kill-more-civilians-says-british-colonel

Where it gets weirder is that Colonel Kemp claims to be in psychic contact with the deceased spirit of Orde Wingate, a man of whom he says was "the greatest Christian Zionist in Britain."

"Kemp also reportedly told his Christians United For Israel (CUFI) audience that he had communicated with the dead. According to the Frontpage Mag report, he had "that morning, spoken to Orde Wingate … 'I spoke to him this morning at Arlington [military cemetery]'.""

Wingate, a member of the Plymouth Brethren (Aleister Crowley's parents had also been members of this bizarre sect) was a British officer who led the Special Night Squad, a militia which was instrumental during the 1930's in crushing Palestinian resistance and preparing the ground for the Jewish invasion and it is rumoured that this group formed and trained the later Haganah group of Jewish terrorists

https://electronicintifada.net/blogs/asa-winstanley/hardcore-christian-zionism-israels-favorite-british-colonel

Again, we see the common-denominator in so much of the material we have already explored here. We see powerful people with a particular agenda for a particular group in contact with and possibly being guided by discarnate beings. On the weight of so much strange and inexplicable evidence is it not perhaps time to consider the possibility that there is some invisible spiritual force 'out there' which seeks to meddle in the affairs of planet Earth to fulfil its own strategic and perhaps, infernal long-term goals?

In the free Tokyo English language ex-pat newspapers and magazines one finds, at least when I lived there, advertisements and notices which raise many questions in themselves. If you were to go there now and thumb through the classifieds and jobs sections, the chances are you will find offers of certain kinds of special employment available exclusively to Filipino women. One such advert I found said something along the lines of: "wanted, psychically gifted Filipinos for ethical work in Tokyo area..." This raises two main questions immediately. Firstly, are there various agencies which know that psychic powers exist and they can use them for some purpose? Secondly if it is necessary for them to make the distinction that the work offered is 'ethical' then what else is going on out there behind the scenes involving 'psychically gifted Filipinos' which is not ethical?

What these 'psychically gifted' women or 'witches' as I would classify the bunch I happened to be sharing a house with, seemed able to do: and a South African Shaman friend of mine later confirmed to me that it was something she could also do, was to be able to project their consciousness into the mind of another person.

In the book The Chasm of Fire, Irene Tweedie documents a woman's experience in India studying under a Sufi shaman. In the account she details the occurrence of her mentor actually entering her mind at night time and projecting all sorts of unsettling and unpleasant images into her mind. Most of the images are of a sexual nature and Tweedie fails to understand the process and why her mentor is doing such a thing to her. Eventually she comes close to a nervous breakdown and becomes very lonely and depressed to such an extent that she abandons the training.

The process which Irene Tweedle had chosen to enrol herself in and later abandoned, was a deliberate attempt by her Sufi mentor to drive her insane through the relentless terror and shock of the visions he was implanting in her mind. To Tweedle this made no sense, but if she had known perhaps that schizophrenia is the key to the Sufi 'enlightenment' and indeed the key goal of all such secret society initiatory programmes, then this knowledge would have allowed her to make sense of what was happening to her, although perhaps knowing the method to the madness may actually impede that goal. It is harder to be scared of the unknown if the unknown becomes known and difficult to remain in a state of confusion about the purpose if one can see that confusion IS the purpose.

But madness or schizophrenia isn't quite the mystery it appears, in fact there is a clear bio-chemical origin behind the transformation from sanity to what is generally termed 'insanity'. Barbara O'Brien reveals in her book that she:

"…became very curious about the psychiatrists who suspected a relationship between schizophrenia and a dysfunction of the adrenal gland."

Under conditions of mental or physical stress the body produces adrenalin. There's no mystery here and this process is well understood by most people. What is slightly more arcane and what has caused a stir in the truth community is adrenochrome. Unfortunately, a lot of what the truth movement is saying about adrenochrome is unfortunately wrong. The elite do not drink it as some kind of elixir of eternal youth, this is all disinformation and nonsense.

Adrenochrome is oxidised adrenalin, that is adrenalin which has gone bad. It is a neurotoxin and free-radical and is not something you want in the body. Adrenalin is produced in the body as a result of stress and anxiety, and it naturally degrades to adrenochrome, however in a healthy body and with a small release of adrenalin, it is safely scavenged by anti-oxidants in the body and excreted. However, if the period of stress, anxiety or prolonged uncertainty, can be sustained over a long time, then the release of adrenalin becomes continuous and the body can no longer safely scavenge the adrenochrome toxin and it starts to build up in the body.

Adrenochrome is a psychoactive compound; its effects are somewhat like LSD but whereas a bad LSD trip will eventually wear off, adrenochrome build up, in a suitably stressed or terrorised individual, will not wear off: leading to a potentially permanent condition of what is effectively intoxication by a powerful psychoactive compound running perpetually through the bloodstream. This condition is known as schizophrenia. Dr Abraham Hoffer's work in identifying adrenochrome as the 'schizophrenia' toxin as well as the possibility of treatment with high doses of niacin also known as vitamin B3, would clear up some of the great mysteries of our times as well as almost instantly solving the world-wide mental illness epidemic; but there are powerful vested interests who perhaps would lose countless millions of dollars in such an event.

Adrenochrome is not an elixir of life, it does not have any positive effects on the body. Hoffer conducted experiments with the ingestion of Adrenochrome and reported his findings in his research paper entitled The Effect of Adrenochrome and Adrenolutin on the Behavior of Animals and the Psychology of Man.

Previously Hoffer had apparently administered adrenochrome to various creatures including spiders, fish, and pigeons to the mammals including rats, cats, dogs, monkeys. One wonders how the spiders felt about being given adrenochrome, one suspects none of the animals had a particularly good trip.

To quote from the paper:

"Some of the changes produced by adrenochrome may persist several days, and in some cases, the effects lead to nearly disastrous results.

The changes in thinking induced by adrenochrome are similar to those observed in schizophrenia. Adrenochrome causes an elective inhibition of the process, which determines the content of associative thinking."

https://www.sciencedirect.com/science/article/pii/S00747774208600252

The mind under a burden of adrenochrome enters a different state of consciousness. Schizophrenia is basically a form of consciousness and it is precisely this state which the UFO cults, the secret societies and Sufi mentors are trying to induce.

The scientific explanation for how it works is complex but basically adrenochrome is antagonistic to GABA fluid. GABA fluid is an electrical brain insulator which keeps the brain synapsis and neurons under control by reducing electrical charge. With adrenochrome the electromagnetic structure of the mind is totally changed. The usual natural dampening mechanisms of the brain's physiology which control the mind, and one might even say, protect the soul from too much awareness in the physical realm, are bypassed leading to a break-down in the mechanism of control over the mental processes of the mind and that sense of estrangement from reality which so familiar to the schizophrenic.

Where things get really strange is that some of the experiences which go along with this altered state of consciousness are not necessarily unreal because they are taking place in altered consciousness. For instance, if you are sleeping you are in a different level of consciousness. What is happening in your dream to your unconsciousness mind is real for that level of consciousness. When you are awake you are in a different level of consciousness, and in effect, a different level of reality.

The adrenochrome experience, actually puts you in a different level of reality and this level of reality is shared by high level Illuminati people and other types who have had specific experiences which have put them in this same level of reality. While in this level of reality they can hear each other's thoughts and are able to perceive demonic and spiritual energies. The Illuminati consider this the peak of human development and call it 'Illumination'. They deliberately induce this state because they find it allows them to have psychic and clairvoyant faculties because the brain is operating beyond its normal limits. We find this curious attitude even within the scientific community as attested by Barbara O'Brien:

"Consider the most extreme of the theories. 'I am almost convinced,' said one biologist, 'that the schizophrenic is an attempt on the part of nature at forming a mutation.'

Historically, the ancient cults believed that there were ways to access altered states of consciousness and in these states, they could communicate with the unseen spirits, or 'Gods'. Every culture in the world has a mythology that the Gods taught them the various crafts, arts and skills which enabled the human race to create the first civilisations within a time frame reaching back to the last 10,000 years, a period which coincides with the end of the last ice-age.

The oracles of the ancient world were usually people who through various methods, existed in a semi-permanent state of altered consciousness which allowed them to see the future and contact the unseen spirit world. Such abilities have always been lauded by the occult and secret-world which has always existed since the very dawn of human civilisation, after all, it would seem that these people were instrumental in gaining such knowledge using occult methods, if the ancient records which come up time and time again are to be believed and since the records all seem to say the same thing regardless of the geographical location, then there must be some truth behind these myths.

"According to the psychoanalyst who treated me, spontaneous recoveries are rare and weird events in advanced schizophrenia and when they occur they present a mysterious spectacle – that of a mind walking out of a fourth dimension into which it has been propelled"

For a schizophrenic to describe their condition as being propelled into the fourth dimension is quite apt, though for some they consider the feeling like being in hell, or even like being in a state of living death. One can see how such an enigmatic and mysterious state of reality might have become the interest and domain of a particular group of people a very long-long time ago in human history. There is even the possibility that the 'curse of Cain' refers to this condition but this is superstition and theorising and nothing more.

Perhaps a brief psychotic episode was also a feature of many of the ancient mystery school initiations: a figurative period in the underworld mired in despair and the fear of death only to pass beyond and out of this realm, back to the realm of life, but this time transformed and with the sure knowledge that there is a whole mysterious hidden realm behind the scenes or normal consciousness; this state being induced either through various trials and tribulations, or through fasting and the ingestion of psycho-active compounds.

Barbara O'Brien seems to see her experience in these terms, almost like a kind of journey through madness and return to normalcy:

"The guidance was clearer than the planning. I had been maneuvered into a hospital when I unconsciously suspected pneumonia; maneuvered into visiting a doctor when I unconsciously suspected a mastoid; maneuvered to a mountain cabin when I was exhausted from bus traveling; provided with a flashlight so that I wouldn't fall on a dark road; rescued from a mountain lion; maneuvered out of the mountain cabin the morning after the mountain lion incident; reminded punctually of meal times and the necessity for eating; reminded punctually (during the last month) of the need for brushing my teeth and other grooming. Whatever mental level the guidance had come from, it was clearly some level other than the this-is-I dry beach, and it had made certain that the organism was kept in good physical condition while the dry beach was incapable of providing the car

The planning was almost as obvious. Even on the first day, the voices had sketched in the picture of things to come. This was an experiment the Operators had told me. My mind was going to be controlled by Operators and I should have to be cooperative for my own sake as well as for theirs. And Nicky had added, as if the success of the experiment were being weighed, I would have one chance in three hundred of escaping the Operators and I would have to be lucky in the bargain. I had been manoeuvred away from home, where publicity of my insanity would have made life difficult after sanity had been regained, and where also there existed a company for which I persisted in working and toward which I had developed long established, difficult-to-change attitudes. I had been induced into riding Greyhound buses, where I could sit in schizophrenic apathy while I lived in my mental world, a state of being almost identical on the surface with the usual bus passenger who stares at the landscape, his mind on inner reflections. I had been coaxed into writing letters that would keep the home folk happy, manoeuvred to California by the Lumberjacks, figures apparently created for that very purpose, and had been induced to stay in California for the final act. And when the fall of the final curtain was sense

It had occurred in an article by a psychiatrist who had cautiously avoided jumping into the lake of guesswork and who, instead, had stood on the center of a seesaw and observed carefully both sides of all the mysteries of schizophrenia. One of these observations was, "Whether the schizophrenic really creates a dream world intentionally and purposefully, or whether he finds himself in one is debatable."

It is possible that she has rationalised it thus since she has the luxury of having sanity to put the experience into some kind of rational framework. Most people having such an experience of schizoid-psychosis of this kind are not so lucky and have to remain permanently in the underworld.

My experiences began in France in the year 2001, I was living amidst the mountains in the middle of France, in the area known as Le Massif Central, a large area of ancient mountains mostly comprised of long extinct volcanoes covered with woodlands, farms and green pastures. The town I lived in, Le Puy en Velay is an amazing mediaeval town; like many of the small towns in the area, there were Romanesque churches, chapels and the remains of sturdy stone fortresses scattered throughout the area, usually perched on top of the hilltops of the extinct volcanoes. The whole area is known as France profonde, or deep France, a place not really on the tourist-track because most non-French people don't really know it's there and the area seems quite happy to be ignored to perhaps retain its identity and to be left to their farming and their strange folkloric cults when on certain days of the year, you can see people going around at night in fancy dress carrying burning torches through the cobbled streets of the mediaeval town.

I was having a great time there lazily teaching English at a small local English cultural centre, and not being made to work too hard, and just generally enjoying French life which is something that is pretty easy to do. However, everything changed and my life of insouciance and lazy ease ended: indeed, it would be no exaggeration to say that my whole life changed, when I was enrolled on a residential training course organised by the French government called the BAFA. It was a ten-day course at a remote location around a 45 minute drive deeper into the mysterious mountains and villages of deep and forgotten France at a strange old mediaeval village mostly made of black volcanic stone called Sauges.

It's a little hard for me to talk about this because it means I have to relive a lot of traumatic and frankly, at the time, terrifying memories, however I have to say that I have no bitterness or regret about anything that happened to me because frankly, it's been a hell of a ride I'm briefly going to let my sepulchral and slightly deranged friend William Burrough's chip in here:

"Now some of you may encounter the Devil's Bargain,
If you get that far.
Any old soul is worth saving,
At least to a priest,
But not every soul is worth buying.
So you can take the offer as a compliment."

Years later, in a house in Haworth, the town famous for the Bronte sisters, in Yorkshire I was very specifically offered the devil's bargain. The offer was to make me a famous writer in return for..... well.....my soul for several lifetimes of servitude in all likelihood. But it all seemed to begin in France, the first steps on the road to joining the Illuminati.

The Illuminati are not just millionaires and billionaires and creepy old men. They're everywhere, you probably even have a friend or two who might even be part of it without you ever knowing. Perhaps they got into it through work, or maybe they joined a special local pagan group who do strange things in the woods at midnight.

The Illuminati is not a group with membership cards and a register of members: it is a frame of mind and the aim of Illuminati recruitment is to slowly draw you in and surround you, slowly revealing themselves and using various psychological techniques, they induce a specific frame of mind in their victim in order to make them into one of them.

The Illuminati are in an all-out recruitment drive and you probably wonder how it's possible for instance to compromise the whole media and politics apparatus so absolutely as we witnessed in 2020 with the electoral coup in America. This is Illuminati infiltration, and the apparent mask of normality which these people may present in public hides a vastly different and shockingly strange inner world which only fellow travellers will be familiar with.

These people are now working as teachers in schools, as police-officers, and in the business-world: anywhere where there is influence over people and power, which in their world means the ability to disseminate the new-agenda to society at all levels. We have seen how in 1967 the agenda was revealed to Raymond Bernard by the group of 12 hooded figures in white-robes with the ability to hypnotise him with a word. The ongoing agenda is the destruction of borders and the end of nations, then apparently we will be fit to receive our alien brothers; though I am pretty sure there are no alien brothers, it is just something being used as a carrot to incite suggestible idealistic people, and we are now living with the idealism of open borders and the destruction of our nation before our very eyes and it seems that high ideals have no-where to hide when faced with the grooming, rape and murder of our children by a group of people inimically to our way of life while the police authorities seemingly cover for them and even arrest their victims. It is clear that whatever that hooded group meeting in the house near a forest with a black and white marble floor represents, they are the people who have written our present nightmare.

But to return to France, the course for the first few days seemed to be what it was supposed to be, a little intense and loaded with information about how to run holiday camps for children and teenagers; learning fun activities to do with the kids and also taking part in the organisation of paper chase around the town and the surrounding hills and woods.

But slowly something strange started happening. First a vague suspicion that things weren't quite as they seemed to be; that I wasn't quite in on what was going on with the people around me. Admittedly I was English and the other 30 odd 'trainees' were French, but there was a gulf beyond that, something else which was hard to define, then slowly it became a little clearer what was happening. The other trainees were not all trainees. Some of them were 'plants' and were in amongst the trainees to watch over, get to know, psychologically assess then slowly destabilise the genuine trainees. I noticed this quite quickly but reasoned that since this was a government course from the monolithic French state which would lead to becoming qualified to be trusted to run holiday camps for children, then they had to look out for dodgy characters. So, feeling like Number 6 in the Village, I was trying to figure out who were the trainees and who were the trainers. I thought I'd figured it out but there was something else going on. Something far bigger and weirder.

We went out for a drink with the other trainees, for a small village on a Tuesday evening the bar was surprisingly busy. It was literally heaving with people, and when I would look around, I found people watching me, not just one or two people but everyone. Then someone decided to order for everyone at the bar. Everyone ordered a different drink and when I asked for a glass of red wine everybody suddenly stopped talking and looked at me, there were noises of disapproval, it was very strange, like one of those weird scenes from a movie, in fact almost exactly like the scene from Vanilla Sky where everybody stops and looks at Tom Cruise's character, while the computerised AI assistant tries to tell Tom that none of this is real and he is in control of everyone in here. In fact, the movie came out the same year and when I watched it, I became surprised at how much of this film might be the strange kind of inexplicable phenomena which could be arranged by gang-stalking and groups of people being orchestrated to behave in certain ways to convince a targeted person that there is something unreal about the present situation.

By far the strangest thing that happened was returning to the dormitory and trying to relax, I started listening to my Walkman, back then we still had tape Walkmans, well, at least I did, and this had a radio integrated. I don't know how they could have known I would bring a radio but when I started listening, I heard the same programme on all the stations. It was a strange kind of trance inducing type of music and there were a few phrases repeated, one of which I remember was 'Open the files on the FBI' and repetition of the phrase 'keep it a secret' repeated regularly.

This was something which the young man enrolled in the University High School also experienced. I expect they had a local transmitter set up which allowed them to dominate the waveband of my radio, at the time it became clear to me that I was involved in something much bigger than just a training programme for running holiday camps for French children.

A few years after I became a TEFL teacher, I attended a job interview for a teaching job in Tokyo in that house in Haworth. During the interview the man who would become my boss, but whom I referred to as the Demon King or DK for short, since he seemed more decaying ghoul than human being, asked me what I wanted out of life, I told him I wanted to be a famous writer, he said 'that could be arranged' and then told me if I took the job I would have 'something better than friends'.

It turned out that the 'school' was a tiny three room converted apartment in a Tokyo office block; there were three people, me the boss and the secretary. In fact, it wasn't actually a school at all, but it was an organisation devoted to training agents of the security services, or spies, and inculcating people into the Illuminati. That's where I found myself. Being trained to be a spy, and being brought into Illuminati consciousness. The man was a Freemason and I was expected to join the Freemasons before I could be fully 'let in' but the things I had seen and the people I had met within the organisation were so repulsive and morally disgusting that I desperately wanted to get out of it somehow.

Years later, back in England I found myself doing another training programme and the same secret organisation made itself known to me and made me a different offer, this time they used successfully passing the course itself as leverage to encourage me to join. During this time many strange things happened to me.

I became increasingly aware that there was some odd invisible force which seemed to be making things happen around me. It was hard to know whether this outside force was something positive or negative; but there seemed to be two elements to it: one which arranged coincidences for me which seemed to benefit me and another which seemed to order certain people to gather and appear at a certain time or place like a kind of flash-mob. Among the group of the latter there were some who were clearly mentally-ill and were street-tramp types or just wandering odd-balls who seemed somehow 'clued in' to me and on one occasion between Convent Garden and Leicester Square one of them loudly shouted to the people around, signalling me 'Don't you know who he is? He's a king!".

There were other people around me who seemed to be part of my new consciousness; there was a sense somehow that we were sharing a reality continuum, instead of being separate individuals. I suspect I may have experienced the Theosophical doctrine of so called 'Oneness' which the New-Age constantly parrot, and tell us is the ultimate goal.

During the course in London, I felt myself changing. I had always been interested in the occult and I couldn't deny the interesting and insinuating offers which had been made to me in the past and I thought myself a kind of occult celebrity: the man they are all trying to recruit. Also, I was daily subjected to strange coincidences which convinced me that I had some great growing power and I also found myself able to achieve strange feats of weather control. Reality become more and more fluid and more and more interesting but I soon learned that I wasn't alone to exist in this semi-magical reality. Some very strange things started happening and suddenly I found myself living in a Jason Bourne style wonderland.

At one point I went out of the house I was living in in Whitechapel on the edge of the City of London for a jog; as I passed through the financial city I went down an alleyway near the main offices of Merrill Lynch, I stopped to catch my breath and suddenly three suited business men turned to face me as I walked down the alley, looking straight at me they said in unison 'Join us!' I knew they were Masons because prior to this my tutor had put pressure on me to join the Masons. I had been told I 'wasn't square enough'. I knew what this meant because since my adventures in Japan I had learned to recognise Masonic key words and insinuations. In retrospect I managed to make sense of all this, just as I had made sense of the strange indoctrination course in the remote French village, but at the time, having people I'd never met before in the street directly addressing me to 'join them' was rather surprising and I wondered what strange parallel universe I had strayed into.

At around the same time I received a phone call from my ex French girlfriend, I'd always suspected that she wasn't always being perfectly frank with me while I lived with her in France (she has since told me that she was indeed a member of something but still stubbornly refuses to tell me what) much more so after the strange BAFA course which had opened my eyes to the potential that some of my relationships where not what they seemed. She phoned me during these couple of weeks when the tension and uncertainty of the past couples of years: the Masons and spies in Tokyo; the odd radio messages during the French teaching course, and the strange fellow trainees on the Paris Celta course who seemed to be wanting me to acquiesce to them in some way and join something in order to be part of the group, all of this had come to some kind of incredible crescendo and all seemed about to be revealed. Now she phoned me and asked me frankly, 'are you going to join the Masons then?' At this point I was not surprised, despite my having mentioned nothing of recent developments to her: but at a certain point with Masonic involvement in your life, you start to assume that anything is possible and everybody knows your business. The final awareness that my former girlfriend too was also involved in this strange international conspiracy came as no surprise and it was in fact quite a relief that finally she was being honest with me.

She then passed me on to her father who is the president of one of the French sports federations, he also asked me if I was going to join, and it seemed to me that the size, organisation and hidden means and methods of this secret group meant that I felt like a very small cog in an immense and all-powerful machine, I told him I didn't think I had much choice. Then, even more bizarrely, he passed me onto my ex's grandparents who happened to be there as well. Her grandmother seemed extremely pleased that I was going to become a Mason, her enthusiasm was almost contagious and it seemed that perhaps becoming a Mason was a good thing. But it all seemed so staged. It was odd that her grandmother should also be at the house as they lived nearly fifty miles away and rarely visited except on special occasions. Was this a special occasion? My final admittance/acquiescence into the Freemasons.

I had encountered people who, one way or another, were able to report on exactly what I was thinking at any time. And so, it occurred to me that, in the manner of The Coming Race by Edward Bulwer-Lytton and The Sky People by Brinsley Poer Trench (a curious book which is ostensibly addressed to psychic people to warn them of the consequences of the rabble finding out about their abilities) that there was an elect group of people who were not like everyone else and that these people hid remarkable powers and ultimately controlled the whole world.

So, one night of 'should I's?' and 'what ifs?' had finally allowed me to put all my doubts about joining the Masons behind me and I was ready to receive what they had to bestow on me. I opened myself to the spirits which had congregated around me and as I lay down in my bed it felt like a Jean-Michel Jarre light show was going off in my brain; with a final sudden flash I knew I was changed. It felt like coming up from a tab of acid.

Initially all this seemed a lot of fun: I felt exhilarated, supercharged and giddily happy, it was as if I was surfing down the street on light itself. I realised that light is in a way, a kind of God fluid which contains eternity and infinity within it and records every moment of reality and can preserve it for ever; it also responds to us if we are mentally connected to it since light and electromagnetic energy is the stuff of our very consciousness. It is possible to tune into the signal of the sun which is a portal from the quantum microcosm from which all the energy in the universe is released.

During the daylight hours my new 'illuminated' consciousness seemed to have few drawbacks: I felt slightly trippy and as I said reality had suddenly become a lot more uncertain and unpredictable.

What slowed me down and put a curb on my enthusiasm was the discovery of all my brothers and sisters in London, particularly in the Square Mile of the city of London.

Total strangers would appear in the street and suddenly ask me questions. People would also look at me and wink knowingly. If I didn't know better, I would say I had entered some kind of communal consciousness and in the London streets on the outskirts of the financial city, there were a lot of fellow Masonic inmates with whom I was now sharing my new reality. A shopkeeper would see me passing and make a private sign of acknowledgement to me. I'd never seen the man in my life but apparently, we had something in common, rather like the film Fight Club where the nameless Edward Norton character sees total strangers in distant cities acknowledging him and cannot understand it, this is exactly what it's like to enter the Freemason domain. When your consciousness undergoes the change in perception there seems to be something about you, perhaps you are mentally broadcasting something, which makes you recognisable to your 'brothers'. Personally speaking, as a private person who values his individuality, I wasn't quite sure I fancied the idea of suddenly being a part of this secret community within a community, particularly as one of the things I liked about London was the ability for one to remain anonymous and vanish into part of the crowd.

Suddenly I was hyper aware and could see the truth of anything and everything instantly. I saw that there were many more people like me out there than I had ever imagined and what's more, they were not the wise and kindly chosen ones but instead grumpy surly and vicious.

At the time I didn't understand quite how this beautiful and remarkable enlightenment could turn people bad but it didn't take long to realise that this psychic world was very strongly policed and by a force who had no qualms about doing anything in order to control you. This ranges from drafting doctors in to question you in the middle of the night while you're on your way somewhere: he held a walkie-talkie and looked me in the eyes as he made a pretence of asking me for directions. It was clear to me that he was testing to see if I was mentally ill, I knew what he was thinking and what his intentions were. I even knew who had sent him. He was part of it. I was surprised but not quite bowled over with shock and at one point I was sure he was going to make a move to apprehend me but something in me wasn't to be cowed, and he thought better of it.

As I say, this was a while back during my 'enlightenment' experience. Rest assured dear reader that your faithful narrator is sound as a pound and as bright as a button these days. Please don't get the impression that you are reading the diaries of a madman or anything, but I daresay, some of what I am saying here does sound a bit peculiar, but anyway, it's out there. You can choose whether to accept it or not.

However, it seems that certain members of this group: people you've never met before in your life, know as much about your private business as you yourself do, as I found in Tokyo when my employer would hold imaginary phone conversations in the next room mentioning things about me and my life while pretending it had nothing to do with me. Subsequently while working at a Catholic school some months later another Mason was talking aloud to no one in particular, but was using coded language and advising me to join the Masons, he said: 'we know all about you so you'd better join or else' without actually addressing me specifically: he would sort of stand near me and speak to me as if there were someone behind me, when of course there was no one. Again, I had never met the man before, but it seemed my reputation preceded me wherever these creepy crawly Masons are lurking about. In another school a Mason addressed me and cryptically asked me: 'are you a rebel of are you part of the Empire?' Of course, I answered 'I'm a rebel' and he said 'well I'm part of the Empire.' I don't know if this was an attempt at intimidation of some kind, but it was genuinely difficult to be intimidated by this rather disgusting and fruity looking fat man who could well have been the school paedophile. There was something oily about the fruity smile that played on his face whenever he was near the kids.

One of the major drawbacks of all this was I felt I was losing my individual will and somehow dissolving into the will of others. And again, as I had experienced in Tokyo, I noticed one or two people around me would talk about me, actually offering me deals and promises if I joined them. What I was experiencing was extreme, distilled coincidence, but with a slightly negative uneasy twinge. I believe that synchronicity as it is called, the odd timing of events which coincide together and seem to create mystical meaning at the oddness of the coincidence, is used by the hidden forces for both positive and negative purposes. With it they can bring people together from miles apart and involve certain people in teaching lessons or initiating someone, totally without the prior knowledge of the person thus targeted or even the person doing the targeting. This explains much of the recent 'gang-stalking' phenomenon.

At one point I must have inadvertently become a 'highly-evolved mystic' because I experienced these so-called 'astral images' but in the same breath I imagine you count the whole population of hallucinating schizophrenics and part-time psychotics among that jolly gang. It was an extraordinary time for me, possibly the most amazing and at the same time, the most confusing and terrifying thing to have ever happened to me. I can look back now in peace and comfort at the experience and thank God that I am no longer half wading through the astral-realm in a half waking half-dreaming hell-reality which is what I might on the spur of the moment describe this Illuminati consciousness as.

These 'astral visions' are waking hallucinations, and as the Martinists claim and as I also believe, they have their origins in the invisible spiritual power which is attempting to negatively control Earth. While I was personally under the spell of the Freemasons, and navigating the 'underworld' I remember looking at the title of the book someone was reading in front of me while on a train, I could only see it reflected in the window next to him and as I tried to decipher the inverted letters it appeared to read 'Remote control humans' and I had an odd feeling of some extra-terrestrial force which is seeming to use and control humans for their own entertainment

The experience I had was a mixture of psychic and physical symptoms, for instance there was often a severe cramping pain in the back of the head concurrent with these visions, this is the part of the brain associated with vision, but what would 'trigger' this pain and the resultant visions? These experiences started in real earnest after submitting to initiation by the 'hidden-masters'. The hidden masters are not the figment of Madame Blavatsky's imagination but they are quite real and the initiate is followed everywhere by a ghostly entourage who are continually whispering dangerous suggestions and indeed, prompting these 'visions' into the person's brain.

Straightaway it doesn't sound quite as much fun does it? If you're in any doubt at this stage that contacting spirits may not be fun then you need only look into the tragic but extremely instructive example of poor Joe Fisher in his book The Siren Call of the Hungry Ghosts in which he details being the victim of very complex and prolonged deception, not at the hands of spiritualists, who he says were just as much dupes as he, but in fact the architects of deception in this instance were the spirits themselves who for some reason, wanted at all costs to be involved in any way in the human realm, to the extent that they would invent personalities and tell people what they wanted to hear, in order to create an existence for themselves.

I'll say nothing more except to profoundly recommend that you read the book. Also be aware that the author became so intimidated by the spirits who apparently became angry at being exposed as being behind some kind of inter-dimensional con game, that he took his own life. So already those contacting the galaxy shenanigans don't seem to be quite so much fun. Turn off the engines Scotty: I'm staying-in tonight.

I can testify to the experience of having spirits take rather an over active interest in one's activities. This was all within the timeframe of my whacky three weeks of enlightened madness. I found myself becoming more and more psychically tuned to a higher frequency; I felt less need to eat, sleep and started feeling giddy and lightheaded. I had all the symptoms of the enlightenment or ascension, or Kundalini awakening and you will be able to find this 'symptom list' in one of the thousand occult themed new-age websites out there in cyber-web land, or at least you used to. I suspect they have achieved their recruitment goals and as a result the New Age movement has gone very quiet lately and gone back underground in order to proceed to the next step of covert world control.

As day turned to night, I began to feel increasingly aware of a stronger and stronger feeling of fear. It was something invisible which seemed to be moving closer to me with the falling darkness. At this time, I became aware of their real agents of control for the first time. Prior to this I has encountered their street theatrics whereby themes prevalent in my life, such as my attachment to the ideals of Jesus and early Christianity would be externalised and I would emerge from the tube station to see someone ranting satirically about Christians going to heaven and non-believers being sent to hell, a kind of ridiculous pastiche of Christianity designed to turn me against ideas of religion. These people were easy to spot: some people can smell a fake, a provocateur and a phoney from a mile off. As I walked out the man winked at me. Such events happened several times during this period. These people constantly watch their own members, they will only let you know if they want you to know and the only people they can afford to let into the secret are their own members who they police mercilessly.

I felt afraid that I was about to become a Freemason despite part of me knowing that perhaps their ethics and morals left a lot to be desired. They were actively trying to recruit me at the school where I I was training, indeed they had been trying to get me to join them for the past eight or so years from France to Japan. But I has always brushed off their hints and insinuations and moved on, now it seemed I was finally cornered and blackmailed that unless I joined, I might fail the course, and I didn't want to fail the course.

As for the policing aspect: for instance, they don't much like their members to be seen running anywhere. I suppose because it draws attention to yourself and they avoid that at all costs. A few times I had been admonished by various of their agents for running in the street. Once indeed I ran across the road between cars, as you do, only to find a man on the other side move into my direction and attempt to push me back into the road. Fortunately, I had enough will power to get through him but a weaker person would have found their earthly adventure terminated right there and then. And this is how they do it, many so-called tragic accidents are often anything but, but are carefully concealed and orchestrated Masonic murders. This is such a new area of research that it is difficult to provide anything which may pass for proof. You can take my word: I feel enough of what I have written here has the ring of truth. If not, you can disbelieve this as unlikely and implausible, I won't hold it against you. Just watch out and be aware that things are not always as they seem and if you ever find yourself in a perilous situation and for some reason a total stranger seems to have it against you and is trying to end your life, don't panic. Just stay mentally strong and keep moving, never freeze or allow confusion to take you because that may be the last feeling to ever cross your mind: often in these cases the biggest paralysing factor is fear, surprise and confusion.

As I said, the enlightenment allows you to 'read' something in people's thoughts. Just as I knew what the intentions of the doctor with the walkie-talkie were. You don't hear their thoughts as such, not in words, but you just know what they're thinking and you receive them as a kind of bundle of instant awareness of what is going through their mind and what their intentions are. This is something I had long suspected about these people and it was a power which seemed so alien and invasive that I had been quite frightened by it. I now realised however that the kind of people who can read your thoughts are not powerful, they are powerless and experiencing a potentially harmful condition of adrenochrome toxicity. It is the extreme heightened mental sensitivity which allows them to know another person's thoughts but this extreme mental sensitivity makes them highly vulnerable.

I had left the house in Whitechapel I was staying in, to return to my parents' house and get some distance between me and what seemed to be happening around me. I later discovered I had been put on the Missing-Persons Register since my parents received a phone-call although when I tried to contact the Missing Persons Register to tell them I was perfectly safe and enquire who it was who had reported me 'missing' they said they had no such record. This is the kind of weird Masonic stuff that tends to grow around you when these people are watching you and you do something unexpected such as suddenly leaving Whitechapel at night and trying to catch a train back to see your parents to clear your head and break free of the strange Illuminati mental spell. This is not something they had accounted for and so because I tried to leave the track or groove they had planned for me, they declared me a missing person, probably providing a description of me and then have doctors with walkie-talkies patrolling to look out for me, and who knows where I would have ended up had I been apprehended especially in my 'illuminated' state-of-mind which could easily be medically classed as a kind of psychosis.

Once I made it to my destination and managed to clear my head a bit and then attempted to find out what was going on the whole network vanished into thin-air. It is quite amazing really and I am glad I saw such an incredible thing that most people not part of the Family will never experience and those that do, probably end up locked into it for life: permanent residents of the Hotel California.

I knew without question however that the process of psychic development was speeding up apace and before long I started to have the 'astral images' which the Martinists talk about. Of all these changes one of the most telling is the total disappearance of the sex drive. This led me to conclude that what I had experienced was the so-called Kundalini enlightenment as this is commonly mentioned as one of the symptoms. Another possible side effect of Kundalini enlightenment is schizophrenia and I personally think schizophrenia is actually the outcome of the various mystical, secret society and Masonic initiations, just as Osiris was dismembered by Set, and re-membered by Isis, his psyche was fractured and put back together but his sexual potency, represented by the phallus, was never found. In the Hindu concept of Kundalini enlightenment, it is said that the Kundalini energy originates in the sacral chakra, or the tail bone at the very base of the spine. This energy is also that which is apparently used for reproduction and to create the life and energy of sperm or ovum.

With the use of certain techniques, such as prolonged periods of stress, uncertainty and sleep deprivation, it is possible for this energy to rise from the sexual centre and, as chi, to energise the higher chakras or glandular centres of the body, making them work harder to produce physical and mental characteristics not normally encountered. This is the Kundalini enlightenment and in itself has the potential to be a force of good. It is possible that Jesus himself had this experience and it was this which allowed him to connect with and know God so completely, however as we now from the story of Jesus, it left him vulnerable to malign elements who would ultimately take his life. Unfortunately, there are a great deal of very bad people around who have hijacked this knowledge for their own use and have taken measures which mean that anyone undergoing enlightenment will, one way or another, fall under their control.

I suggest that our mental hospitals are full of shamans who see too much and might be in danger of revealing their insights, were they not handily dismissed as 'nut-jobs' and locked up for our 'protection'. However, there are schizophrenics who do represent a genuine danger to the public, yet these people are often released back into the community to kill/stab again. They themselves are part of an unofficial occult police force and it is for this reason that we often find schizophrenics involved in murders and attempted murders where either 'the devil told me to do it', 'God told me to do it' or 'a voice told me to do it'. I also noticed a 2010 press release in a tabloid paper (I think the now defunct News of the World which explains the lack of available source) which detailed the case of a newly released schizophrenic who murdered an elderly man in an apparently unmotivated attack. The one puzzling fact about the case is that the murderer said to his victim 'I know you' before he brutally murdered him.

'I know you!', like 'how's your mother?' and 'how old are you?' not to mention 'Are you Mark?', are all typically cryptic forms of Masonic greeting and identification. Like secret-agent passwords and counter signs, but these phrases are designed to blend into normal conversation and appear completely innocuous, or at most, like a case of mistaken identity. I suggest therefore that the schizophrenic murdered the elderly gentleman as part of a targeted occult murder. I mentioned this to a family member who also knows a great deal about the Freemasons and he told me that this sheds light on the recent death of a very prominent local Freemason's son out in China. It appears that the Mason in question, despite being the grand Poobah of the region was also universally unpopular with other Masons. Therefore, it was hypothesised that his son's mysterious death abroad could be attributed to some kind of Masonic vengeance. Whatever the truth, it is clear that signing the Devil's bargain has seriously unpleasant consequences for those rash enough to sign it. If you want a long and happy life then don't join the Masons, if however, you long for a life of pain and uncertainty, confusion, degradation and slavery then the Masons will make your every dream come true.

The UFO cult began in earnest in the 19th century, amidst the spiritualism movement which began in the 1840's in New York, partially or even wholly inspired by the work of Emmanuel Swedenborg and Franz Mesmer. Swedenborg was a Freemason who lived throughout the 18th Century and believed he could communicate with spirits while awake and claims to have visited heaven and hell, he also believed that Jesus Christ himself visited him and told him to reform Christianity to prepare for his arrival.

The founder of Methodism John Wesley called Swedenborg "one of the most ingenious, lively, and entertaining madmen that ever set pen to paper" and in their book, Kingdom of the Cults (2003) Martin and Zacharias write of Swedenborg:

"He was deceived by dreams and visions and the machinations of him whom the Scriptures describe as the 'spirit that now worketh in the children of disobedience'". The Christian writers John Ankerberg and John Weldon say that he "fell prey to deceiving spirits and ignored the Bible's warnings against spirit contact because he believed 'good' spirits had taught him the truth."

In Swedenborg's Spiritual Diary we can read fascinating accounts of Swedenborg's experience of the spirit world and his communication with what may or may not be the genuine spirits of the dead and recently dead, including King George II the King of England who has been dead for a month when Swedenborg apparently spoke to his ghost as well as Pope Benedict XIV three weeks after his death. He also spoke to Aristotle who appeared to him in rather a rough and forlorn state because all of his works had only given rise to scientism without faith and had drawn men away from God, what Swedenborg terms "learned dust" but it was only the delight from drawing forth his thoughts into words and philosophy which redeemed Aristotle who was still what Swedenborg termed a 'good spirit', though apparently his followers and those who imbued his philosophy receive no such benefit.

Swedenborg's Spiritual Diary is an interesting document to read but one doesn't quite know what to make of it. There are some instances where Swedenborg might be accused of settling personal scores (sometimes with whole nations) with the people he knew in his lifetime since nearly everyone he knew in life who was considered a fine upstanding member of the community or church, or a man of genius and intelligence, is almost always presented as finding themselves in a forlorn and hopeless state in the next world where their apparent gifts can no longer avail them, or their piety in life was revealed in death to be just a sham.

One can't quite help feeling that the cards seem a little too stacked against the soul in the next world, especially if you happened to be an acquaintance of Swedenborg's. For instance he met the spirit of the eminent philosopher Christian Wolff whom he describes in the spirit world "now lives among fools and simpletons.. He has the appearance of a chimney-sweep, his learning turned into suffocating dust." Or of the Dutch whom he saw in the next world and states that they "Live in a vomit stench" because apparently some societies of the Dutch at that time had allowed their wives to rule over their husbands and that "they collected vessels full of vomit, and held the nostrils over them, and reveled in the stench." This sounds more like some kind anti-Dutch score-settling and Swedenborg, as a Jacobite secret-agent and supporter of the English pretender to the throne James II may have had many enemies during his time spent engaging in espionage in the Low Countries.

At one point Swedenborg says he is possessed by an evil spirit who is later revealed to be a well-known deceased figure of the church:

"There had been a certain spirit with me for some time in secret, who had connected himself [with me] from the delight of ruling and of perverting truths… He was the Archbishop Spegel."

So, if he were so easily possessed by an evil spirit is it not possible that a great deal of Swedenborg's spirit contact might not be from the same source designed specifically to mislead him? Could we not echo the words of that lady in the audience at the presentation by H.I.M. who asked "How do you know that you're not being deceived by demonic forces?"

It just seems too easy to endlessly dismiss everyone and besmirch everyone not to mention statistically improbable that everyone Swedenborg knew in life was languishing in death as a hypocrite and fraud. Swedenborg himself may have believed that the spirit was the Archbishop Spegel who had become a demonic spirit in death but in life the man was apparently tireless in his efforts of educating the people and encouraged every peasant to learn to read.

Some of his visions do not appear to be consistent and perhaps they are not absolute in themselves but co-dependent on Swedenborg's shifting personal opinions. For instance, in one of the entries in his Spiritual Diary he claims that in death, Mohammed has become a Christian and his followers are all shut out from heaven until they can accept Jesus as being God on Earth.

"As respects Mohammed, he is not among the Mohammedans, but among the Christians…The Mohammedans said that he is in that place because he has acceded to the Christian religion."

However, in some later entries Mohammed is now in chains and his followers vainly attempt to free him from a kind of stockade which they can't gain access to. As result of not being able to have 'their Mohammed' they choose another, a man from Germany to be their new Mohammed.

"The second Mohammed, who was in chains, and for whom they sought, was led forth; and it was discovered who he had been in the world, that, namely, he was born in Saxony."

Then apparently, they chose a third Mohammed:

"There was also another Mohammed, who was a Christian from Greece, who had a place behind that one and he, because he sometimes undertook his duties and worked diligently, was proclaimed [Mohammed] by the former one, and acknowledged by some among them who have thought of many Mohammeds."

This seems a little farcical even by the standards of organised religion and one can't help but think the whole thing is some kind of dark satire which had been designed to fascinate and captivate Swedenborg's attention and perhaps some of his own thoughts and fancies were brought to the fore, in the same way that Evelyn Waugh was captivated and also menaced, generally with mis-represented events from his own life. Furthermore, some of the things he is told show a lack of understanding about certain things, for instance I suspect that Swedenborg's knowledge of Jewish beliefs, were somewhat limited since we find the following entry in the Spiritual Diary:

"Thus Mohammedans who are saved acknowledge the Lord to be one with the Father, and almost hate Christians because they make three gods. In like manner the Jews laugh at Christians; especially because they make three gods..."

This is a peculiar thing to say since I have often contended that the origins of the Trinity come from the Zohar and indeed, Jews in the middle-ages being questioned by the Inquisition were said to have confessed that they too allow the Trinity in Jewish belief in the hope of trying to placate the inquisitors. From the Zohar:

"Come and see the mystery of the word YHVH: there are three steps, each existing by itself: nevertheless they are One, and so united that one cannot be separated from the other. The Ancient Holy One is revealed with three heads, which are united into one, and that head is three exalted.."

Swedenborg also had a pretty poor opinion of Swedes, the people not the vegetable, and recounts how he looked upon a street in Stockholm and the houses appeared to have no windows and the angels informed him that those who lived there were spiritually dead.

I do not think things are ever so simple as to classify whole groups of people or indeed, anyone as spiritually dead. The Quakers for instance have the belief that everyone is trying to do the best they can with what they have been given, it would seem unlikely to me that a being as exalted as an angel would be so quick to write people off as spiritually dead, such a sentence does not allow much chance of redemption or salvation which is, in Christian theory, continually on offer to all who repent of their sins and turn to God.

However, there are things which Swedenborg gets right, for instance when Swedenborg suggests a kind of defence against demonic or spiritual attack and it is one, I can also endorse:

"It was perceived that when the most deceitful spirits above the head spoke among themselves, wishing even to destroy me, they said they could not do it, because there was nothing of me to be found, but if there had been anything, they could have done it…But when it was represented that I was, as it were, nothing, then they seemed to themselves, to have no power over that which thus appeared as nothing, for they would then have nothing to assault. Thus he is safe who in true faith believes himself to be nothing."

It reminds me of the incident of the Nile delta farmer I had met in Egypt and how he always seemed to say exactly what I was thinking as if he was lifting his conversation straight from my own head.

I realised something weird was going on and started to feel a little peculiar, not quite in a panic but there was certainly some rising fear as if I had suddenly strayed into new and potentially dangerous territory, I can't imagine anyone would be particularly thrilled by the prospect of meeting someone who could read your mind. Perhaps you might start to think the 'man' wasn't a man at all but some kind of advanced alien extra-terrestrial, or perhaps some kind of demon or even an angel in human-form. It would certainly put you at a noticeable disadvantage and also potential embarrassment that whatever secrets you might want to keep would be almost impossible to seal up and might come bubbling to the surface for this uncanny fellow to sift up.

My practice has always been during intense periods of metaphysical flux and mental anxiety or disorder to enter a Zen state. I advise everybody in the world to learn to acquire the Zen state, it instantly 'switches off' anything which might be mentally dangerous or troubling and reminds you that you are not your thoughts, not even your personality, you are much more than this and your core consciousness is unassailable.

It is possible that Swedenborg is being given a blend of truth and lies and perhaps it is up to our discernment to find what we can find of use from his writings and discard that which seems a little too fevered. He also talks of dreams and like Barbara O'Brien and Pythagoras, the supposed author of the Pythagorean Commentaries, believes they are something that can be created by the spirits, something which European cultural folklore has long held to be true in any case and the word 'nightmare' includes the word 'mare' which is an Old English word for a kind of demonic goblin which rides on people's chests when they are asleep and gives them bad dreams.

All European languages have this same meaning for 'nightmare' in their respective languages and the concept has its origins in the earliest Proto-Indo-European root language which informs us that such beliefs stretch back to the very earliest days of settlement and civilisation of the European continent.

"I dreamt during the night and upon waking spoke with spirits who said that they had been watching around me, and that they had occasioned the dream, and had expressly induced everything that I remembered and related. From this it is still more manifest to me that dreams are from the world of spirits."

In the spirit world there are things which the spirits are not permitted to do under threat of punishment; the punishment seems to be carried out by other spirits of a malicious inclination who are constantly seeking some pretext to exert violence on other spirits, so a kind of rough justice, or honour among thieves seems to be established in this realm.

"Upon awaking I heard the spirits who were awake above me, and who wished to be present with me in my sleep; but sinking shortly afterwards into slumber, I had a disagreeable dream, and upon awaking it was said that it was those spirits who introduced the dream. Punishers were then, to my astonishment, immediately present, who afflicted them most miserably, by mentally inducing upon them a body and bodily senses, and by a continual rolling backwards and forwards, attended with resisting struggles, so that they were torn or wrenched.."

"I wondered that the punishers were so suddenly present, but it was perceived that it arose from the necessity of man's sleeping in security, as otherwise the human race would perish; such a punishment, therefore, follows from necessity, and that the punishers were so immediately present with a knowledge of their being authorized to act in this manner, was from the atrocity of the malice viewed in relation to this necessity."

Swedenborg observes the following which may explain the present problems we face in our day and age and how evil only seems to grow in power from year to year. According to Swedenborg, the origin of these evils on Earth is the ever growing evil of the spirit-world:

"...the world of spirits is so bad that it turns everything to evil, and becomes itself worse and worse, so that the equilibrium preponderates on their side; and seeing the world of spirits is such, it cannot be but that man himself should become worse by means of its influx..."

It is also noteworthy that his Spiritual Diary seems to comprise principally of Swedenborg making reference to spirits which had possessed him without his knowing it, or of evil spirits trying to throw him under the wheels of carriages; or he would wake up in the middle-of-the-night with the feeling of small snakes in his hair which had been plotting against him. This seems to be the tenor of his work and experience and at times seems hardly different from the psychotic experiences of Gilbert Pinfold and Barbara O'Brien.

There is however much of wisdom in what Swedenborg says, he is no doubt correct in his understanding about the nature of the demonic spirits which run amok, the problem however is that he opened the doors to this particular area to the Freemasons who did what only Freemasons can do, that is, keep it a secret and use it to their own advantage. If a genuine effort had been made to fully democratise this knowledge and inform everyone about this hidden aspect of life it would no doubt have led to a wonderful Christian revival and much of our understanding of the world and the nature of reality would been changed for the better. We would realise for instance that anger, negative thoughts and destructive behaviours to ourselves and others did not come from our authentic self but were the result of an infestation of demonic spirits and we would be in a far better position to improve ourselves by being able to distance ourselves from these thoughts and transcend them as something shameful from elsewhere, rather than own them and act on them as people are wont to do.

Swedenborg perhaps correctly observes that evil spirits continually attack men and are always busy influencing their thoughts, mostly undetected and unsuspected:

"The deceitful [spirits] who are above the head have flowed in for a considerable time and in some cases with so much subtlety that I knew not that it proceeded from them. For some time past a mere manifest reflection has been given me, and today a clearer still, so that I could observe how they flow into the subtle thought of man, which influx is such that man could never perceive the source of it. From close observation granted me by the Lord, I perceived this so manifestly as to notice each one of their common influxes, and if that close observation had not been granted, I should by no means have perceived whence the [influx flowed], still less that it was from those above the head, but [could have taken it to be] in myself and from myself, as other men think and even believe. But that it is from spirits I am now able to know more distinctly than ever before. When they apperceived that I was reflecting upon their influx they became highly indignant and wished, as they said, to withdraw, but they knew not whither."

Something that I have noticed personally is that when engaging in some task in the kitchen, the chances of injury or mischief are much greater if one allows oneself to become distracted by a stray thought. I call this the 'karma kitchen' as often while cooking, using sharp blades or high temperatures, I would sometimes find a painful or moderately embarrassingly memory intrude upon me, and I would often find that if I engaged in any delicate or potentially dangerous task, I ran the risk of cutting, burning or otherwise hurting myself. It is only in the kitchen that this happens, I do not get these unwelcome thoughts anywhere else and I wonder if indeed there is some malicious entities which awaits the very moment when we are most at risk of having an accident to attack us. Generally however, it makes sense that if we are continually assailed by these beings then there must be something which protects us. I myself have had this feeling several times, that there was always something which managed to prevent the worst outcome or stop an accident before it happened, through luck or a sudden fortuitous impulse.

"Today I particularly observed that they were in such a perpetual endeavour, for it was given to perceive it when they thus made the attempt, and indeed that the sphere of their endeavour is continually such that it is their life; and I perceived that man is continually preserved by the Lord, and their endeavours frustrated. Hence it appears that unless the Lord in every, even the smallest moment, preserved man, yea, even the least of his steps, he would immediately perish; such is the effort of the world of spirits."

I'm sure we can all think of personal examples from our lives where we have found ourselves miraculously protected or preserved from a bad outcome and we might marvel at these 'coincidences' that were put in place to protect us. I can think of many examples but one in particular always comes to my mind. When I was a student and rather hard-up living in East London, I had fallen behind on my rent. I tended to stay at home throughout this period, being quite comfortable and perhaps smoking a little too much cannabis to permit much external activity. However, one day I decided to take what seemed at the time an epic trip across London to spend the day at Hampstead Heath with my then girlfriend. London is of such a size that one tends to stick to one's neighbourhood since travel times across the city can be the equivalent of travelling fifty miles or so in the country. While out in Hampstead Heath, to our surprise we met our neighbours. It was indeed a remarkable coincidence to find that we had both decided to travel out all the way from East London to Hampstead Heath on such a day and I wondered if it had any meaning.

When we returned home later that day, we found our housemates then told us that the landlady had sent a couple of heavies around to try to squeeze the rent out of me. I have no idea what they would have done but from reports of my housemates they didn't seem very happy and were highly anxious to meet me. My great aunt had a pet-store near Hampstead Heath railway station and by chance a room was available in the house her son was renting in nearby Gospel Oak. I therefore quickly vacated the house in East London and moved my girlfriend, my chattels, and pot-plants out to Gospel Oak: I remember the tense overground rail journey during which I ferried the plants, hidden beneath a black bin bag but exuding such a strong distinctive aroma, it was impossible to not know what they were. I believe I had to make the trip three times to ferry all my plants across.

I was heartily glad that 'something' had inspired me to leave the house early in the day and spend the whole rest of the day far away from what could have been an unfortunate scene, it seemed to me that meeting our neighbours out there and subsequently and immediately finding a room available and living at the foot of Hampstead Heath, reinforced the impression that all this had been arranged by a higher power, dedicated, much to my gratitude, to keeping me out of mischief to the best of its ability. Swedenborg comments on this phenomenon:

"I perceived that no disasters or fortuitous evils, as they are called, can happen to a man with whom the Lord is: for when by the agency of evil spirits who were present, a restive horse threatened injury [to his rider], those spirits were suddenly cast down. They that were with me observed, that from such things it might be perceived what kind of spirits they are who bring misfortunes with them, which was afterwards confirmed."

These 'spirits' as well as being the spirits of the dead he also describes the activities of the Nephilim, which he describes as spiritual beings in hell and the original inhabitants of Canaan and the Garden of Eden who became corrupted and lost their love of God for the following of their own pleasures and using their will to dominate others. The etymology of the word Nephilim Swedenborg gives as relating to the Hebrew word Naphal: to fall, so it either means 'fallen ones' or 'those who fall on others'.

According to Swedenborg, not all the Nephilim perished in the great flood and some went on to father what he describes as, "the seven profane tribes which are known as the Avim, the Anakim, the Horim, the Emim, the Zuzim, the Zamzummim, and the Rephaim."

As for the presence of these tribes in the present day, I would say it is clear that they exist in some form and their descendants literally walk among us, but the last traces scholars have made of them are as follows:

Avim: David Rohl suggests Ahhotep II who drove the Greater Hyksos Caphtorim out of Egypt, was an important descendant of this earlier Palestinian group and became the inspiration behind the legend of Io.

Anak, the Anak were described as very tall and may be one of the origins of the Nephilim being described as 'giants'. The word Anak is also the Hebrew word for giant. Robert Graves identifies the Anakim with Anax, the giant ruler of the Anactorians in Greek mythology. They inhabited the area later known as Edom and Moab.

Horim: later became a Bronze Age people known as the Hurrians who settled extensively throughout Iraq, Syria and Anatolia (modern day Turkey) the present-day people of Armenia are the only national remnant of this people and they are intermixed with the Uratians. The term 'Horim' means 'free-people'.

Emim: Their name means 'dreaded ones' and the root is from the Hebrew word 'Eyma' which means 'terror'. "The Emims dwelt therein in times past, a people great, and many, and tall, as the Anakim" (Deuteronomy 2:10).

Zazu: According to the Hebrew Bible, the Zuzim or Zuzites (meaning "restless" or "roaming") were a tribe who lived in Ham, a land east of the Jordan River between Bashan and Moab. The Zuzim were conquered by the Elamite King Chedorlaomer (Genesis 14:5). Many scholars identify the Zuzim with the Zamzummim, a tribe of the Rephaim living in the same region as the Zuzim and later occupied by the Ammonites. In Hebrew "Zuz" represents the root "z'z" which means, "to move" and is likely associated with the Ancient Egyptian "s's" meaning, "to move on foot" as in the "ssw" or Shasu. The Shasu and Zuzim may be one and the same if one considers their close proximity to the Horites "Kharu" and Hebrews "Habiru" as they are described in Egyptian lists.

Egyptologist and archaeologist, Donald B. Redford has argued that the earliest Israelites, semi-nomadic highlanders in central Palestine mentioned on the Merneptah Stele at the end of the 13th century BC with reference made to Yahweh as: "Yahu in the land of the Šosū-nomad" are to be identified as a Shasu enclave. Since later Biblical tradition portrays Yahweh "coming forth from Se'ir", the Shasu, originally from Moab and northern Edom/Se'ir, went on to form one major element in the amalgam that would constitute the "Israel" which later established the Kingdom of Israel.

Rephaim: Again, these were a taller than average sized people. The term is used to describe what were an Iron Age people living in what later became the Kingdom of Israel, yet the term is also used to describe what are considered the 'residents of the underworld' or wandering earthbound spirits. These could be the beings largely identified as Gods, demons and Djins. The Phoenicians considered the Rephaim 'the divine ones' and it is possible that many of the Gods of the ancient world are derived from the activity of the Rephaim. The etymology of the term 'Rephaim' has never been satisfactorily deduced.

Og of Bashan was one of the Rephaim whom Moses slayed and his capital was called Ashtaroth, also known as Ashtartu, Ashtara and means "Astarte of the Horns", Astarte being the name of a Canaanite Goddess. Ashtaroth is the name of a demon in Jewish demonology.

Swedenborg believed that mankind used to be able to openly communicate with spirits but lost this faculty in the time of Noah. If this is true then it may offer some explanation to many of the events of the Old Testament as perhaps still a few of the prophets still had this ability, such as Moses hearing the voice of God and even catching a glimpse of his form or Samuel hearing God's commandment to "blot out the remembrance of Amalek from under heaven" or Joshua's army following his orders from 'God': "They completely destroyed with the sword every living thing in the city -- men and women, young and old, cattle, sheep, and donkeys."

Swedenborg's Spiritual Diary was written between 1747 to 1765 and we can observe that in his early entries he seemed to see the truth of the spirits and how their only interest was to lie and mislead, yet he persisted and allowed himself to be misled, ultimately Swedenborg discovers the ultimate motivation and goal of the spirits:

"THAT EVIL SPIRITS ARE INSANE, AND THAT THEY STRIVE WITH ALL THEIR MIGHT TO LEAD OTHERS TO THEIR OWN HELL, AND THUS TO TORMENT THEM. I spoke with evil spirits who continually infested me, and who infest men and upright spirits in like manner; and because they are insane themselves they would fain strive to make all others infernal also, by leading them away from good and mutual love into the love of self, thus into hatreds towards all; and the more they are who are wrought upon in this way, the greater is the number of those who torment them; so that they are continually procuring hell to themselves. - 1749, July 27."

"When spirits begin to speak with a man, he ought to beware that he believes nothing whatever from them; for they say almost anything. Things are fabricated by them, and they lie…. They would tell so many lies and indeed with solemn affirmation that a man would be astonished…. If a man listens and believes they press on, and deceive, and seduce in [many] ways…. Let men beware therefore [and not believe them]."

Another early entry in his Spiritual Diary complains of the constant presence of evil spirits:

"EVIL SPIRITS ATTEMPTING TO INFEST ME. When I retired to bed the evil spirits above the head formed a design to destroy me, and for this end took measures for calling out all hell, and every evil and pernicious spirit. They first drew the dragon over to their side, but because he had been evil entreated by them it was given him to extricate himself. They then endeavored to summon all hell, and thus to surround and to attack me in a body, and at length to destroy me, which they had so often in vain attempted before. I seemed to be lifted up among them, as there were many of them above the head, who

raised me up by phantasy among them, that I might thus be on all sides beset by them...
- 1748, November 4.”

Such a description is indistinguishable perhaps from the mania of someone suffering from schizophrenia or under the influence of drugs having a very bad trip. Perhaps Swedenborg was a public example of the Illuminated consciousness wrestling with the reality of having breeched the barrier of contact between this world and the astral world, and the confusion and danger which this brings, but also of the celebrity and renown amongst his Masonic brothers which those who achieve this exalted Illumination receive.

Swedenborg asserted that the Old Testament contains a hidden meaning and he devoted his Arcana Coelestia to re-interpreting much of the Bible in the way of the Kabbalists. He states for example that the flood was not a literal flood of water but a metaphorical flood of evils upon the world. This clearly doesn't make much sense and throws the entire rest of the historical narrative of the Bible into disarray. For him the Serpent of the Garden of Eden was not a literal devil but another metaphor, this time meaning man's lower nature, and the fall of man was the state of a reliance on the physical senses and turning away from the inner world.

The remarkable thing is that these 'insights' are very similar to the kind of Rabbinical Old Testament commentaries which comprise the Kabbalah where we find the very sense and words of the Bible are redefined until they sometimes mean the exact opposite of what was intended. Is clear to me that Emmanuel Swedenborg was perhaps a well-meaning dupe of 'The Manipulators' and we are now living in a world ruled by a secret religious organisation which communicates with demons and spirits as part of its sacred rites, they even offer human sacrifice to these beings in exchange for their favour and intercession.

Swedenborg is greatly revered amongst Freemasonry and metaphysics and perhaps it is here that we can see how intellectual laziness and a lack of analytical skill, perhaps added to some wishful thinking and perhaps even some innate evil inclinations, can lead people to become led-astray. We have seen how even a Grand Master of the Rosicrucians can be a puppet and dupe to some unknown secret organisation and it is no different to the Freemasons, they are simply foolish and intellectually lacking dupes. The tragedy is however, it is they who rule our world.

Perhaps the one glimmer of light in this is that the Christian world at large was never fooled by Swedenborg and he failed to create his New Church on behalf of Jesus Christ which was his greatest wish, contrary to genuine rational minded men like John Wesley and George Fox whose reformative movements still live on around the world and continue to influence the world for the better rather than Swedenborg whose main contribution has been to open wide the doors to non-physical entities to fully invade Earth via the Masonic Lodges and the minds of gullible and foolish men seeking self-aggrandisement and not heeding their Bibles when it says:

"Do not turn to mediums or necromancers; do not seek them out, and so make yourselves unclean by them: I am the Lord your God."

In a biography of Swedenborg, I discovered a hint about what may have been one of the 'Manipulators' of his time. Hayyim Samuel Jacob Falk was an 18th Century Kabbalist who narrowly avoided being burned at the stake in Westphalia after being charged with sorcery.

In her research paper entitled: Dr. Samuel Jacob Falk: A Sabbatian Adventurer in the Masonic Underground, Marsha Schuchard provides us with some interesting information:

"Falk spent his early years in Podhayce and Fürth, centers of secret Sabbatianism, where he had access to the antinomian Kabbalism of Baruchia Russo, who advocated 'holy sinning'--especially in sexual and ritual matters--in order to bring about a millenarial reversal of reality. Falk was said to be gifted in: 'practical magic, hypnotic techniques, alchemical metallurgy, and folk medicine.'" Furthermore:

"Falk boldly defended the Jewish religion, predicted a universal war, and an approaching messianic consummation."

The online Blake Quarterly describes Falk as:

"..a Jewish alchemist and Cabalist, who became revered and feared as one of the "Unknown Superiors" of illuminist Masonry. Falk instructed Swedenborg in Cabalistic trance techniques and sexual magic, which they believed would usher in a spiritual and political millennium."

The following incident involving, reported in Nesta Webster's book, involving Falk and a hypnotised Swedenborg recalls the strange events of the Rosicrucian Grand Master Raymond Bernard and mysteriously falling into hypnotised unconsciousness in the company of the twelve men in white robes:

"According to a later Swedenborgian freemason, Swedenborg was in the company of some unnamed Jews when he went into a trance or ecstasis, and they allegedly stole his watch....Swedenborg defended 'these good Israelites', and he developed messianic fantasies of preaching in their synagogue about the return of regenerated Jews and Christians to Jerusalem."

The latter is something we are now having to deal with and the messianic fantasies and fancies of people such as Swedenborg in their high-minded meddling have unleashed on our present age and we have seen that none of this seems in any way beneficial to anybody except the Jews who presently appear to be the very masters of the Earth: dictating American foreign policy, given a free-hand in Israel and using British and American armies to dispatch their enemies and also dictating an agenda of mass-immigration, censorship and demonisation of white identity.

In an article entitled: "Kabbalist or Charlatan? The Life and Times of Dr Samuel Falk The 'Baal Shem of London' on the Jewishhomela website Rabbi Pini Dunner gives us some insight into the mysterious Dr Falk which may explain his apparently mysterious rise to eminence:

"For a few years he struggled, and his faithful assistant records that his personal life was fraught with difficulties as he and his wife constantly argued about finances. Eventually things began to change for the better. People were surprised at his sudden change of fortune. How was it possible that someone who had been so insolvent that he was forced to pawn all his belongings had suddenly achieved such incredible material success? Rumors began to spread that he possessed mystical powers that he used to attain wealth. The truth was more mundane. Falk was an exceptionally charismatic individual and particularly attractive to the type of people who are drawn to enigmatic personalities. Two of those people were the affluent Jewish banker Aaron Goldsmid, and his son George."

So it would appear that Falk, who went on to become one of the secret masters of Freemasonry, was bankrolled by Jewish bankers, according to Marsha Schuchard "He also met the bankers Tobias and Simon Boas who were both Scottish Rite Freemasons."

There is oblique reference to some 'peculiar rituals' and such activity appeared to be common knowledge amongst the Jewish community in which Falk operated, also from Rabbi Dunner's article:

"Remarkably, although he was not considered a scholar, this in no way detracted from his reputation as a Kabbalist, nor did the fact that he performed extremely peculiar rituals prevent senior community leaders – including Chief Rabbi David Tevele Schiff – from considering him their friend."

One of these peculiar rituals is referenced in Nesta Webster's classic book: Secret Societies and Subversive Movements and refers to a letter published in the September 1762 edition of The Gentleman. The editor relates that they are publishing the letter just as they received it, noting that several peculiarities of style indicate that the letter was written by a foreigner. What is fascinating indeed about this letter is that it gives us a first-hand account of somebody who was enthralled by a character we can strongly presume to be Samuel Falk, as the particular description of the man recently arriving from Germany align with the events in the life of Falk. Here we may see some of the mysteries of the Kabbalist and his practices exposed and seen clearly for what they really are.

The letter begins with a man going to a tavern where he encountered several people discussing the existence of witchcraft and whether it exists or not. One of the men, a man of reputation asserts that Cabbala and magic are 'pretended arts' and 'contrivances of tricks and frauds, which pick the pockets of fools..and always end in bankruptcies'.

At which point the author of the letter recalls a story told to him three months ago, over a bottle of wine, by someone who experienced the same thing. The narrator recounts how, four years ago a gentlemen came from Germany with his numerous family, and claimed to be the greatest physician and cabalist. The man he said, was a Christened Jew and 'the biggest rogue and villain in the world' who has been imprisoned everywhere and banished out of Germany and at some time publicly whipped 'that his back lost all the old skin and became new again'.

The rogue attempted to become acquainted with the man who describes himself as 'enchanted' and was no more master of his senses. The Cabalist told him that he had spent 16 months with three adepts and has learned all the mysteries and secrets of nature. He had sworn an oath to the adepts not to reveal any of the secrets for a certain length of time, but that time apparently was soon coming to an end. Naturally this made the man very curious as he says, and he forgot all precautions and fell in with all his proposals to the extent that he ended up buying several secrets from the Cabalist which amounted to more than a 1000 pounds, which in the 18th century was an extraordinary sum, and he declares that all the 'said secrets were nothing but cheats and deceits'. The man grew angry at being cheated whereupon the Cabalist offered to teach him the secrets he had been taught by the adepts and of which the period of secrecy was soon coming to an end. The condition was that he must avoid all churches and public worship as 'unclean' for half a year, and the Cabalist said that for this reason he and his family had never once attended church since their arrival in England, in order that he always be ready to begin the so called 'Godly mysteries'.

He also told the man to tell everyone in his house to swear an oath that they will speak nothing of what they witness. He then told the man that he must procure a Hebrew Bible stolen from a zealous protestant, whom the man duly robbed, the Cabalist then asked for a Bible in English, it happened that the man he robbed had a Bible in English and one in Hebrew and so he robbed him of all his personal effects by some kind of cunning ruse, leaving him destitute which the Cabalist demanded of him. He then asked the man to procure one pound of the blood of an honest protestant. He was in some consternation at this for he had the suspicion that the Cabalist was trying to incite him to murder. He then reasoned that he himself was an honest Protestant and so he bled himself and once he had roughly three quarters of a pound he gave this to the Cabalist. The Cabalist then demanded another 400 pounds which the man had to borrow, once he had procured the sum he paid it into his hands. The Cabalist then sent everyone out of the house except for themselves.

The next night at 11pm they went out into the man's garden and the Cabalist then put a cross tainted with the man's own blood at each corner of the house, and in the middle of the garden the Cabalist put a threefold circle made of paper, about three yards in diameter. In the first circle all the names of God in Hebrew; in the second all the names of the angels; and in the third the first chapter of the holy gospel of Saint John, again all written in blood.

The Cabalist laid both Bibles in the circle which created a protection which the devil could not enter. The Magician then brought a billy goat which he had prepared and led him backwards through the circles. The man noticed that the belly of the goat was extremely big and looked as if it would burst open, but the man reasoned that the Cabalist must have somehow filled the beast's belly full of wind with some kind of blow pipe. He then covered the goat in crosses drawn in blood and tied his legs together and at that the wind came out of his belly in strange murmuring tunes. Then the Cabalist began to speak strange words and conjured the devil to appear and satisfy their desires and demands. Then the man began to hear strange sounds and voices coming from the region of the crosses in the corner of the garden, which he afterwards reasoned was performed by the conjurer's children who had hidden themselves without his knowledge, but at that time he was feeling his hairs standing on end. The night was cloudy and suddenly lightning flashed and thunder roared and he lost his senses. Then the ground under his feet started to shake and his body trembled violently and he thought it was the last minute of his life and the devil would come and take him, the goat and the cabalist and break all their necks at once.

It was impossible for him to stay there any longer and he ran out of the garden and into his house and shut the door behind him. A short while later the Cabbalist came in too and the man asked him if he had been successful. The Cabalist answered no, but that he had seen the demon and it had a beautiful look, shining like glittering gold and diamonds, and the spirit told him that he had done everything correctly except that the blood was not of an honest protestant but of a rogue and a villain. At this the man lost his temper and he beat the magician and drove him out of his house. Therefore, the man was defrauded and he dared not prosecute the Cabalist because then everything would become known, so he had to remain silent and hide everything and not quarrel with that damned rogue. The man was utterly ruined and had to cheat his creditors.

The following description about Falk comes from the Jewishhomela website and one cannot help but notice the description of men in white robes, could these be of the same cult which Raymond Bernard would encounter 200 years later?

"On one occasion he withdrew into his home for six weeks, and allowed it to be known that he was not eating or sleeping for the entire period. After six weeks had passed, he sent for a group of ten men to join him – but only after they had immersed themselves in a mikvah. The men arrived at midnight and were asked to clothe themselves in white robes, and also to remove their shoes. With that they were invited into a large room lit only by flickering candlelight.

One of the ten men later wrote in a letter to his son that upon entering the room, "the saintly man was seated on his throne arrayed like an angel of heaven, diademed with a golden miter, a golden chain round his neck reaching to his waist, from which hung a great star, and holy names were engraved on the star. His face was covered with a star-shaped veil, and his headgear was marvellously fashioned out of parchment, with holy names written on it. A star of pure gold was fastened on each corner of his turban, and names were engraved on them. Who could possibly describe the beauty of the painting on the tapestries that were hung on the walls, with sacred figures, as on the heavenly throne in Ezekiel's vision....

The letter describes the strange 'throne room' as having been divided into an inner section and an outer section delineated by silver chains. Falk instructed five men to sit within the chains, and the other five to sit outside of them, following which he took out an engraved shofar and an engraved trumpet, and presumably blew on them. The letter writer and his nine companions were overwhelmed by this melodramatic scene, and became Falk's avid devotees."

The description of being 'overwhelmed' and becoming 'avid devotees' suggests something of the techniques of cult mind control and a form of hypnosis. The whole performance was staged within the context of the Judaic rite of purification by taking a mikvah bath and also the blowing of the Shofar horn which is traditionally only blown at the start of the Jewish new-year, at the end of the holiest day of the Jewish year Yom Kippur. The ritual significance of the Shofar cannot be understated and goes back the Exodus of the Jews and was heard coming from the thick clouds on Mount Sinai and kept the Israelites rapt in awe.

It seems the whole performance was designed precisely to create the transformative effect and so instil the idea that Falk was more than just a man and the religious trappings were clearly intended to convey the idea that Falk was something like part of the line of Patriarchs and perhaps the latest incarnation of a leading figurehead for Jews in the world.

However the opinion that Falk was just a charlatan and a conman was one that was even held by certain Jewish Rabbis themselves. In a letter to a colleague, leading German Rabbi, Rabbi Yakov Emden who extolled Orthodox Judaism and was critical of the growing Sabbatean movement wrote of Falk:

"Some rich non-Jews also believed in him, thinking that he could discover treasure for them. Using trickery he succeeded in entrapping one wealthy non-Jewish captain, who spent his entire fortune on him and has now been reduced to poverty, and he is only able to survive as a result of Falk's charity. Incredibly this captain continues to praise him among wealthy Christians, so that they give him a lot of money. In this way the Baal

Shem is enabled to live as a man of wealth, and he uses his money to bribe his close followers so that they continue to spread his fame."

I would suggest that in order to understand the present we need to discover the secrets of the past. There has been an agenda unfolding throughout the years for the establishment of a Jewish homeland and Freemasonry has been its prime motor of action. We can understand how this has been achieved, by the activities of Jewish Kabbalists and Sabbateans infiltrating into Freemasonry during the 18th century, and people like Emmanuel Swedenborg were their disciples. Freemasonry has long been suspected of actually being a secret society with Judaic origins:

"Chevalier Ramsay delivered his famous Ramsay's oration, which described Freemasonry as an originally Jewish fraternity, whose secrets were discovered by the crusading knights of the Temple and then transmitted to operative masons in France and the British Isles."

If we are to understand more about this manipulation, we need to understand everything we can about the arch manipulator Falk, but such men, whom one moment are under threat of being burned at the stake for witchcraft and the next are called by Count Cogliostro "the greatest man in Europe, the famous Falk in London" one would hardly expect to find clear footprints of all their movements.

In a report of the Vatican inquisition dated 1791:

'Cagliostro perceived that their [Freemasons'] ceremonies were disfigured and disgraced by magic and superstition; the principles of Swedenborg, a Swedish preacher; and those of M. Falc, a Jew rabbi, are regarded as chiefs by the illuminated.'

In her article: Jacobite and Visionary: the Masonic Journey of Emanuel Swedenborg, Marsha Schuchard writes:

"That Scottish Freemasonry had long traditions of 'second sight' was relevant, and some Swedish freemasons would later claim that Swedenborg possessed that peculiar gift of clairvoyance. See Tafel, 'New Documents', New Church Magazine, 4 (1885), p. 381, for Dr Husband Messiter's belief that Swedenborg possessed second sight."

Falk was one of the Ba'alei shems: a master of the divine name, a Ba'al shems is a Kabbalist who can write Kabbalistic amulets using the supposed name of God, and they were said to be able to conjure angels, predict the future, and offer protection from demons and disasters. Falk was said to engage in magical rituals in Epping forest and along the shores of the Thames. He became known as the 'unknown superior' of the Freemasons.

As member of the French Anti-Masonic league and founder of several anti-Masonic newspapers and writer of several books on Freemasonry, Andre Baron, pointed out the links between Freemasonry, Martinism, and Adam Weishaupt's Bavarian Illuminati and wrote the famous maxim: "Remember that the constant rule of the secret societies is that the real authors never show themselves."

Catherine the Great, the Empress of Russia was deeply critical and suspicious of Freemasonry and wrote a trilogy of plays satirising Freemasonry and specifically lampooning Count Cagliostro. In his paper entitled Catherine II and her Plays, Adam Drozdek relates the plot details of one of her anti-masonic plays The Deceiver:

"In The deceiver, Kalifalkzherston pretends to be able to double the size of diamonds, to speak with invisible Alexander the Great who during his lifetime visited him and gullible Samblin believed him. Kalifalkzherston promised Dodin to win for him Samblin's daughter Sophia. He was also able to cure an imaginary illness of Samblina, which was pronounced to be a miracle. He promised Samblin to multiply Samblin's riches by cooking money and small diamonds, but he fled with diamonds he got from Samblin for such a cooking; however, Dodin captured him, whereby he won over Sophia. The last words spoken by Dodin are addressed to the audience: 'Such a deception is not new in the world, I think ... it only takes up different forms in [different] times – this I give you for your consideration.'"

The character Kalifalkzherston is clearly intended to represent Cogliostro and the incident of stealing diamonds which were claimed to be used to cook to make bigger is echoed by real life event of the theft of a diamond necklace which had been loaned to him on the basis of a claim that he could use it to produce bigger diamonds. He was also involved in a much more sinister affair involving a diamond necklace which may have been the spark to start the French Revolution. The affair of the diamond necklace, which involved a jeweller on the verge of bankruptcy in need of selling an expensive diamond necklace he had made for Louis XV who had ordered it for one of his favourite courtesans, but had died before its completion and the courtesan subsequently out of favour in the new court, banished, leaving the jeweller out of pocket for the diamonds he had purchased for the creation of the necklace.

It seems then that several disgruntled parties united in a conspiracy against the new queen Marie Antoinette in an extra-ordinarily serpentine plot which seemed to unite several different strands of discontent and deftly weave them together to form a net to catch the Queen and promote resentment among the French sans culottes towards the French monarchy; events which would ultimately lead to the French Revolution.

Briefly the story is that the self-styled Comtesse de la Motte, Jeanne de Valois-Saint-Rémy, having aristocratic ancestry but whose father was a dissolute drunkard, wanted to augment the stipend she received from the royal court to allow her to live in a manner which she felt befitted her. She found a dupe in the form of Cardinal Rohan who was out of favour with Marie-Antoinette but was desperate to ingratiate herself with the queen. La Motte apparently pretended that she was a close confidante of the Queen and gave Rohan letters forged by her lover Retaux de Villette, expressing not only her appreciation of his qualities, but later, her love for him. La Motte even arranged a meeting between Rohan and a prostitute who resembled Marie Antoinette. In exchange La Motte borrowed large sums of money from Rohan which she told him was for the Queen's charitable activities but which was in reality to fund her own lifestyle.

La Motte was then approached by the jewellers to be an accessory to help them sell the diamond necklace in exchange for a commission. Retaux forged letters from the Queen to Cardinal Rohan with an order to buy the necklace, saying that she wanted to buy the necklace secretly in order to avoid any negative publicity over spending such a large sum (equivalent of 10 million pounds in today's money) at a time when so many French citizens were living in poverty and struggling for subsistence.

Jeanne accused Count Cagliostro of being the one who persuaded the Cardinal to purchase the necklace and thus was potentially, the manufacturer of the necklace plot. It is curious that while Cardinal Rohan was immediately arrested, and who was ultimately only a poor dupe, one of the main agents of the whole affair, the so-called Comtesse de la Motte was not arrested until three days later, giving her ample time to destroy all correspondence and evidence implicating those also involved, such as the Freemason Count Cagliostro.

Despite Marie Antoinette being entirely blameless and indeed, the very acme of a victim of a tawdry and base conspiracy, public opinion went against her, no doubt the manner in which the affair was handled by the press may have had an effect. Cardinal Rohan's acquittal also seemed to infer his innocence and the guilt of the Queen who, it was believed, had used the Comtesse de la Motte in her own conspiracy against Cardinal Rohan.

Jeanne de la Motte although found guilty and imprisoned, later escaped and fled to England where she published her memoirs where she attacked the wronged Queen and portrayed herself as an innocent victim of her courtly intrigues. The hand of providential justice in her case however, was not long in catching up with her, and whether it was through the agent of avenging angels and a God who had decided to withdraw divine protection, or agents of Cagliostro eager to cauterise any loose ends, she ended up falling from her hotel room window while apparently hiding from debt collectors, although her husband claimed it was agents of the revolutionaire Duc d'Orleans, grand master of the Grand Orient de France Freemasonic lodge, who may have been one of the agents trying to cauterise said loose end.

As reported in The Times she was found 'terribly mangled, her left eye cut out, one of her arms and both her legs are broken," and the woman she maligned and played her part in her ultimate downfall, Marie Antoinette, died two years after her on the guillotine in 1793.

The Duke of Orleans himself, as cousin to King Louis XVI, was a member of the royal elite who had become a revolutionary and had even voted in favour of a death sentence for the King. Like so many of the revolutionaries like the bloodthirsty Robespierre, he found himself hoist with his own petard, suffering the same ignominious death at the sharp quick kiss of madam Guillotine. What we see here is the casting off of the puppet, or useful idiots and dupes: those Freemasons which have outlived their usefulness and who 'know too much' while those operating and manipulating from behind the scenes, alone survive the horror they have unleashed.

From Webster's Secret Societies and Subversive Movements:

"But all these secret sources of instruction are wrapped in mystery. Whilst Saint-Germain and Cagliostro--who is referred to in this correspondence in terms of light derision--emerge into the limelight, the real initiates remain concealed in the background. Falk 'is almost inaccessible!' Yet one more almost forgotten document of the period may throw some light on the important part he played behind the scenes in Masonry."

And quoting the Jewish Encyclopædia:

"Falk ... is ... believed to have given the Duc d'Orléans, to ensure his succession to the throne, a talisman consisting of a ring, which Philippe Egalité before mounting the scaffold is said to have sent to a Jewess, Juliet Goudchaux, who passed it on to his son, subsequently Louis Philippe."

Nesta Webster makes the connection between Falk and the Duke of Orleans explicit:

"One fact, then, looms out of the darkness that envelops the secret power behind the Orléanist conspiracy, one fact of supreme importance, and based moreover on purely Jewish evidence: the Duke was in touch with Falk when in London and Falk supported his scheme of usurpation. Thus behind the arch-conspirator of the revolution stood 'the Chief of all the Jews.' Is it here perhaps, in Falk's 'chests of gold,' that we might find the source of some of those loans raised in London by the Due d'Orléans to finance the riots of the Revolution, so absurdly described as 'l'or de Pitt'?

The direct connexion between the attack on the French monarchy and Jewish circles in London is further shown by the curious sequel to the Gordon Riots. In 1780 the half-witted Lord George Gordon (as a Jewish writer describes him), the head of the so-called 'Protestant' mob, marched on the House of Commons to protest against the bill for the relief of Roman Catholic disabilities and then proceeded to carry out his plan of burning down London. During the five days' rioting that ensued, property to the amount of £180,000 was destroyed. After this 'the scion of the ducal house of Gordon proved the durability of his love for Protestantism by professing the Hebrew faith,' and was received with the highest honours into the Synagogue.

The same Jewish writer, who has described him earlier as half-witted, quotes this panegyric on his orthodoxy: 'He was very regular in his Jewish observances; every morning he was seen with the philacteries between his eyes, and opposite his heart.... His Saturday's bread was baked according to the manner of the Jews, his wine was Jewish, his meat was Jewish, and he was the best Jew in the congregation of Israel.' And it was immediately after his conversion to Judaism that he published in The Public Advertiser the libel against Marie Antoinette which brought about his imprisonment in Newgate."

So behind all of the movements and personalities instrumental to fomenting the French Revolution we find this man Falk. He is unlikely to have been the sole 'manipulator' of all the Masonic puppets but he is one whose name has been revealed to us through history and one we should not forget because if we do not learn from the mistakes of the past, we will be doomed to repeat them, and that seems to be the course for humanity because we do not have enough people who know any of this information or indeed, have the remotest interest in it. Yet if it were to appear clearly to their eyes that knowing this information and acting on it would protect them, their children, friends and loved ones, from the outrages of war and revolution that these people are continually manoeuvring us into, then they would act, at least one would hope so. But I sadly just cannot see any of this happening so this information will have to remain with those who have the sense to protect and preserve themselves and their loved ones, and will be able to see the same tell-tale signs, which have been endlessly repeated through history, which most people will be oblivious to until they are consumed. The wise will have made contingencies to remove themselves from the scene of devastation, watchful with eyes wide open and fleet of foot, and not, dozing in front of the television while the news reporter rings the toll of their doom.

So to return to Falk, who was one of the mysterious hidden rulers of Freemasonry, a Sabbatean Kabbalist and beloved of Jewish financiers, and linked to some of the worst excesses of bloodshed of the 18th Century in the form of the French Revolution, I am astonished to find that he was my neighbour for nearly a year since his rotten mouldering bones lay probably not much further than 100 metres from where I slept at Stock's Court for my first year down the Globe Road, for the man is actually buried around the corner from my old Halls of Residence at Stepney Green of my old University Queen Mary College in Mile End.

He is still remembered and commemorated as his grave stone has a raised platform with a metal box beneath it containing many small tea-lights which no doubt are lit to commemorate him.

The epitaph on his tomb reads:

"Here is interred ... the aged and honourable man, a great personage who came from the East, an accomplished sage, an adept in Cabbalah.... His name was known to the ends of the earth and distant isles."

The university was built around and incorporated several old parcels of Jewish cemetery, one such, somewhat incongruously sandwiched between the faculty of English building I attended for three years, and the medical sciences building and I am surprised that knowledge of a man whose activities would solve so many of the riddles of the past and present, had been lying right under my nose for the several years of my time at Queen Mary College.

His body lies in the Old Velho Jewish cemetery of Mile End behind a building called Albert Stern house, named after Jewish engineer in charge of British tank production during World War One, which when compared to the relatively recent towering halls of residence around it, seems almost hidden by its comparatively small size and old grey stone construction against the garish materials of the newer buildings. This building is also a halls of residence for students and even has a couple of plaques in Hebrew and English on the front commemorating the cemetery, the Jewish hospital which used to be on the site and the cemetery behind it and also a plaque commemorating Edward Lumbrozo Mocatta, from the Jewish family of financiers originally from Portugal, who died in 1915. Dennis Wheatley in his 1930's novel The Devil Rides out features an odious and greasy character called Mocatta who is the foreign leader of a Satanic cult who has the ability to conjure demons.

I once used to spend time in that building smoking weed and listening to Pink Floyd with a ginger haired former public school-girl called Natasha and known as Flash to her friends, who was on my Astrophysics course, which I abandoned in favour of English literature. It's at times like this that I think of backwards causality, where events in the past can be influenced by events in the future, or at least that they can be connected in some way which indicates an ordering outside of time. Indeed, Jacques Vallee comes upon a similar theory which he terms: 'the Associative Universe' where he postulates the theory that the universe is not ordered in space and time but by associations; that is there is a mechanism of order which tries to group associative events, this is what we call 'coincidence' and it reveals an innate associative order of the universe which exists beyond our perception of linear time:

"I believe there is a system around us that transcends time as it transcends space. I remain confident that human knowledge is capable of understanding this larger reality. I suspect that some humans have already understood it, and are showing their hand in several aspects of the UFO encounters. If there is no time dimension as we usually assume there is, we may be traversing events by association. Perhaps I had unconsciously posted such a request on some psychic bulletin board with the keyword 'Melchizedek.' If we live in the associative universe of the software scientist rather than the sequential universe of the spacetime physicist, then miracles are no longer irrational events. Instead, consciousness should be defined as the process by which informational associations are retrieved and traversed. The illusion of time and space would be merely a side effect of consciousness as it traverses associations."

I discovered this same phenomenon independently and I term it as 'creating a coherent unit of reality' and wrote about it in my book "Light in the Darkness: 4D Investigations":

"A pattern in 4d reality is the ordering of events and phenomena into recognizable and meaningful patterns of reality. This is what a coincidence is. It is the arrangement of people and events into a meaningful coherent unit of reality.

The perception of time and the sequencing of events in time, gives us the impression that there are different moments in reality. That last year IS a different moment in reality, that ten minutes ago was something else which has now passed and that tomorrow likewise will be a different 'moment' in reality. However, these aren't really different moments but part of the same ongoing continuum which we perceive sequentially and separated by time, but this separation is only a human perception. There is no reason why yesterday cannot be connected to tomorrow, not just forward in time, but also backwards in time because fundamentally there IS no time, there is only one eternal moment. That ongoing perception SIGNAL which we are all connected to."

I always wondered about the Russian revolution and in what way could the interests of a people and nation ever be said to have been served by the deaths of millions of people and the innumerable terrible atrocities committed against Russians by fellow Russians. It made no sense to me but I knew that there must be a reason for it because it happened after all and for something to take place some groups of very rich and powerful people must have a specific desire to make it occur.

The main thing that strikes me about the Russian revolution is that it seemed to hate Russians. It cut them down mercilessly, executed the best of the officers and generals, imprisoned the best of intellectuals and sent them to far off Siberian gulags where their intelligence could be safely contained and not a threat to the new regime.

The revolution seemed determined to kill the best of people, and had no compunction about bloodying its hands and without shame to achieve its goals and to a disinterested observer those goals appeared to be to murder Russians and strip their country of anything noble, valuable, intelligent and worthwhile. If one reaches the understanding and follows the evidence that indicates that the Russian revolution was not planned, funded and largely carried out by Russians, nor was it carried out for their interests but planned, funded and carried out by non-Russians who had their own reasons for destroying Christian Tsarist Russia, then working backwards one can examine all so called revolutionary movements: the French Revolution and even the English Civil war and the execution of King Charles I, we realise that there has always been some 'other' group operating on the world-stage, using their puppets, whether Oliver Cromwell one minute, a Duke of Orleans the next, then Lenin. In the case of Cromwell and Lenin, there is the lingering suspicion that their deaths were not entirely natural but were carried out once the puppets had served their turn and had literally outlived their usefulness. All of these revolutions were said to involve international banking interests. In Cromwell's case, his great great grandfather, Morgan Williams married Thomas Cromwell's sister. Thomas Cromwell as chief minister to Henry VIII is known for being the instrument of the schism from the church of Rome.

Thomas Cromwell, as a boy, left his family to travel to the continent and found himself joining the French mercenary army at 13. Leaving the army and starving on the streets of Florence he escaped destitution by taking up service in the household of Florentine banker Francesco Frescobaldi, whose family were said to have once financially conquered England:

"not only in holding the purse-strings of the kings of England, but also in controlling sales of English wool which was vital to continental workshops and in particular to the Arte della Lana of Florence." Braudel, The Wheels of Commerce ('Civilization and Capitalism').

The Frescobaldi family financed the wars of King Edward I and were also receivers of customs in England from 1307 and they were also collectors of the papal tax and helped finance the crusades. Amedeo de Frescobaldi absorbed many of the debts incurred by the King and after his death and negotiated all of the customs duty on wool from Ireland and Scotland, no doubt in service to the late King's debts. However, with the fall of King Edward II and suspicion of foreigners he was eventually arrested and had all his goods seized. He fled England and the royal debt was never paid and the Frescobaldi's went bankrupt. It seems curious then that such a man as Thomas Cromwell, on the verge of absolute destitution should be 'rescued' by a member of the family who once had had such a powerful hand in the Kingdom of England only to lose everything, on the turn of politics. Did they sponsor Thomas Cromwell to return to England and manoeuvre him into setting up a continental mercantile and legal network and to return to London a very influential man with extensive contacts, destined for power by his own evident usefulness. In a sense was the advent of Thomas Cromwell the first time the bankers had wrestled control of the course of England and its destiny, whispering policy into the ears of the king. If so then what do the bankers want? What is their policy?

If we look at what Thomas Cromwell ultimately did to England, we might be able to trace a course which might outline their ultimate agenda and motivations. Renowned English historian Dominic Selwood, Fellow of the Royal Society of Antiquaries, in his book Spies, Sadists and Sorcerers states that Thomas Cromwell pursued an agenda of destruction:

"No one can be sure of the exact figure, but it is estimated that the destruction started and legalized by Cromwell amounted to 90% of the English art then in existence. Statues were hacked down. Frescoes were smashed to bits. Mosaics were pulverized. Illuminated manuscripts were shredded. Wooden carvings were burned. Precious metalwork was melted down. Shrines were reduced to rubble. This vandalism went way beyond a religious reform. It was a frenzy, obliterating the artistic patrimony of centuries of indigenous craftsmanship with an intensity of hatred for imagery and depicting the divine that has strong and resonant parallels today."

This was a period of time when the so called 'dark-ages' were perhaps still brightly illuminated in the cultural memory, a time before what I would term the European banker Conquistador: William the Conqueror. What would be the purpose of effacing more than a thousand years of history leaving nothing but darkness and giving the impression that British history began in 1066?

The first Jews arrived in the country in 1066 and the first written record of a Jewish settlement in the country dates to 1070: there is no record of Jews in England before this time. During the reign of Henry I, Jews tended to represent the King's financial interest and they had supremacy over Christians: a Jewish person's oath was worth that of twelve Christians, so in effect, Jewish people during this period had a kind of diplomatic immunity and Jews were to be treat with special consideration as if they were the King's own property.

One of the oldest town-houses, if not the oldest town house in England is known as the Jew's House in Lincoln and was built in the 12th Century. It was in Lincoln in 1255 that one of the first instances of the ritual murder of a Christian child occurred. Nine-year-old Hugh disappeared from his home on 31st July and was discovered in a well on 29th August. He had been tortured and crucified in a re-enactment of the crucifixion of Jesus according to the confessions of those found guilty. There have been at least 150 accounts of children sacrificed by Jews as part of a ritual murder; though now all such accounts are now classed as 'blood libel' and antisemitic canards, as if these children never existed and their murders never happened.

From a logical and rational perspective, not to mention a scholarly and academic one, it is one of the axioms of historical research that the closer you are to the time the events took place the more accurate the recording of the facts. Conversely how can we be expected to believe an analysis that these events never happened 800 years after the facts? On this sound logical basis alone the canard of 'blood-libel' should be summarily dismissed as some kind of deliberate mental distortion of reality.

The accounts of these murders have endured for hundreds of years and such reports pervade history throughout the centuries and the different countries of a whole continent. To imagine that tens of thousands of people, for the past thousand years in all the countries of Europe where these blood-sacrifices have been reported have all been engaged in some huge and coordinated plot against Jews is possibly the most paranoid conspiracy theory anyone could imagine, but the Jews are permitted their paranoid conspiracy theories and even questioning them has become a criminal offence in many countries throughout the world.

Blood libel is a contemporary concept which has been summarily invented in order to efface these truths which expose the nature of a people who are not only actively opposed to our best interests, but are hostile to us and will seek to kill our people at any opportunity, whether they pick off a lost child or manage to slay millions in an organised a murderous organisation of engineered social revolution and destruction of institutions and civilisation. It is a common evil to be murdered by an antagonistic force, but to demonise the victims and victimise the demons, this elevates the whole story to a kind of infernal satire and such a level of evil to be permitted in this world convinces me indeed that this world is literally under the thrall of a supernatural diabolical force of malicious evil constantly seeking human blood through revolutions, genocides and wars which seems to have sided with a particular human group claiming ethnic and religious privilege and supremacy, at the expense of everybody else on Earth whose blood is let as remorselessly and without a second thought, as the butchering of animals.

There is an enormous effort to conceal and obfuscate these crimes and call them 'blood-libel' and insinuate that they are not true, or were invented in order for certain royal elements to profit by the confiscation of Jewish property. This alone is interesting and a fact worthy of note, and perhaps indicates how deeply our culture and society is controlled by elements which do not share our wellbeing and interests but instead the preservation and supremacy of their own. If reality can be rewritten to the extent that historical torture and murder of children by known parties can be spun into some kind of bizarre accusation of antisemitism then we are living in a world where a caste system obviously exists and we are not at the top of that system. It might be the kind of behaviour one might expect in a strange parallel world where a literal slave-race comprising 99.8 percent of the world exists, while the other 0.2 percent are the master-race. Any crime reported by the slaves against the master-race would face the full force of the master-race's machinery of control to silence the complaints of the slave-race.

Thomas Cromwell weakened Europe by encouraging the great schism which would riven it in two and lead to hundreds of years of wars, intrigues and conflict. If there were another force, neither part of England nor of Europe which did not have their interests in mind, then it would likely want to encourage a policy in England of supporting the Protestant reformation and weakening the power-base of the Roman Catholic Church.

It seems strange that on his execution, the man who had been so instrumental in taking England out of the Roman Catholic Empire would declare:

"And now I praie you that be here, to beare me record, I die in the Catholicke faithe, not doubtyng in any article of my faith, no nor doubtyng in any Sacrament of the Chirche."

Dominic Selwoood in his book Spies, Sadists and Sorcerers is very critical and states frankly that: "Thomas Cromwell was the Islamic State of his day".

He says of Cromwell whom he describes as Henry VIII's 'chief enforcer':

"..one whose record for looting, murder and destruction ought to have us apoplectic with rage."

He goes on to describe some of the outrages against history and culture which Thomas Cromwell committed and with this analysis, which we being remote in the far distance of history, can see that what Thomas Cromwell achieved was hardly different from the work of the French or Russian Revolution and indeed, could well be seen as part of a single continuum or ongoing project against the religion, culture and lives of the state's citizens.

As hypothesised before one wonders whether Thomas Cromwell was acting as an agent of the Frescabaldi banking family all along; it is certain that their returns on their investment in the person of Thomas Cromwell had proved highly profitable, aside from any ideological and political agendas they may or may not have had the sequestering of the whole wealth of the Roman church in England must represent one of the world's greatest booties, and any losses the family may have incurred as a result of the Barons acting against what they considered corrupting foreign elements in the English court had been well and truly repaid with interest, I therefore consider Thomas Cromwell to be an instrument of banker-vengeance:

"Flushed with the success of engineering Henry's divorce from Catherine of Aragon and his marriage to Anne Boleyn, Cromwell moved on to confiscating the Church's money. Before long, he was dissolving monasteries as fast as he could, which meant seizing anything that was not nailed down and keeping it for himself, for Henry, and for their circle of friends. It was the biggest land-grab and asset-strip in English history, and Cromwell sat at the centre of the operation, at the heart of a widely-loathed, absolutist, and tyrannical regime. When Anne Boleyn pointed out that the money should be going to charity or good works, he fitted her up on charges of adultery, and watched as she was beheaded."

And whether there is something innate in human nature or something innate in the 'revolutionary' system which has historically always been sponsored by international banking fraternities, the same casual attitude to the liquidation of perceived political opponents with the detached nonchalance of the administrator or clerical functionary.

"With lazy strokes of his pen, he condemned royalty, nobles, peasants, nuns, and monks to horrific summary executions. We are not talking half a dozen. He dispatched hundreds under his highly politicized 'treason' laws."

It is also strange that the barbarousness of the French Revolution is closer to us in time and there are more cultural connections with our present day since there are constant cultural reminders through Dickens' Tale of Two Cities or musicals like Les Miserables which evoke the post-revolutionary period, there has been a recent interest in the Tudor period through the work of popularising historians such as Dr David Starkey and the television programme Wolf Hall, but these media portrayals serve only to show how remote and estranged from our present period these distant bloodthirsty and quarrelsome Tudors were, it's almost as if a certain level of barbarity is expected of our mediaeval kings and queens, but what if they were only following the instructions of their advisors and chief ministers, what if the barbarity of tortures and summary beheadings were really the work of some other group with their own interests. This is what I believe.

I do not believe that monarchs have the level of intelligence or malice necessary to have created the deep rivers of blood which have led us to our present moment, nor do I believe their motivations would be so great to kill so many people. Most people are content enough to get through their life with the least possible grief as long as they receive a reasonable degree of respect, understanding and value from other people. A monarch has little to prove to acquire that respect, but they have every chance of losing it by acting poorly, what if they were guided into acting poorly? Then faced with the consequences of popular discontent, the monarch feels alienated from his people, resentful, even possibly fearful, then his minister is on hand to suggest the correct punitive dissuasive remedies.

Thomas Cromwell was an example of one of the 'Manipulators' of his day using a puppet king to do his bidding and the bidding of his owners. We can only speculate as to what kind of international merchant banking fraternity might have existed in the middle-ages, or whether he was indeed really employed in some way by the Frescabaldi family nursing old grievances and eager to exploit an opportunity to train and infiltrate an agent into the very highest echelons of the English royal court. What is known is that both Edward I and Edward III defaulted on their loans and led to the bankruptcy of several large Italian banking firms; Edward I had sought more loans from the banker Ricciardi of Lucca for his war with France in 1294 but they were either unable or unwilling to extend him more credit whereupon he seized their English assets, bankrupting them.

King Edward III defaulted on a debt of 900,000 gold florins to the Peruzzi banking family and 600,000 to the Bardi banking family, this led to the collapse of several Italian banks, along with the ruination of the wealthy patrons who held their money with the collapsed banks. It is argued that this led to a general Europe-wide economic decline, also termed a 'great depression' which began in 1340. Considering the toll three terms of English Monarchs had had on the Florentine banking industry and the vast quantity of unpaid debts is it really so unusual to make the suggestion that a member of this deposed banking empire uses an English agent to belatedly settle the bill with ample interest. It's just an idea, but it is a strongly persuasive one, at least to my reasoning. In history a 'coincidence' is often a sign that there is a conspiracy, and can it be a conspiracy that we have witnessed several bloodthirsty attacks on Christian nations in which the priority seems to be the destruction of the church and the murder of fellow Christians? The French Revolutionary moto was based on the phrase of French philosopher and Freemason, Denis Diderot 'hang the last noble with the entrails of the last priest'.

Lazar Moiseyevich Kaganovich was a Jewish communist and Stalin's 'chief enforcer' responsible for the deaths of millions of Christian Russians and Ukrainians in the Holodomor along with the destruction of Christian monuments, churches and over a thousand years' of Russian history, perhaps most notably the great Cathedral of Christ the Saviour in Moscow when he proclaimed "Mother Russia is cast down. We have ripped away her skirts." This is clearly a victory cry of triumph against Russia and the Russian people, along with her culture and history by the outside element which is antithetical to their existence and will employ all the machinery of the modern age to create horrors of bloodshed and destruction.

Like the Guillotine of the French Revolution, named after a French Freemason who was not the actual inventor of the machine, as guillotines had been in use as a means of execution in England since 1280, but as the man who first suggested its use in the Revolution, we find the endless need for piles upon piles of heads of Christians in these revolutions.

This is echoed back in the time some two hundred years previously where Selwood describes, what I would term the 'revolutionary legacy' of Thomas Cromwell:

"We only have to survey the smashed up medieval buildings the length and breadth of the country, or contemplate Cromwell's record of public beheadings and other barbarous executions."

Thomas Cromwell was eventually beheaded at Tower Hill on the 28th July 1540 prior to his execution he begged the king for mercy, perhaps he asked for the same mercy he had shown those he had executed for there was none and for once justice was done, although Henry apparently regretted killing such a useful and important minister. It is curious that on the same day as his death one of his protegees, Lord Hungerford of Heytesbury, who had reached his position through the patronage of Cromwell, was also executed, ostensibly for buggery but he was also known to have been part of a seditious group which had even practiced magic to attempt to shorten King Henry's life and ascertain the chances of success of a Catholic rebellion in Lincolnshire.

This brings us to another strange element to this story which might cause us to wonder that perhaps Cromwell was just employed to disrupt the Kingdom and had no particular deep ideological reasons for causing the split from the Roman Church since he (and even King Henry himself) confessed that they had remained Catholic.

The man who was executed: Lord Hungerford, whom Cromwell brought to prominence and patronised, was connected to people sympathetic to The Pilgrimage of Grace rebellion against Henry's break with the Roman church and the policies of

Thomas Cromwell himself. This uprising began not far from where I was born in Lincolnshire in a pleasant market town called Louth at the Saint James church and as many as 40,000 people marched on Lincoln to demand the freedom to practice as Catholics (just like King Henry and Thomas Cromwell himself) and protection for the Church treasures of Lincolnshire.

Ultimately Hungerford was executed for his suspected involvement or sympathy with the Pilgrimage of Grace rebellion since he employed William Bird his chaplain, and it was claimed that Hungerford knew the man to be a traitor, and such associations, along with the Rector of Fittleton and the Vicar of Bradford, cast doubts on his loyalty to the king.

Oliver Cromwell, like his great great grand-uncle, was a pawn and puppet of international finance. Why was King Charles murdered? Follow the money. He had angered the merchants and bankers by seizing gold coins from the Royal Mint which were destined to the merchants and creditors of Government debt and just as the King Henry had ordered Cromwell's death, Oliver Cromwell ordered King Charles' death. There are no coincidences in history, instead, evidence of an underlying agenda.

In an edition of Plain English dated the 3rd September 1921, a weekly review edited by Lord Alfred Douglas, who is known for his part in the downfall of Oscar Wilde, the following letter appeared:

"The Learned Elders have been in existence for a much longer period than they have perhaps suspected. My friend, Mr. L. D. van Valckert, of Amsterdam, has recently sent me a letter containing two extracts from the Synagogue at Mulheim. The volume in which they are contained was lost at some period during the Napoleonic Wars, and has recently come into Mr. van Valckert's possession. It is written in German, and contains extracts of letters sent and received by the authorities of the Mulheim Synagogue. The first entry he sends me is of a letter received:- 16th June, 1647. From O.C. (i.e. Oliver Cromwell), by Ebenezer Pratt. 'In return for financial support will advocate admission of Jews to England: This however impossible while Charles living. Charles cannot be executed without trial, adequate grounds for which do not at present exist. Therefore advise that Charles be assassinated, but will have nothing to do with arrangements for procuring an assassin, though willing to help in his escape.' In reply was dispatched the following:- 12th July, 1647. To O.C. by E. Pratt. 'Will grant financial aid as soon as Charles removed and Jews admitted. Assassination too dangerous. Charles shall be given opportunity to escape: His recapture will make trial and execution possible. The support will be liberal, but useless to discuss terms until trial commences.'"

Conventional historians have dismissed the letters as fraudulent, in the same way they have dismissed the Protocols of Zion, but if the Protocols are fake then they must have been written by either a time-traveller or a soothsayer since despite having apparently been written at the very dawn of the 20th century they have so far completely predicted the unfolding events of the proceeding 120 years.

In 1655, six years after the execution of Charles I, Portuguese Jewish merchant and Kabbalist Mannasseh Bin Israel petitioned Oliver Cromwell for the return of the Jews to England years 365 years after their expulsion in 1290 for a series of recorded ritual murders against children.

The Portuguese merchant Antonio Fernandez Carvajal settled in London in about 1635 and, with the advent of Oliver Cromwell, became the first endenized English Jew and in 1656, under Cromwell's protection, Jews were readmitted to England. Carvajal is described as the 'founder of the modern Jewish community in Britain' He too is buried behind Albert Stern House in the Old Velho Jewish cemetery of Mile End.

Carvajal had served Cromwell as a money lender and as a spy, providing information of Royalist activities in Holland. It seems clear from the diary of Member of Parliament for Westmorland, Thomas Burton dated February 4th 1657 that there was a definitive quid-pro-quo between Cromwell and the Jews who had funded him and provided him with intelligence:

"The Jews, those able and general intelligencers whose intercourse with the Continent Cromwell had before turned to profitable account, he now conciliated by a seasonable benefaction to their principal agent [Carvajal] resident in England."

Carvajal brought into the country silver amounting the sum of £100,000 per annum. No doubt it was with such Jewish money that the English Revolution had been financed and the New Model Army of the Parliamentarian had been funded.

Similarly, James II was deposed by the Dutch William of Orange with the help of 2 million guilders from Jewish banker Francisco Lopes Suasso who also arranged transportation for Swedish and Pomeranian mercenaries to assist William in conquering England and deposing its rightful king.

Although attempts had been made to readmit the Jews fully to England there had been resistance amongst the population and it was only with the ascent to power of William of Orange that the Jews fully enjoyed all the privileges, rights and opportunities which citizenship would allow. The Jewish Naturalisation act of 1753 was a reward for the loyalty, assistance and funding of the Jews in combatting the Jacobite rebellion; so we can see that at every single major turning point in English history, Jews have been involved as financiers, advisers and secret agents, always steering the destiny of the Kingdom to suit their long-term goal. The problem is that few had any suspicion that the Jews had any long-term goals or if they did then they had been fed a delusion that their long-term goals could coincide with the best interests of the Christian world. Cromwell like Swedenborg seems to have believed that helping the Jews would usher in a new Christian messianic age and may have believed that bringing the Jews to England would aid in their conversion to Christianity, at which point Christ would apparently return to Earth. It was believed that this would happen in the year 1666 and was nurtured by Manneseh Ben Israel in his letter to Cromwell and the Rump Parliament as a reason to readmit the Jews:

"[T]he opinions of many Christians and mine do concur herein, that we both believe that the restoring time of our Nation into their native country is very near at hand."

It would seem that a myth and mania had been created and dispersed throughout the Puritan movement in order to serve an unsuspected secondary agenda. In a sense the UFO and aliens mania is just a modern version of this kind of cultural manipulation which ultimately once it has served its concealed purpose to benefit the originators and manipulating agents, will be cast off and merely remembered as a historical curiosity, perhaps a hundred years from now, once the UFO agenda has served its purpose it will be seen as just another folly of history, pursued by the gullible and naïve, under the powerful delusion of wishful thinking and carefully released disinformation designed to nourish and strengthen those delusions.

The Jews ultimately betrayed Cromwell and his revolution by funding the restoration of the Stuart dynasty with Charles II who was backed by Jewish benefactors Andrea Mendes da Costa, Antonio Mendes and Augustine Coronel-Chacon. The populace rejoiced at the restoration of monarchy and the end of the dour and joyless puritans, little suspecting that everything that had transpired had been a stratagem of the Jews to ensure their return and ultimately, financial and political domination of England and beyond.

Their return to England marks the turning point in the fortunes of the Jews, prior to this they had been repeatedly expulsed and rejected from manipulating the machinery of the state. Sir John Clapham was invited to write The Bank of England: a History, at the invitation of the bank to celebrate its 250th anniversary. He noticed that there seemed to be a large number of Spanish and Portuguese Jews among the bank's owners in its earliest years. He noted that the foundation of the bank of Amsterdam also had a disproportionate number of Jews amongst the bank's owners and stock holders.

These Jews had been largely ancestrally settled in Spain until the expulsion of 1492, when they had moved on to Portugal but by the middle of the 16th Century Portugal too had started to root out the corrupting Jewish element which had hidden itself as false converts to Christianity. The majority of Jews thus fled Portugal and relocated to Holland and it is likely that Holland's rise to importance as global banking and trading hub was a result of Jewish activity.

Among the owners of Bank of England stock was one Solomon de Medina, the first Jew to be knighted and who had come to England with William of Orange as army contractor to William III. He too possessed an extensive intelligence network which was much better than the government's. John Churchill, ancestor of Winston Churchill was said to be much in debt to Solomon's intelligence network for his victories against the French King Louis XIV and his extensive campaigns in Europe, in addition to receiving funding for his campaigns and provisions for his troops from him. Like the Cromwell's family ongoing relationship with international merchants and bankers the Churchill family, culminating of course in the life of Winston Churchill, effectively became servants of internationalist Zionist interests to the detriment of European and British interests.

The result of what historian David Irving calls 'Churchill's War' was the loss of the British empire, and the destruction of Europe and massive loss of life and the creation of the state of Israel. Hitler had sued for peace and promised he was committed to the continuance of the British Empire and would use his armies to defend it provided he would be given a free-hand in the East to deal with the international threat of Communism, but the war had been arranged by the very forces behind the creation of Communism and the timeline of revolution, the murder of Christian monarchs, the destruction of the Christian religion and the massacres of large numbers of Christian people under one pretext or the other.

William D Rubinstein in an article for the Jewish Historical Society of England describes Churchill as:

"..among the best friends the Jews ever had as a British political leader.." which is high praise since the bar of British leaders historically serving Jewish interests is pretty high indeed. He is further described as: "an absolutely consistent supporter of the Jews and of Zionism throughout his lengthy career." Churchill's father Lord Randolph Churchill was friends with the Rothschild banking dynasty and his son Winston was friends with James and Dorothy de Rothschild.

In his book Churchill and the Jews, Martin Gilbert quotes a popular clubland jibe of the time that Randolph Churchill only had Jewish friends and goes on to portray how closely intertwined the Churchill and Rothschild families had become: the young Churchill being classmates with the young Nathaniel Rothschild at Harrow school and it seemed that throughout his early life the Rothschild families were to be relied upon to help Winston and he wrote in a letter to his mother how he wished to work as a newspaper war-correspondent: 'Lord Rothschild would be the person to arrange this for me'. His finances were also managed and investments made for him by another Jew, Sir Ernest Cassel at no charge. Throughout his early life Cassel continually made gifts to Churchill of money, shares and even a library for his London flat. It is clear from this relationship that Churchill even at this early stage in is life was a kept-man and totally dependent on Jews for his career and finances.

At 27 Churchill became MP for North West Manchester where he represented a constituency with a majority of Jews and campaigned vociferously and wrote a letter against a bill to prevent Jewish exiles coming from Tsarist Russia. The Sun newspaper at the time alleged that Churchill had been specifically instructed by his friend Lord Rothschild to write the letter. Major Williams Evans-Gordon, one of the Grand Committee members on the creation of the bill stated that Churchill: "was faithfully carrying out the instructions he had received for the party for which he was acting."

Despite having a habit of losing elections, and moving from the Conservative to Liberal party and later, back again, in order to fuel his ambitions, Churchill found himself being shuffled into a safe Liberal seat and in 1910 was made home-secretary. There is something of the hidden hand moving the Winston Churchill chess-piece into ever higher positions of power despite having no qualifications or apparent aptitude for any of the roles except, and solely perhaps, his adoration and defence of the Jewish people along with his friendship with the Rothschilds.

Churchill's conveniently positioned hand seemed to be present at every stage in the growing effort to establish a Jewish homeland in the Middle-East. For instance, he ensured that the arch-Zionist Theodor Herzl's son Hans was naturalised a British citizen at the start of World War 1; Churchill had also signed the naturalisation papers of Chaim Weizmann, a Jewish chemist who was instrumental in the creation of the state of Israel by creating new techniques of agriculture and went on to become the first president of Israel and according to conventional history, it was he who convinced the United States to recognise the state of Israel. It is far more likely that this is just historical embroidery to add to his image since we can surmise that by this time, after world revolutions and two deliberately engineered world wars the creation of Israel was already a foregone conclusion, it only needed the tireless activity of bought and paid for agents like Churchill to make it happen.

Lenin was almost the only leader of the central committee to not be of explicitly Jewish origin although declassified KGB files revealed that Lenin's maternal grandfather was Jewish. Martin Gilbert does not shy away from the prominent part the Jews had played in the rise of Bolshevism and the Russian Revolution and quotes Churchill stating 'Bolshevism is a Jewish movement' and Gilbert writes "he knew the significant part individual Jews had played in establishing and maintain the Bolshevik regime." Churchill also wrote in a 1920 article for British newspaper The Illustrated Sunday Herald entitled: Zionism versus Bolshevism, a Struggle for the Soul of the Jewish People, that Jews held a prominent role in the Soviet machinery and listed the Jews who held real power and the names of those non-Jews whom they presided over and that the 'prominent, if not indeed the principal, part in the system of terrorism applied by the Extraordinary Commissions for Combatting Counter-Revolution (the CHEKA) has been taken by Jews, and in some notable cases, by Jewesses.' Although Felix Dzerkinsky, the head of the CHEKA and one of the architects of the Red Terror, was only half Jewish through his father, although like so many of the primary Soviets like Stalin, his wife Zofia was Jewish.

Churchill also noted that Jewish businesses and places of worship had been exempted from the fury the Bolsheviks had meted out to Christian Russians and noted that there was a danger that people may begin to associate Jews with the crimes of Bolshevism. Churchill was strongly under the impression that there were 'good Jews and bad Jews' and indeed, this was one of the subheadings of his article; he didn't see, or chose not to see, that all of their activities were actually part of one continuous all-encompassing world agenda. Had this not been the case then perhaps the Soviet Union would not have been the first country to officially recognise the state of Israel.

In 1922 the Liberal Party lost the general election and Churchill lost his hitherto safe Liberal seat at Dundee and was reduced to scrabbling around trying to make himself relevant again and finding a way back into the House of Commons. At this time, he had acquired the well-earned reputation that during the war he had done the bidding of rich Jews for nefarious purposes. Lord Alfred Douglas accused Churchill of being involved in a scam to misrepresent the results of the Battle of Jutland in 1916 in order to drive down the stock market and purchase stock; Churchill then delivered a second message representing the outcome of the battle in much more positive terms, driving up the price of the stocks which had lately been driven down and purchased by Churchill's Jewish conspirators and then sold for enormous profit.

Churchill was saved from total political eclipse by his Jewish owners when vice-president of the Board of Deputies of British Jews and chairman of British Shell, Robert Waley Cohen chose him to act as an intermediary with the government between the merger of two oil companies, one of which was owned by the British government (indeed it was Churchill who had ten years previously negotiated its purchase): the Anglo-Persian Oil Company.

No doubt everybody got kickbacks and was happy and Churchill found himself back in favour and after losing yet another election, was gifted the safe Conservative seat of Epping and was promptly made Chancellor of the Exchequer. One can now understand what might have qualified Winston Churchill, and perhaps any Chancellor of the Exchequer of the United Kingdom, to this high-office: a close and intimate friendship with the Rothschilds. Former Chancellor George Osborne had a close friendship with Nat Rothschild, so too did Peter Mendelsohn, the Minister without portfolio under Tony Blair's Labour administration who, like Churchill with his repeated failures and scandals, was somehow always placed back on the politics chessboard despite being universally unpopular and even suspected of some of the worst possible crimes against children.

There was a period during the first term of Blair's New Labour government during which there was said to have been a paedophile minister in the Blair government but all subsequent reporting had been hit with a government D notice making it a matter of national security that the story be squashed. Incidentally Mendelsohn was also close friends with disgraced Jewish paedophile and blackmailer Jeffrey Epstein.

Norman Lamont before becoming Chancellor under John Major's Conservative premiership had worked for NM Rothschild bank in London and became director of Rothschild Asset Management. It seems clear to me that the role of Chancellor of Exchequer is to serve as a medium between the Rothschilds and the British government and to ensure that Jewish money continues to flow into the Bank of England. Prior to this, and the earliest Chancellor I remember from my lifetime was Nigel Lawson, himself born to a wealthy Jewish family heavily involved in world finance with his father the owner of a London commodity trading firm and his mother from a family of stockbrokers. Perhaps this might be the easiest way to convince people of the Jewish domination of the British economy, have them spend a cursory couple of minutes researching the background and career of the average British Chancellor of the Exchequer.

It was Mayer Amschel Rothschild who in 1815 said:

"Permit me to issue and control the money of a nation, and I care not who makes its laws!" because of course he knew that if he had control of the nation's money supply he could use this power to dictate its laws since the threat of removing the money supply from a country would lead to a complete social and economic breakdown and who knows what kind of promises and favours and agendas are even now being secretly followed in order to ensure that the Jewish bankers continue to supply the countries with the sustenance they need to effectively maintain social continuity and not lapse into chaos and anarchy.

Prime-ministers must effectively appeal to the Chancellor to approve their spending plans, and although Chancellors do tend to be financially wealthy themselves, it is not their money which they are spending, it is money which must be approved by the Bank of England which means we return to the realm of mysterious and unknown stockholders, if we recall, many of whom were Jewish at the time of the Bank's creation.

This relationship was exposed in an investigation into David Cameron potentially illegally lobbying current Chancellor Rishi Sunak to provide loans to bail-out a failing investment company Greensill Capital which Cameron worked for as an 'advisor'.

The text message revealed the workings of the UK economy and how indeed the Chancellor of the Exchequer is an agent for the Bank of England and presumably can only make spending and loan requests to them for approval:

Mr Sunak's second reply to David Cameron dated 23 April:

"Hi David, apologies for the delay. I think the proposals in the end did require a change to the Market Notice but I have pushed the team to explore an alternative with the Bank that might work. No guarantees, but the Bank are currently looking at it and Charles should be in touch. Best, Rishi."

In 1929 the Conservatives lost the election to Labour and Churchill was out on his ear again but he devoted the next three months to a propaganda tour of America and Canada trying to drum up support for a Jewish national home in Palestine, through speeches, lunch engagements, newspaper and magazine articles.

Churchill worked tirelessly for the creation of the state of Israel and appealed to the House of Commons to reverse a decision by the House of Lords not to pursue the Balfour declaration as a matter of government policy: the Balfour Declaration had been enshrined in a white paper which Churchill himself had drawn up and submitted to the League of Nations. Martin Gilbert summarises the importance of Churchill's central role in the creation of the state of Israel:

"With Churchill's active and persistent support, the establishment of a Jewish national home in Palestine had become a reality."

David Irving reveals further details of Churchill's financing by the Czechs, as well as the facts of Churchill's financial rescue by a wealthy banker of Austro-Jewish origins: Sir Henry Strakosch, who, in Irving's words, emerged 'out of the woodwork of the City of London, that great pure international financial institution.' When Churchill was bankrupted overnight in the American stock market crash of 1937-1938, it was Strakosch (who was instrumental in setting up the central banks of South Africa and India), who bought up all Churchill's debts. When Strakosch died in 1943, the details of his will, published in the London Times, included a bequest of £20,000 to the then Prime Minister, eliminating the entire debt.

Official history records the first Freemasonic lodge was founded on the 24th June 1717 at the Goose and Gridiron alehouse in London but there has been a presence of Freemasonry prior to this date for several hundred years, perhaps it is only in 1717 that Freemasonry effectively began its slow emergence from the subterranean underground it had hitherto inhabited and commenced the next stage of its long term, millennial plan.

In his book about 'The Hiram Key' Freemason Christopher Knight states plainly that: "there appears to have been a significant Freemasonic infrastructure in place in London, well before 1646."

1646 is a significant date because it is on this date that the first documented record of someone being initiated into Freemasonry was made. On 16th October 1646, antiquarian and member of the Royal Society and later founder of the Oxford Ashmolean Museum of Art and Archaeology at Oxford, Elias Ashmole in his dairy records:

"I was made a Free Mason at Warrington in Lancashire, with Coll: Henry Mainwaring of Karincham in Cheshire."

At this date during the English Civil War Warrington was a stronghold of the Parliamentarians and Colonel Henry Mainwaring was a Roundhead Parliamentarian friend of Ashmole's father-in-law. Ashmole was interested in Hermetic studies and Alchemy and published several books on the subject.

The following is from the website of the Societas Rosicruciana in Anglia which seems to be some kind of international rival to the largest Rosicrucian organisation in the word, the mighty AMORC founded in 1915 and preceded by the Societas Rosicruciana which was founded in 1865 by Robert Wentworth Little and recruits from among Master Masons while AMORC is a group which seems to require little more than the completion of an online application from and the payment of annual dues of £246. They seem to organise open-evenings at UK Friends House, UK headquarters of the Quakers opposite Euston Station in London and as a Quaker myself I am surprised that they are happy to throw their lot in with a quasi-Satanic Kabbalistic organisations like this one, but I also saw Benjamin Crème at Friends House going on about his daft Maitreya but I suppose he had to pay the Quakers for the use of the room and presumably they put the money to good use.

Quoting from the Societas Rosicruciana website:

"Some Masonic historians believe that modern Speculative Freemasonry owes much to the Rosicrucian movement. Certainly, the earliest recorded speculative Freemasons in England, Sir Robert Moray and Elias Ashmole, if not themselves Rosicrucians, were deeply interested in Rosicrucian philosophy and ideals – ideals that perhaps provided their motive for establishing The Royal Society. The Rosicrucian Society of England was founded in 1867 by the freemason Robert Wentworth Little and six other brethren following the discovery of certain manuscripts in the archives of Grand Lodge. Many eminent and scholarly masons have been members of the Order."

Initiated into Freemasonry in 1771 the German poet Gotthold Ephraim Lessing in 1778 wrote five dialogues on Freemasonry entitled: "Ernst und Falk: Conversations for Freemasons."

From Secret Societies and Subversive Movements:

"The dialogues between Ernst and Falk throw a curious light on the influences at work behind Freemasonry at this period and gain immensely in interest when the identity of the two men in question is understood. Thus Ernst, by whom Lessing evidently represents himself, is at the beginning not a Freemason, and, whilst sitting with Falk in a wood, questions the high initiate on the aims of the Order. Falk explains that Freemasonry has always existed, but not under this name. Its real purpose has never been revealed. On the surface it appears to be a purely philanthropic association, but in reality philanthropy forms no part of its scheme, its object being to bring about a state of things which will render philanthropy unnecessary…As an illustration Falk points to an ant-heap at the foot of the tree beneath which the two men are seated. 'Why,' he asks, 'should not human beings exist without government like the ants or bees?' Falk then goes on to describe his idea of a Universal State, or rather a federation of States, in which men will no longer be divided by national, social, or religious prejudices, and where greater equality will exist."

What is interesting again is that same refrain, the same tune and the same words, whether it be spoken by elite Jewish Freemasons or messages apparently beamed into people's heads by aliens.

In the dialogues is the hint that Freemasonry is controlled by something far older and most Freemasons have no idea what is really happening or what they are involved with. And that as Falk himself as a Jew, does not attend Masonic lodges and that Freemasonry does not exist in an 'outward form' and he says:

"A lodge bears the same relation to Freemasonry as a church to belief."

And Webster Nesta's comments:

"In other words, the real initiates do not appear upon the scene. Here then we see the role of the "Concealed Superiors."

It seems clear then that it is made explicit that Falk, as a Kabbalist Jew, is one of the elect 'concealed superiors' of Freemasonry, however he does not attend the lodges and exist as a 'hidden master'.

The Freemason Andrew Michael Ramsey states that Freemasonry was created by the Crusader knights, stating that medieval crusaders, likely the Knights Templar, founded Freemasonry. But there is a myth of an even earlier foundation according to Freemason Henrik Bogdan in his paper entitled An Introduction to the High Degrees of Freemasonry:

"The name Heredon, more commonly spelled as Heredom (and sometimes as Harodim), is the name given to a mythical mountain supposed to exist north of Kilwinning, Scotland. According to a Masonic myth, associated particularly with Ecossais Masonry, the Masons were driven away from Jerusalem after the destruction of the Temple of Jerusalem and subsequently found their way to this mountain in Scotland. They remained on this mountain until the time of the Crusades."

Lodge Mother Kilwinning is generally held to be the oldest Masonic lodge in the world and has its origins in the 12th Century, almost 500 years prior to Freemasonry's supposed creation in London at the Apple Tree Tavern in 1716. Freemasonry in Scotland supposedly developed under the reign of King David I and the Heredom degree with a Rosy Cross degree originating in 1314 following the Battle of Bannockburn which has long been rumoured to have been decisively won in Scotland's favour due to the intercession of a band of mysterious knights who may have been the Knights Templar.

One of the earliest known reference to the Rosicrucians was in a poem The Muses Threnodie from 1638 by Scotsman Henry Adamson:

"For we be brethren of the Rosie Crosse,

 We have the Mason word, and second sight,

Things for to come we can foretell aright.."

Robert Fludd wrote several works on the Rosy Cross in the early 17th century; Fludd has also been called 'the Father of Freemasonry'. Robert Fludd spent time studying with the Jesuits in Pyrenees. His theory of the 'tripartite' nature of creation where he believes that 'the divine light' was the active agent responsible for creation and that the sun literally contains the 'Spirit of the Lord' and that this same 'spirit' circulates through man is interesting and predates my own and other theories of the true nature of light as the transcendent God element of reality and my own writing where I indicate that the sun is a portal connecting this higher subatomic realm of infinite God energy and sending it out into our material realm to populate the universe with life.

A very early Rosicrucian illustration from 1604 shows the 'Tree of Sophia' and bears a strong concordance with the Kabbalistic Tree of Life is also annotated with Hebrew characters. Robert Fludd was also said to have been a Kabbalist. The famous satirist writer of Gulliver's Travels and Freemason Jonathan Swift writes of the history of Masonry in Scotland:

"The famous old Scottish lodge of Kilwinnin of which all the Kings of Scotland have been from Time to Time Grand Masters without interruption, down from the days of Fergus, who reigned more than 2000 years ago, long before the Knights of St. John of Jerusalem or the Knights of Malta, to which lodges I nevertheless allow the Honour of having adorned the Antient Jewish and Pagan Masonry with Religious and Christian Rules."

He also makes an allusion to Rosicrucians and expressly associates it with Kabbalah:

"Fergus…was carefully instructed in all the Arts and Sciences, especially in the Natural Magick, and the Caballistical Philosophy (afterwards called the Rosecrution) by the Pagan Druids of Ireland and Mona, the only true Caballists then Extant in the Western World… I am told by Men of Learning that the Occult as well as Moral Philosophy of all the Pagans was well besprinkled and enrich'd from the Caballistical School of the Patriarchs…and Rabbins."

Laurence Dermott Irish Grand Secretary of the 'antient' movement of Freemasonry of the middle of the 18th century also refers to a Kabbalistic tradition endemic and perhaps fundamental to Freemasonry.

"…that at Solomon's Temple (and not before) it received the Name of Free-Masonry, because the Masons at Jerusalem and Tyre were the greatest Cabalists* then in the World; that the Mystery has been, for the most Part, practiced amongst Builders since Solomon's Time."

From the excellent researcher Marsha Schuchard in her article about Scottish Kabbalistic Freemasonry:

"….his reference to Ramon Lull provides a good starting point for my narrative, which will chronologically trace some "ancient" sources of the 'Antients.' Why did Swift assert that the teachings of Lull, the 13th-century Spanish mystic and polymath, could provide a key to the very essence of Masonry? Lull had drawn on Cabalistic and Sufi mystical teachings to develop mnemonic and meditation techniques that made possible encyclopedic learning and architectural visualization, which he believed were useful accomplishments for stonemasons and other craftsmen, and for his friends among the crusading Knights Templar, who could thus become 'illuminated' knights.

To develop the Art of Memory, Lull drew upon the meditation techniques of Jewish Merkabah mysticism and the Sepher Yetzirah, in which the adept rebuilds the Temple of Jerusalem in his imagination. As the Art developed, it involved the visualization of a building, palace, or temple in which images of intellectual concepts, historical facts, and/or geometrical relations were placed in special rooms, which facilitated their permanent placement in the initiate's memory and mind. In a condensed and simplified form, it was useful to the operative mason's ability to visualize complex geometrical and structural relations through architectural imaging. The intense mental concentration sometimes produced a trance state, in which some practitioners believed that they achieved prophetic vision or 'second sight.'"

We find something like an 'agenda' of the Rosicrucians made explicit in the Confessio Fraternitatis printed in 1615:

"What think you, loving people, and how seem you affected, seeing that you now understand and know, that we acknowledge ourselves truly and sincerely to profess Christ, condemn the Pope, addict ourselves to the true Philosophy, lead a Christian life, and daily call, entreat and invite many more unto our Fraternity, unto whom the same Light of God likewise appeareth?"

The anti-Catholic tenor ought to intrigue us and perhaps could be part of the demonstrated movement to destroy Christianity piecemeal by first dividing it with schism and then opposing the arms of Catholics and Protestants against each other, at least this is what we can ascertain if we plot the activities of the international merchant class from the period of Henry VIII and Thomas Cromwell through the various revolutionary movements culminating, at least for now in the Russian Revolution.

Martin Luther's personal insignia was a rose with a cross inside indicating that he too was a Rosicrucian. Just to make it clear I am not a Catholic and have no particular allegiance, I am however a Christian. What I query is that although the protestant reformation led to many good things for Christian expression it also very severely weakened Christianity as a global force able to defend its nations and empires. We are now, unfortunately, living in a world where we have been subjected totally by the banking fraternity and have had no institution to defend against them for a couple of hundred years. Now that their financial and political dominance over us is absolute, they are now attacking our social and moral values, and again, we have no institution able to defend our moral values, our culture and history from attack. None of this would have been possible without the first cracks being made into the edifice of the Church and the final fatal splitting of schism. It is my belief that the Rosicrucian agenda was precisely this and it is they, as precursors to the Freemasons and as Kabbalists taught by Jews, whose purpose it was to undertake the first steps in the long-term goal of subjugating the West by first encouraging division in the church. Although with the benefit of hindsight we can clearly see that the Catholic Church has behaved in the tyrannical and despotic manner of an institution whose primary goal is the maintenance of its own power base and orthodoxy at all cost, even at the expense of directly contradicting Jesus and his Earthly ministry.

We can find further clues connecting Rosicrucianism with Jewish identity in the Chymical Wedding of Christian Rosenkreutz. The story begins at the end of Passover followed by Chag HaMatzoty the seven days of unleavened bread and the chemical wedding coincides with the end of this period and the roasting of the Paschal lamb.

The story is full of allegory and numerological codes and while it superficially presents itself from a Judeo-Christian perspective it is secretly extolling the Kabbalah. The seven days before the 'wedding', which had been identified as a Christian allegory of the creation of the world and the 'wedding' to superficial appearance is a Christian allegory based on the wedding at Canaan and Jesus describing himself as the bridegroom, but in this case the number seven refers to the seven movements along the Kabbalistic tree of life and the 'wedding' is a reference to the union of the 'bride' or Malkuth, the human station of the Tree of Life, with an aspect of the divine emanation, mentioned in the key Kabbalistic text the Zohar.

Rosicrucian Jack Courtis goes into great detail analysing the Chymical Wedding and his commentary can be found at: https://www.crcsite.org/rosicrucian-library/chymical-wedding-guide8/

Chymical as in 'chemical' refers to alchemy; it is unknown at what point in history chemists had the idea that they could draw parallels between the outer manifestation and results of their chemistry experiments and the inner changes of mind and consciousness which these early scientists experienced as part of their occult practices.

Zosimus of Panopolis was an Egyptian Gnostic mystic born in the late 3rd Century. In him we perhaps see the release of some of the great alchemical secrets of the Ancient Egyptian Priesthood. Zosimos provided one of the first definitions of alchemy as the study of "the composition of waters, movement, growth, embodying and disembodying, drawing the spirits from bodies and bonding the spirits within bodies."

He also wrote in ambiguous terms typical of the study of alchemy:

"The symbol of chemistry is drawn from the creation by its adepts, who cleanse and save the divine soul bound in the elements, and who free the divine spirit from its mixture with the flesh."

This book Azoth of the Philosophers by the legendary German alchemist Basil Valentine, appeared in the 16th Century but was ostensibly written by a 15th century German Benedictine Canon. There is some doubt as to the true identity of the writer of the Azoth of the Philosophers but it would accord with the ancient trend of not a scientific priesthood which is what we have in the present age, but a priesthood of scientists fusing spiritual and material phenomenon in fascinating and remarkable ways.

This is also one of the reasons why we the modern scholar finds Alchemy so seemingly obstruse, because we are used to the separation of church and science.

As the originator of Alchemical lore in the West his work is crucial in setting the standard and influence the develop of both physical and hermetic science all throughout the middle-ages and even until the dawn of the Enlightenment at which point science had started to become industrialised and was beginning to separate from the hermetic lore into the study solely of the physical characteristics of matter apart from any spiritual influence. It is interesting that this break seemed universal, splitting at the seams where the spiritual domain meets the material and it was largely through the work of heretical scientists such as Giordano Bruno, Gallileo and Tycho Brahe, all whom were hermetic scientists who markedly signalled their break with the orthodoxy of the church.

It is only in fairly modern times that science has removed itself from the spiritual psychic realm and historically speaking, this is very much an aberration from what had been normal understanding of reality for thousands of years. Science, until the modern area of industrialisation: where scientific experiments started to be produced and reproduced without any of the trappings of spiritual exhortations or divine intervention, was usually part of the religious world so in Ancient Egypt for instance, Sekhmet was the patron of doctors and they were her priests. Science was usually knowledge, discovered by and carefully guarded and used by ancient religious cults.

Ammonium for instance, takes its name from the Ancient Egyptian horned God Amun in whose name a Temple was constructed which Alexander the Great famously visited to consult the oracle there and had his 'divinity' and his legitimacy as Pharoah confirmed. The temple is at the oasis area around the town of Siwa in the far west of Egypt on the border of Libya, in the midst of the desert, and since ammonium was also extracted by the Arabs from camel dung it was thought that the presence of ammonium chloride in the sands of Siwa was a result of the micturition of innumerable camels throughout history as their owners prayed at the shrine. The more likely reality is that Siwa is located in a depression of the Earth in an area in which water flows abundantly from the ground and ammonium chloride and other salts are washed out of the deep earth and are a geological feature independent of the presence of thousands of urinating camels stretching back through the corridors of time.

Ammonia chloride was considered by the alchemists to be one of the four alchemical 'spirits' because of its corrosive properties and suggested an ability to melt metals from one form to another. It was also used by the priests in their various rites of Amun, and since ammonium is highly flammable and commonly used in explosive and rocket fuel, one can well imagine what kind of apparently magical use the priests might have made of it to awe and astonish those attending their rituals.

The priests also used their knowledge of chemistry in initiation rites and 'the mysteries'. They used the deadly toxin Anthrax daubed on statues of Sekhmet, to strike down with a curse, anyone so profane to importune the formidable Goddess.

In the Ancient Greek rites of Eleusis, the one to be initiated: the mystae, would be instructed to fast prior to the unveiling of the mystery and was given a strongly psychoactive brew called kykeon on an empty stomach, before witnessing whatever special effects show the priests had prepared for them, in order to convince him he had witnessed the activities of the Gods.

The kykeon was made from water, barley, mint and most likely ergot fungus, from which LSD was later synthesised by Albert Hoffman in 1938, and the initiate would likely have had little understanding of the bio-chemical composition of the brew and little suspected he was being drugged, and even if he were aware of the importance of the kykeon to the experience he would probably not have been able to scientifically understand the process since even alcohol was imbibed with the belief that intoxication was possession by the spirit of Dionysus and was still a quasi-spiritual experience so even if the initiate did suspect that the kykeon had caused a change in his perception of reality he would still be expected to ascribe it to some kind of divine agency, perhaps this is why alcohol is known as spirits, well actually I know that this isn't the reason, but it ought to be.

While the mystae would be caught up in the transformative experience and was no doubt struggling with his new reality of Gods, Goddesses and whatever else was being transmitted to him by the mystery play, the priesthood understood the process scientifically and it had probably been accidentally discovered in the unrecorded forgotten tides of history that certain barley grains with a strange little spur of fungus on them could produce specific effects on the perception of reality of the person it was administered to.

The mystae likely took it all at face value, since to not do so would be to profane the mysteries and render the whole thing ineffectual: since the intention was to create a permanent change in the mind of the initiate and convince him that he had genuinely witnessed supernatural events and the otherworldly feelings of derealisation which the psychoactive compounds in the kykeon provoke, may have convinced him that he himself had undergone some change of state: that he may have died for instance and entered hell. Dr Abram Hoffer's research into schizophrenia indicates that schizophrenia is caused by adrenochrome, which is a psycho-active psychedelic compound and the symptoms of schizophrenia or psychotic episodes are indistinguishable from a psychedelic experience. It is a common delusion amongst schizophrenics that they exist in a different state of reality to other people; that for some reason they are being dragged into hell. The Cotard delusion is the belief that they have already died in some literal sense and although they appear to be alive, they themselves believe they have died and are living in some kind of post-mortem purgatory.

Such people are dangerous for civilised society as demonstrated by a fairly high-profile example of the Cotard delusion in the person of Norwegian black-metal singer 'Dead' alias Per Ohlin. He had a fascination with death and would throw rotting pig heads into the crowd at their live shows to drive away what they considered poseurs. He would bury his clothes underground so they started to rot and he would wear these 'grave clothes' and he would also keep dead and rotting animals at home under his bed. He committed suicide at 22 and his suicide note read:

"I am not a human being. This is just a dream, and soon I will wake up."

This act resulted in his fans and supporters committing a wave of arsons of old wooden Stave churches across Norway including the Fantoft Stave Church which was nearly a thousand years old and was burned to the ground by black metal artist Varg Vikernes, his real name, the much less Nordic Louis Cachet and by 1996 there had been 50 such attacks as well as a series of murders.

It seems peculiar that these black-metal followers would burn down churches. What threat do they represent in these days? Clearly none, so there is obviously something else, an ideological reason: Satanism. Who benefits from burning down churches? If there is a genuine spiritual battle taking place on Earth and if one is in the service of a Satanic force which is antagonistic to humanity and its well-being, then burning down a beautiful and unique ancient wooden church would make sense.

This is a demonstration of the kind of obvious dangers which depersonalisation delusions can provoke, and so any religious organisation or cult which practices such a thing is playing with a very dangerous material: the human mind, and since such rituals have been taking place for thousands of years and continue to take place within Freemasonry and appendant cults, then how many of these 'depersonalised', deluded people, who believe they are in hell or living as a dead man in an unreal world of illusions, might be among us?

Such rituals have been used over the ages to create a certain kind of person. One specific cult which used drugs and elaborate staged performances to convince the mystae that he had died were those carried out by Hassan Ibn Sabbah's Assassins. Marco Polo wrote that Sabbah created a garden of paradise in a hidden valley with real streams or milk, wine and honey, flowing in every direction from secret conduits built inside palaces, and also the availability of beautiful women which no doubt provided some kind of motivation to believe the delusion and convince the mystae that he had died and was in heaven and that Lord Hassan had power over him.

Masonry is said to be a science, from the Latin 'scire' to know, and for many years was probably the most overt demonstration of art and technological development in society. The construction of the great gothic churches required the mastery of many elements of what we call science: primarily of mathematics, engineering, and mechanical physics. This wedding of science to religion which had been common in the ancient world continued into the early middle-ages to the late middle-ages with clergy-scientists such as father of the scientific method Roger Bacon, Copernicus and Ramon Lull, who is said to have been the originator of computation theory where he designed the first truth-tables which are the basis of a computational logic-gate based system which he later made into a analogue computer made of paper, on how to win religious arguments against Muslims.

In the modern age I would include Nikola Tesla as a scientist who was directly inspired by the spiritual realm and this is something he himself acknowledged. The similarity between his methods and those used by the early Masons being the creation a 'mind-palace' in which to visualise the construction as a mental prototype, except to Nikola Tesla the devices he created appeared to arrive fully formed straight into his mind delivered fresh from the realm of light. Tesla had been musing on the setting sun and was reminded of a poetic passage from Goethe's Faust describing the new voyages of the retreating sun which he started quoting for his friend with whom he was walking:

"As I uttered these inspiring words the idea came like a flash of lightning and in an instant the truth was revealed. I drew with a stick on the sand the diagrams shown six years later in my address before the American Institute of Electrical Engineers, and my companion understood them perfectly. The images I saw were wonderfully sharp and clear and had the solidity of metal and stone, so much so that I told him: 'See my motor here; watch me reverse it.' I cannot begin to describe my emotions. Pygmalion seeing his statue come to life could not have been more deeply moved. A thousand secrets of nature which I might have stumbled upon accidentally I would have given for that one which I had wrested from her against all odds and at the peril of my existence."

It is interesting that Tesla was musing on the sun and quoting Faust, in a manner of speaking he was making an invocation to the sun, the source of all light and was answered with his greatest wish: the secrets of the electrical AC motor which remains his greatest achievement and perhaps the greatest invention of the 20th Century, were given to him in a flash of light. Perhaps in this instance we witness the ancient scientific methods of divine inspiration rewarding the faithful adepts who know how to give the Gods their due praise.

Tesla claimed he was born during a lightning storm and throughout his whole life he would be subject to attacks of intense bright flashes of light invading his mind and causing hallucinations; it is possible that in some sense, Tesla was highly charged with EM energy, as we all are since EM energy is what animates us: driving the processes of our body, keeping our heart pumping and being the very stuff of our thoughts and our minds. The Miller-Urey experiment demonstrated that life on Earth was likely a result of electro-static discharges impacting inorganic gasses such as methane, ammonia and hydrogen which resulted in the production of the building blocks of life: amino acids, which are the first level of organic compounds. This demonstrates that the animating organic factor of life comes from electricity which is a form of light.

Admittedly the title of this chapter is somewhat portentous but I can think of no better way to describe the machinations of the secret societies which slowly emerged from the shadows of mediaeval mysticism into the light of our world during the period of the renaissance. It seems to me that the work of the secret societies is a mystery not only to the public outside the guarded veil of their inner courts but also to those members who form the main body of adepts who serve it. It has always been a question of initiates brought into the society, being given high-sounding platitudes and upon discovering themselves agents of the changes and tectonic movements they see unfolding in the world outside have no clearer idea of the final goal except for the catch-phrases of 'universal brotherhood' and 'equality' which form the chewable and partially digested cud which for the adept becomes his God. A mere word or idea upon which all sacrifices are to be made. The means were bloody no doubt: the revolutions, the murders of men both innocent and guilty and the ultimate crime against ancient tradition: striking against God itself through repeated regicides, for even Jesus told us to 'rend unto Caesar'.

And now after the bloodshed, the guillotines, the ethnic cleansings and genocides, the creation of the modern world and its borders and powers, we stand at the summit of the dream of the secret societies and we ought to now see that they have only created a vicious nightmare where we stand now, as a race, knee deep in blood with the promise of more to come, and science, perfected in infamy, now a brood-mare for pestilence and destruction on a thousand fronts.

And the secret wisdom of all ages was always a dangling carrot for the ass. In order to perfect the art of deception the ultimate coup is to make a man serve under the pretext that something is the exact opposite of what common sense clearly show it to be.

With this hindsight, which much to our cost and sorrow serves us little, we can flutter back through the centuries to observe what is considered the re-emergence of the mystery school tradition of the ancient world disingenuously repackaged through strict necessity as a Christian fraternity. We have already remarked that Rosicrucianism was regarded as the true originator of Freemasonry so what clues can we discover about the secret meaning of Rosicrucianism? What can we find of its aims and rituals from the few published writings about this most mysterious secret society which may very well form the key to the mystery of our world and its rulers.

According to Rosicrucian Max Heindel, the Rosicrucians have their origins in the late 14th Century, being formed in 1313, at which point they were fully a society operating in secret; it wasn't until the 16th Century, still early in terms of the growth of the current post-Renaissance World Order, that Rosicrucianism announced itself to the world and went on a massive international recruitment drive with the publication of a trilogy of Rosicrucian texts, designed to stimulate interest and spread the word, amongst the intelligentsia and scientific community of Europe:

"So, according to the will and meaning of Fra. C.R.C., we his brethren request again all the learned in Europe who shall read (sent forth in five languages) this our Fama and Confessio."

In his book The Rosicrucian Cosmo Conception, Heindel identifies the Craftsmen or Freemasons as 'the sons of Cain' who are opposed by the Sons of Seth and by some dubious etymology he calls them Phree Messen which is said to be Ancient Egyptian for Children of the Sun, but frankly this seems unlikely.

It is worth pointing out that the Rosicrucians have long been rumoured to operate as an astral society, that is, contact being made with future initiates through dreams or other such astral dimensions of consciousness. It may be easy for some to scoff at and reject such notions as fantasy but the important thing is that there are testimonies of such events and these soon become an important part of the ongoing lore and literature of the Rosicrucians, whether they are real or not, they might as well be because of the level of influence such accounts have on the real world as a whole. Heindel himself was visited by the astral body of a spiritual being identifying itself as an Elder Brother of the Rosicrucian Order and he was later given instructions on how to reach the Etheric temple of the Rose Cross near the German border. The thing about the Rosicrucians is that a society which seems to exist as much in the astral non-material world, as much as the physical world, possibly leaves a very wide margin of error for people's own fancies and delusions, the thing is however that every adept who claims to have contacted some other worldly Rosicrucian ghost brother does no harm to the organisation, on the contrary, he justifies it completely and perpetuates the mythos, possibly even he reinvents in completely and the only person who could challenge his insights would have to have had his own testimony of being visited by a ghostly astral Rosicrucian Brother and since such occurrence are quite rare one can immediately see that competition to control the Rosicrucian narrative is not going to be particularly fierce. One can't help being of the suspicion however that whatever the Rosicrucians really are, they are continually at the mercy of whatever passing ghostly entity wants a bit of attention and has the ability to manufacture a vaguely convincing back-story.

That such people can so dramatically rise to positions of influence in the post Renaissance world is perhaps a testimony to how far the Masonic Swedenborgian ethos has permeated the elite of our world that anyone who has contacted spirits is obviously a very important person with great insights to share, and not, as is more likely a deluded dupe being used a plaything by entities maliciously antagonist to human well-being and development.

Head of the German Theosophical society Rudolf Steiner, like the Rosicrucians, the Templars and many other nefarious organisations in the past, dissimulated their true goals and ideals behind the figure of Jesus Christ, using him as a human shield to obscure their true intentions. In the time of the Rosicrucians it is more understandable since were they to present themselves without any Christian context they would rightfully be found to be heretics and worse: traffickers with spirits. But in the modern age Steiner uses the cover of Christianity to soften up his audience that there is nothing to fear. There is something in human nature that makes us unfortunately, easily ready to defer to the appearance of power and authority, and also a curiosity which although it has no doubt been instrumental in our human development has also been used to enslave us by the secret societies.

According to Steiner, being a Christian is the 'search for balance between polarizing extremes and the ability to manifest love in freedom' just the kind of high-sounding self-serving nonsense that has nothing to do with Christianity but which is so framed that it is hard to disagree with. Who wants to disagree with freedom? But Christianity is not about freedom in the sense of unbridled license, but who will stand up and make the case? Central points of Steiner's thesis include the idea that 'Christ' is central to all religions, though just given a different name. This clearly isn't true. Also, that every religion is true for the time and cultural context in which it was born. This isn't true either. All this does is seek to make Christianity and Christ some kind of temporal political phenomenon and again, the inference is that something better than Jesus will come along in due course. Also, that historical forms of Christianity need to be transformed in order to meet the evolution of humanity. This is wrong on so many levels, that God should somehow serve mankind and his 'evolution' as if humanity is the highest state of reality. Again, we see yet another attempt at destroying Christianity by rendering it 'relative' or just 'one among many systems of thought' and that it needs to 'change to suit our modern lifestyles'.

It is important to note here that the Theosophical society's logo features a swastika above a star of David. The Swastika apparently representing the fiery energies of nature, while the star, or seal of Solomon, represents
the descent of spirit into matter and the eventual evolution of spirit back to its divine origin.

Steiner apparently received spiritual visitations throughout his life and this led him to the development of a system of thought called Anthroposophy. Anthroposophy believes that everyone on Earth must reincarnate through the races, apparently from all shades of black and brown until one becomes a white Aryan. This is clearly quackery of the worst sort and seems to be informed by the harmful Hindu beliefs in a caste system. But why would spirits want to spread this kind of backwards nonsense amongst the civilised and intelligent west if not to precisely corrupt and infiltrate the spiritual intelligentsia with retrograde third world thinking? Steiner also believed that disease was a part of a patient's karma and eschewed inoculations and treatment of disease on the grounds that to do so would not address the underlying spiritual problems of the patient which would have to be reckoned with in a future life. He is quoted as saying "If we destroy the susceptibility to smallpox, we are concentrating only on the external side of karmic activity."

It is easy to mock and ridicule such people in these times when so many of the actions of disease and their treatments are well understood, but the dangerous and worrying reality is that Rudolf's cult of Anthroposophy operates as an invisible international secret organisation to this day in as many as 10,000 international organisations including education and environmental groups such as the World-Wide Fund for Nature and Greenpeace, which have lately become extremely influential.

Also, there are various intermediary training and social change organisations which operate from Anthroposophy principles and work with some of the largest multinational companies in the world such as Lumo in Brazil which works with Santander bank; Walt Disney Company; the French medical giant Sanofi Aventis, Bayer, Monsanto and Johnson and Johnson among many others. The company seems to have been influenced in its ethos by the work of Bernard Lievegoed who has been described as Holland's most advanced management thinker, and implementing what I would term, initiatory sciences of human development into the corporate environment.

Between 1968 and 1976 Lievegoed was chair of a Dutch government commission on transforming the education system in Holland. You see, no matter that people such as Rudolf Steiner and his theories can be easily discredited the message tends not to get through to the institutions who adopt their methods and surreptitiously integrate them into the framework of the institutions of the state. Why would they do this? Is it because these people, no matter what nonsense they are fed by the voices or spirits which encourage them to create their cults, can be assured of their success and celebrity and there are duly awarded their driving seat at the engine of human destiny, simply by virtue of being a member of the appropriate secret society and being guided by the voices of the hidden masters?

Rudolf Steiner advanced techniques on how to contact non-physical entities and perceive non-physical realities but why? What purpose does this serve? Is this not the very thing we have been warned about by our Christian heritage: the occult, hidden arts and necromancy? As we have seen from the example of the schizophrenic Barbara O'Brien and the temporarily demented drug fiend Evelyn Waugh and even Emanuel Swedenborg, contacting non-physical beings and other realities tends not to be a particularly edifying or beneficial experience.

The Fama Fraternitatis, or Fame of the Brotherhood is an anonymous tract which appeared in Germany in 1614 and is the first open manifestation of, if Rudolf Steiner is to be believed, a society which was formed in the early 14th century. The tract claims:

"..we do attain more and more to the perfect knowledge of his Son Jesus Christ and of Nature, that justly we may boast of the happy time, wherein there is not only discovered unto us the half part of the world, which was heretofore unknown and hidden, but He hath also made manifest unto us many wonderful, and never-heretofore seen works and creatures of Nature, and, moreover, hath raised men, imbued with great wisdom, who might partly renew and reduce all arts (in this our spotted and imperfect age) to perfection, so that finally man might thereby understand his own nobleness and worth, and why he is called Microcosmus, and how far his knowledge extendeth in Nature."

This is interesting because it is not a Christian idea to strive to master scientific arts and discover the unknown world. The ministry of Jesus was all about transcendence from the world and it is clear that Jesus Christ is merely added to the tract, as we suspected, as a human shield to hide the fact that they are engaging in what at the time, could have been considered occultic arts.

The second Rosicrucian tract, the Confesseio Fraternitatis in which the author declares in answer to their critics who are rightfully dubious that they are a Christian organisation:

"What think you, loving people, and how seem you affected, seeing that you now understand and know, that we acknowledge ourselves truly and sincerely to profess Christ"

At the same time, they make a statement strongly supportive of the Christian reformation, going even so far as to call the Pope 'antichrist' and to hint at further revelations:

"And as we do now securely call the Pope Antichrist, which was formerly a capital offence in every place, so we know certainly that what we here keep secret we shall in the future thunder forth with uplifted voice, the which, reader, with us desire with all thy heart that it may happen most speedily."

They also answer the charges of heresy and conspiracy which vigilant critics had duly suspected them of:

"...we follow the will of our most excellent Father, nor can by any be suspected of heresy, nor of any attempt against the commonwealth, we hereby do condemn the East and the West (meaning the Pope and Mahomet) for their blasphemies against our Lord Jesus Christ, and offer to the chief head of the Roman Empire our prayers, secrets, and great treasures of gold."

The most developed and interesting publications from the Rosicrucians is the Chymical Wedding of Christian Rosenkreutz. This tract has much of interest about it, in that it seems to reveal the resurgence of the ancient mystery initiation rituals of the Greeks and Romans. This time the couching in Christian imagery is only the merest and thinnest façade and the pretence is very quicky dropped, perhaps showing a confidence in the ability of their organisation to maintain the necessary levels of secrecy it needed to operate as a pagan initiatory organisation within the context of a nominally Christian Europe.

We have to consider to what extent these mysteries truly are Christian and whether seeking the kind of personal transformation into a kind of enlightened Jesus figure, might not be in of itself, considered impious since Jesus is generally regarded as a unique personage and indeed the Son of God and one might wonder indeed at what kind of ignoble blasphemous excesses might be wrought by magicians and dabbling noblemen become Rosicrucian spiritual alchemists and managing to convince themselves that they too have become like Jesus.

The Chymical Wedding details the initiation ceremony of a member of some kind of mystical order to a higher inner grade, apparently the vision of his initiation was communicated to him seven years prior to the events described in the tract. Again, this theme of 'astral' communication which would later become a central part of the UFO mythos appears.

There are several very peculiar elements of the rites laid out in the Chymical Wedding and although the text is generally ascribed to Johannes Valentinius Andrea who claims authorship and described it as a 'lampoon', this is not a satisfactory explanation for what was to become one of the foundation works for Rosicrucianism and modern initiatory systems in the west including Freemasonry. The tract shows too much understanding of contemporary chemistry and far too much detail about the kind of things which have been reported to have occurred during the mysteries of ancient Greece. The events described in the tract, although perhaps exaggerated to some extent and some of which dressed in allegory so that the reality becomes unrecognisable contains enough salient details to actually reflect what was mostly a real occurrence. Additionally, Andrea would have been only 19 years old at the time he claimed to have written what he described as a fake document and it would simply be impossible for someone of just 19 years of age to effectively invent a whole course of initiatory science. The only explanation is that there is something else at work here, perhaps an attempt to claw back some of the secrecy of the Rosicrucians by denying the authenticity of the Chymical Wedding which exposes rather more of this secret society than might be prudent; even now Freemasons regularly flatly deny evidently provable elements of their society. For instance, during my time debating Freemasons on internet forums they would baldly deny that there were any more than three Masonic degrees when their own Masonic writers make no secret of the existence of at least 33 degrees.

Another strategy of the Freemasons is the attempt to deny the past membership or authenticity of anyone whom history has demonstrably shown to be either a fraud or a highly unsavoury personage. There are many unsavoury Freemasons throughout history, indeed Freemasonry by definition is unsavoury, but most people's reputation can be protected unless they fail so spectacularly or indeed, go out of their way to be obnoxious, then when Freemasons cannot salvage their reputation, they deny all knowledge and find ways to distance themselves from their errant sons. An example is Aleister Crowley, whose Masonic membership ensured he would take a high place in the British establishment, including the secret services and work in America during World War 1 as a double agent under the guise of an Irish nationalist writing invective anti-British propaganda which had him later labelled by many as a traitor despite his protestations that it was all part of a ploy by British Intelligence to use hyperbole and exaggeration to make the Germans appear ridiculous; there were also rumours of occult work to help the British war effort. But Freemasons now declare that Crowley was a member only of several 'irregular' Masonic lodges. What this actually means is that Crowley was a member of high-level Freemasonry since calling these lodges 'irregular' allows rank and file 'knife and fork' masons to pretend that their Junior school Freemasonry is the real thing. Additionally, the United Grand Lodge of England does not recognise 'Continental Freemasonry' as 'regular' so the majority of French Masonic lodges under the Grand Orient de France are not recognised by English Freemasonry.

This plausible deniability is how the Freemasons cut themselves off from someone considered beyond the pale, even though Crowley was initiated into the Golden Dawn at the Mark Mason's Hall of Great Queen Street, the same location where the present-day headquarters of the United Grand Lodge of England are found. He also attended lodges in America which were not then recognised by the English Grand Lodge. In order to highlight how much of a capricious matter of convenience the distancing of Crowley as a member of 'irregular' lodges is consider that by these standards Mozart, Voltaire, Goethe and most European Freemasons would be considered 'irregular' in the eyes of the UGLE either because those lodges were not then recognised by the UGLE or still are not; but there are no such qualms when it comes to admitting these more highly esteemed members to the great alumni of discarnate Freemason spectres.

Another whom world Freemasonry has attempted to distance itself from is Johann Georg Schröpfer. He has been described as an 'independent' Freemason and much effort is made on his Wikipedia page to create the fiction that the man apparently was never accepted as a Freemason and created his own Masonic lodge despite never having visited a Freemasonic lodge. This is because Johann Georg Schröpfer has been recorded in history as a charlatan and a conman and the Masons of the present day are busy rewriting history in order to put as much distance between them and he as possible. In fact, it would appear that Johann Georg Schröpfer was an extremely well-connected member of the Masonic fraternity during the 18th Century

The academic researcher Marsha Schuchard recounts a recit by a French spy in the service of the French royal court Charles Théveneau de Morande where he describes an Illuminati lodge where a supposed séance takes place. It is interesting to observe de Morande's Wikipedia page where he is described in the lowest terms as a blackmailer and a 'gutter journalist' which is a highly subjective point of view and it is to be suspected that his history has been written in such black books because of his service to the French King and his continual attempts throughout his life to expose the Illuminati agents in Britain agitating to overthrow the King of France and plunge the country in the bloodshed of revolutionary carnage.

"Then, on 26 October Morande published an extremely rare account of the behind-the-scenes trickery of certain illuminist….Morande gave a detailed exposition of an illuminist seance. Picture, he exhorted his readers, an interior room surrounded by benches, where about thirty spectators are seated. The room is lit by a single lamp, placed on a table at the extreme end and enclosed in a type of magic lantern, which collects all the rays and shoots them through a convex glass three inches in diameter. In the middle of the room, the Evocateur stands, dressed in white with an enormous hat and an apron decorated with bones of the dead. All the initiates are dressed similarly, except for the hat. 'Voila ce-qui s'appelle une grande loge d'Illumines.' Schroepfer begins to make a thousand grimaces and monkey-like tricks ('mille singeries'). He circles the room with his wand and draws a triple circle around himself. He falls on his knees before the lamp and is bathed in light, making a resplendent impression. In the middle of his ritualistic movements, he adroitly pulls a string attached to the inner peak of his hat which focuses a light on a transparent design pasted into the hat. A hidden light shines through a magnifying lens on to the transparency, which emits through a hole a projected vision of the late Duke of Courland (reflected from his full-length portrait on the transparency). The spirit appears like an eerily tinted cloud. By manipulating the lens and light, Schroepfer makes it grow from a small figure on the floor to a gigantic vision that reaches to the roof. Using ventriloquism, he makes the apparition speak in a muffled, rumbling voice. After reducing the apparition and making it melt into the abyss, his assistant lights drops of liquid phosphorous that fill the room with luminous clouds and then suddenly plunge it in darkness. This gives Schroepfer time to change his hat and remove the evidence of his trickery…. Morande concluded his expose by warning 'les Illumines de bonne foi' who are 'honnetes gens' to guard against the continuing impostures of Cagliostro and the Egyptian Lodges in London."

That Schröpfer worked with Count Cagliostro to create fake ghostly apparitions for his Egyptian rites demonstrates that Schröpfer was connected to the major Illuminati Masonic movers and shakers of the time. Interestingly, if we recall the rites of Eleusis and the pre-requisite of fasting before ingesting the psychoactive kykeon we can observe similar techniques to those of the ancient Greek mystery schools. Viewed in this light, it is difficult to consider either Cagliostro or Schröpfer to be charlatans and imposters any more than the priesthood of ancient Greece or even Egypt were imposters when they unveiled the Gods to the unsuspecting initiates which they knew to be a combination of lighting effects and actors. The techniques deployed by the charlatan Schröpfer were hardly different to those used in the Eleusinian mysteries, where according to the research of Matt Gaton in his paper entitled 'The Eleusinian Projector: The hierophant's optical method of conjuring the goddess' at the culmination of the harrowing mysteries an apparition of the Goddess filled the telesterion or initiation hall, probably by the use of a fire and figures of the goddess in a small rectangular stone structure at the centre of the telesterion called the anaktoron projecting the illuminates image into the hall. Small figurines have even been recovered from the site which seems to prove this theory.

"For a typical night of necromantic activity Schroepfer's followers would fast for 24 hours and were served an Italian salad (possibly drugged) and much punch before the midnight start of séances in a darkened room with a black-draped altar. A robed Schroepfer performed the rituals and demanded his followers to remain seated at a table or face terrible dangers if they didn't. He made use of a mixture of Masonic, Catholic and Kabbalistic symbolism, including skulls, a chalk circle on the floor, holy water, incense and crucifixes. He started with a long prayer that addressed Jesus Christ, God and the Holy Trinity, asking for the protection of good spirits. He usually raised three different ghosts: one good soul in beautiful white, one neutral in subdued white and one evil in awful brown and black. The arrival of ghosts was mostly accompanied by a sound like that of wet fingers on glass, which sometimes grew louder and could continue for about an hour. The spirits he raised were said to be clearly visible with recognizable features, hovering in the air with their arms crossed in front of their chests. They seemed to be vaporous, not made of flesh, and at times they screamed terribly. Ghosts could answer his questions and their voices sounded hollow. Apparitions reportedly raised by Schroepfer over the years included Frederick the Wise, August III, the beheaded Danish "traitors" Johann Friedrich Struensee and Enevold Brandt with their heads in their hands, Count Brühl, Maurice de Saxe and the Knights Templar's last Grand Master Jacques de Molay."

Most spectators of Schröpfer's séances were convinced that the apparitions they saw were real. No clear evidence of deceit seems to ever have been found, but critics have described several suspicions. A local merchant who frequented Schröpfer 's lodge claimed in his diary that he once barred the door behind them before the seance had started. Consequently, the expected ghost was heard fiddling with the lock, but failed to enter. Another time he hid under the table and recognized the shoes of a ghost as the shoes he had sold the day before to Schröpfer 's oldest stooge. Schröpfer had once rather suspiciously refused to raise the spirit of the famous poet Christian Fürchtegott Gellert who had been known in person by some of the spectators. Among the techniques that Schröpfer reportedly used for his elaborate effects were actors performing as ghosts, ventriloquism, hidden speaking tubes, glass harmonica sounds, aromatic smoke, camera obscura projections, magic lantern projections on smoke and concave mirror projections.

From Marsha Schuchard's research paper into 18th Century Illuminism and Freemasonry in England entitled: William Blake and the Promiscuous Baboons:

"It is also clear from the diaries of various Freemasons that human actors were often employed to imitate good and evil spirits, and they may have donned animal costumes in order to represent the bestial elements of man's unregenerated nature. While performing his theurgic rituals, Cagliostro employed a transparent screen to partially obscure his assistants, who may have impersonated baboons and angels.

Morande kept up his attacks on the Cophta's disciples who maintained their loyalty to illuminist Freemasonry..he charged that members of the Egyptian Rite in London were in league with the radical political illuminati in Germany, who exploited the mystical illuminists in order to promote their own seditious and atheistic schemes. One successful stratagem, repeatedly used to seduce gullible Masons, was the staged production of an 'apparition' - 'un ombre sous forme d'un nuage color? - which then emitted supernatural pronouncements. But, Morande warned, 'cette apparition etoit un effet d'optique'.. Morande also pointed out that Monsieur Le Dru, known as Comus, performed similar astounding feats while performing magnetic cures. Comus had been publicly linked with the Swedenborgians by the Marquis de Thome, a radical illuminist who helped organize the Swedenborg society in London.' Morande's revelation of the tricks of optical illusion also raises questions about the role of the artist Loutherbourg, who collaborated in Masonic rituals with the Swedenborgians and Cagliostro.

The Inquisition would later publish a Cagliostroan ritual in which Loutherbourg and the seven celestial angels appeared in a vision. Loutherbourg was a master of illusionistic effects achieved through theatrical lighting, coloured transparencies, and chemical reactions. A learned Cabalist and practising magnetizer, he also understood many of the techniques of trance-induction and group hypnosis. Working with Cagliostro and the Swedenborgians, Loutherbourg made a series of symbolic watercolour drawings to be used during initiation into the Egyptian Rite. Cosway, a mutual friend of Loutherbourg and Blake, was also fascinated by Cagliostro, and he described his meeting with 'the Wandering Jew' (the epithet applied to Cagliostro by London newspapers) and 'the wonders beyond conception' that he had seen but was 'forbidden to communicate'. At this time (c. 1787) Blake not only evoked the spirit of his dead brother Robert but he also sketched spiritualistic subjects taken from Swedenborg's writings. In one drawing, he showed 'an Incantation', in which a magus-figure raises his arms before an altar; in another, he showed a woman wearing an 'Egyptian head-dress. Even more relevant to Cagliostro's rituals was Blake's drawing of three naked children 'crouched round a bowl-like source of light'. Blake was evidently aware that the Grand Cophta frequently used children as mediums, who kneeled around a specially lit crystal bowl of water and gazed into it until they went into a state of visionary trance. The children then 'pretended to hold a communication with the seven angels, who ascended and descended behind the screen."

In the Rosicrucian foundational text which appeared in Germany at the start of the 17th century: The Chymical Wedding of Christian Rosenkreutz, we find a curious evocation of early Communism in the form of a proclamation which the protagonist, known only as 'RC', hears in a dream prior to the commencement of his voyage to the Rosicrucian castle to take part in the Chymical wedding.

"The joyful time is drawing on,
When every one shall equal be,
None wealthy, none in penury.
Who er'e receiveth great Commands
Hath work enough to fill his Hands."

We have seen how the secret societies have been behind violent social-change in the name of 'equality' often with the result that those judged part of the reactionary former controlling establishment and those who had been successful within the previous system, were violently executed.

During the performances described in the text of the Chymical Wedding we find something somewhat disturbingly and rather unambiguously described as the ritual execution of six individuals described as kings.

"Mean time a little Bell was tolled, at which all the Royal Persons waxed so mighty bleak, that we were ready utterly to despair. They quickly put off their white Garments again, and put on entirely black ones.

Finally, there steps in a very coal-black tall Man, who bare in his hand a sharp Axe. Now after that the old King had been first brought to the Seat, his Head was instantly whipt off, and wrapped up in a black Cloth, but the Blood was received into a great golden Goblet, and placed with him in this Coffin that stood by, which being covered, was set aside. Thus it went with the rest also, so that I thought it would at length have come to me too, but it did not; For as soon as the six Royal Persons were Beheaded, the black Man went out again; after whom another followed, who Beheaded him too just before the Door, and brought back his Head together with the Axe, which were laid in a little Chest."

The 'mysteries' which are described in the Chymical Wedding are attended by a throng of what are called 'virgins'. It is likely that this word is chosen because of the evocation of purity and even a certain sense of Christian sanctity, but it is deliberately used to convey a false impression. The fact that these events unfold within the ministry of some sixty 'beautiful virgins' and other epithets are used, like 'gentle virgin' as well as certain theatrical effects being employed such as being drawn on "a gloriously gilded

Triumphant Self-moving Throne' and wearing "a snow-white glittering Robe, which sparkled of pure Gold, and cast such a lustre that we durst not steadily behold it," all worked in concert to create "a beautiful and moving spectacle'. But if the description used was merely 'women' and if we choose not to be emotionally swayed by the apparent grandeur and appearance of grace of the ritual and strip down the facts to the ritual murder by beheading of six people, followed by the beheading of the executioner himself, aided and abetted by a large group of women in cultic attire, then we can clearly observe that what the text really describes is something like a kind of early Satanic ritual murder whose affect is to traumatise and transform, and also implicate, those in attendance in the guise of initiates.

There are hints too at some kind of sexual element behind the Chymical Wedding, although of course since this text appeared in the early 17th century and was also a description of essentially secret rites, the hints are obscure, but a certain ongoing sexual tension is certainly evident and this is used specifically to tease RC who is depicted as a man somewhat advanced in years:

"As soon as we were come again into the Hall; one of the Virgins began: 'I wonder, Sister, that you durst adventure yourself amongst so many Persons': 'My Sister,' replied our President, 'I am fearful of none so much as of this Man,' pointing at me; This speech went to the Heart of me: For I well understood that she mocked at my Age, and indeed I was the oldest of them all. Yet she comforted me again with promise. That in case I behaved myself well towards her, she would easily rid me of this burden."

Is there a hint then that the 'virgin' will willingly engage in sexual intercourse with RC if he behaves 'well towards her'? Yet another passage makes some kind of insinuation about 'sports' between the men and the 'virgins', which cannot be divulged owing to secrecy.

"Mean time a Collation was again brought in, and every one's Virgin seated by him, who well knew how to shorten the time with handsome discourses: But what their discourses and sports were I dare not blab out of School."

It is likely that one of the 'rewards' of being involved in the Rosicrucian mysteries was sexual gratification just as it is a key part of such Wiccan and Satanic ceremonies. Though they do not apparently give themselves up without a little literal ritual humiliation:

"This the Virgin perceived, and therefore began, 'I dare lay anything, if I lye with him to night, he shall be pleasanter in the morning.' Hereupon they began to laugh, and albeit I blushed all over, yet I was fain to laugh too at my own ill-luck. Now there was one there that had a mind to return my disgrace again upon the Virgin; whereupon he said, 'I hope not only we, but the Virgins too themselves will bear witness in behalf of our Brother, that our Lady President hath promised herself to be his Bedfellow to Night': 'I should be well content with it,' replied the Virgin, 'if I had no reason to be afraid of these my Sisters, there would be no hold with them should I cause the best and handsomest for myself, against their will.'

The women then contrive a casting of lots to decide who will spend the night with whom:

"But now first arose a dispute how the business should be carried, but this was only a premediated device, for the Virgin instantly made the proposal that we should mix ourselves together in a Ring, and that she beginning to count from herself, the seventh, was to be content with the following seventh, whether it were a Virgin, or man; for our parts we were not aware of any craft, and therefore permitted it so to be; but when we thought we had very well mingled ourselves, the Virgins nevertheless were so subtle, that each one knew her station before-hand: The Virgin began to reckon, the seventh next her was again a Virgin, the third seventh a Virgin likewise, and this happened so long till (to our amazement) all the Virgins came forth, and none of us was hit; Thus we poor pitiful Wretches remained standing alone, and were moreover forced to suffer our selves to be jeered too, and confess we were very handsomely couzened."

It is revealed then that the drawing of lots for be partners is a set-up, probably something which the women had pre-arranged in order to mock and humiliate the men, all within the long-term goals of the initiatory ordeal.

The initiate RC says "This indeed to me seemed a bloody Wedding, but because I could not tell what would yet be the event, I was fain for that time to captivate my understanding until I were further resolved." In effect RC is refusing to make a conscious judgement about what he has seen, so he is entering a kind of hypnotised state where he is no longer capable of making value judgements about reality. This is very interesting and is the key to such rituals. That the person suspends their judgement and allow themselves to be guided. One can imagine what kind of atrocities might be possible by someone who surrenders their will and judgement to whatever occult influence has an interest in guiding it to suit their purposes.

Many of the ancient mysteries of Greece depicted ritualised murders and we can only guess whether actual murders took place or whether they were carefully staged enactments designed to resemble real murders. The Crata Repoa is a Masonic text from the 18th Century which supposedly depicts the mysteries of Ancient Egyptian Masonry but which resembles more a pastiche of haunted house adventures. This Egyptian revival formed part of the so-called Egyptian rite of Freemasonry and Manly P Hall, the celebrated 33 degree Masonic historian apparently chose to lend the Crata Repoa credibility by publishing it in his book Freemasonry of the Ancient Egyptians.

It is clear that the Crata Repoa is a lot of nonsense but it does reflect both what Freemasons believed might have taken place during Ancient Egyptian initiations and they could have drawn this conclusion by drawing on the broad themes of contemporary Masonic rites and what knowledge and rumour might have reached them about Greek mysteries, much of which has actually made its way into the current sphere of knowledge and is what are known as the great myths. One of the best examples of this is the myth of the Minotaur which in all likelihood, was probably a character in a ritual initiation which was said to be associated with King Minas' palace of Knosos but may have taken place at the ancient quarries some 20 miles away on the same island of Crete where there was the Labyrinth Cave near Gortyn with a history of human settlement going back 7000 years; many islanders to this day consider the caves to be the labyrinth mentioned in the myth of the Minotaur.

All based on this ancient principle of staging a spectacle in order to invoke or provoke specific thoughts, feelings, and specific changes in mentality of the initiate we have the far more overtly sinister and destructive recent phenomenon of what is known as Trauma Based Mind Control.

As one of the 'virgins' tells RC: "this Death shall make many alive." By which we can infer the meaning to be
that the ritual deaths are designed to provoke the mind of the initiates in some way, to make them 'alive' that is, mentally transformed.

The following excerpt comes from a former Illuminati trainer known as Svali who was fairly active in conspiracy theory circles and gave several interviews within this community, but lately some of this specific information seems at risk of being lost in light of the wave of mass censorship which risks washing away all truth and ability to identify the evil hidden forces behind the stage of our society:

"I have seen set ups (oh, yes, they set up fake deaths, etc.) where a person was "burned alive" to teach the children not to tell. They are told that this is a traitor who disclosed, and now he is being punished. The person wasn't really a traitor and is in a flame proof vest, but the vision of a person on fire and screaming remains with 3 and 4 year old children for a lifetime. And, when they are adults, even if they DO leave, scenes such as this mean they won't tell many people for fear of being traced and punished.

Because I helped create a lot of set ups as an adult trainer, I became somewhat cynical and have chosen to disclose as a result, although I do fight intense fear even now at times. Try being buried in a wooden box for a period of time (it may have been minutes, but to a four year old it is an eternity), and then when the lid is lifted being told, "if you ever tell, we'll put you back in forever". The child will scream hysterically that they will NEVER EVER tell. I was that child, and now I am breaking that vow made under psychological duress. Because I don't want any other children to go through what I did or have seen done to others."

The crude and terrible purpose behind Satanic rituals fulfils many goals at once. In addition to implicating members in terrible and astonishingly evil crimes which guarantee to estrange them from decent society and bring them deeper into the Satanic fold, the purpose of mental and psychological transformation is rapidly completed. The brain-chemistry transformation which may take years to complete in conventional mystical secret society programmes can be achieved in a matter of days with the right shockingly unpleasant display in which the individual themselves may play a part. It is almost impossible to explain such a transformation to someone who has not experienced it but something like the desperate and profound personal transformation can be glimpsed in Dostoevsky's great novel Crime and Punishment. It is likely that Dostoevsky himself could write so well about such a profound mental transformation since he himself was placed in an almost initiatory programme within the context of his impending execution for discussing banned books critical of Tsarist Russia, a sentence from which he was reprieved at the 11th hour.

The Chymical Wedding is assuredly a 'transformative' programme and we can observe the various moments of extreme stress and uncertainty the protagonist, a knight of the order of the Golden Stone known as RC, is placed under for prolonged periods, only for a slow reversal of the conditions and instead find himself in a kind of worthy glory, only to have other pressures piled upon him, more uncertainties and even mockery, all of which is designed to make him question himself, place him in personal insecurity and slowly destroy his ego leaving him, somewhat like the alchemical allegory of the Phoenix, ready to be 'reborn' into a new reality and fresh identity.

The term 'wedding' in the transformative sense of wedding the soul to some kind of higher reality first appears in Plutarch's essay On the Soul:

"Thus death and initiation closely correspond; even the words (teleutana and teleisthai) correspond, and so do the things.
At first there are wanderings and toilsome running about in circles and journeys through the dark over uncertain roads and culs de sac;
then, just before the end, there are all kinds of terrors,
with shivering, trembling, sweating, and utter amazement.
After this, a strange and wonderful light meets the wanderer;
he is admitted into clean and verdant meadows,
where he discerns gentle voices, and choric dances,
and the majesty of holy sounds and sacred visions.

That the wedding and close union of the soul with the body
is a thing really contrary to nature may clearly be seen from all this."

So we find passages such as this where RC is placed in uncertainty, discomfort and the feeling of 'imminent danger':

"…he bound each of us in a several place, and so went away with our small Tapers, and left us poor Wretches in Darkness. Then first began some to perceive the imminent danger, and I myself could not refrain Tears. For although we were not forbidden to speak, yet anguish and affliction suffered none of us to utter one word. For the Cords were so wonderfully made, yet none could cut them, much less get them off his Feet: yet this comforted me, that still the future gain, of many a one, who had now betaken himself to rest, would prove very little to his satisfaction."

Or indeed the psychological results of witnessing the ritual beheading of the six kings, which, understandably, prevents him from sleeping:

".. his intention was to lull me asleep, which at last I well observed, whereupon I made as though I was fast asleep, but no sleep came into my Eyes, and I could not put the Beheaded out of my mind."

Whether Johann Valentin Andreae wrote The Chymical Wedding is debatable, especially as in his later life Andreas considers alchemy to be a subject of ridicule and astrology not to be serious science, and this does not accord with the Chymical Wedding which is resplendent with opaque and obscure references to astrology and alchemy but then so the Fama Fraternitatis itself is also critical of many aspects of so called alchemy as perhaps a serious scientific community might be who wanted to distance themselves from quacks and charlatans:

"But now concerning, and chiefly in this our age, the ungodly and accursed gold-making, which hath gotten so much the upper hand, whereby under colour of it, many runagates and roguish people do use great villanies and cozen and abuse the credit which is given them; yea, now adays men of discretion do hold the transmutation of metals to be the highest point and fastigium in philosophy."

It is possible that Andreas wrote the tract as a detail of his experience but again this seems unlikely since the story is written from the perspective of an old man and it would be a stretch for Andreas to reframe what must be a personal narrative in this way.

Alchemy, although more often associated with the search for the Philosopher's stone and the transmutation of base metal into gold is actually just a previous incarnation of what we call chemistry. The alchemy in the Chymical Wedding, which is wrapped up in allegorical and metaphorical references to the Greek Phoenix, seems to be the description of an authentic scientific experiment with various chemical reactions which at that time were seen as something mystical and the scientific lexicon at that time being lacking, were described in unfamiliar terms which uses the language of metaphor. The experiment described in the tract is carried out with all the gravity of a religious liturgy including music and 'virgins' shrouded in white linen.

The nature of the experiment and the accuracy of the narrative cannot be certain, but the facts laid out by the narrator are: that the coffins of the six kings and the black executioner, apparently executed the previous day are brought to a tower containing a series of laboratories at each floor of the tower. That the narrator and his fellows enter a laboratory where they distil the essences from various plants and minerals and put these into glasses, believing that the experiment would be able to restore the bodies to life, meanwhile, the women wash the bodies of the men. RC sees seven flames rolling across the sea, which he believes to be the spirits of the departed men, these flames advance to the top pinnacle of the tower in which the laboratory is located.

The next morning, they awake, having slept on mattresses in the laboratory at the bottom of the tower, there they discuss what might happen next: whether the men would be returned to life, or whether the experiment would produce an elixir which would give longer life to all, or indeed whether the men had really been killed at all and someone had been killed in their place. They then make their way up to the next room in the tower above them which they have to do with the use of a ladder, ropes or wings, where they are greeted by one of the women and the narrator believes a container is brought in which contain the six bodies of the beheaded men.

A round object wrapped in taffeta which is believed to be the head of the moor who executed the six kings, is placed in a kettle and covered it with a lid full of holes.

One of the compounds they had distilled, presumably something strongly caustic is poured into the kettle which is then brought to the boil and from the holes the liquid rises out and reaches the bodies below where it dissolves them into a liquid. A tap at the bottom of the container containing the dissolved bodies was turned and a very red liquid was removed from the casket and filled a large golden globe. Then the casket containing the bodies was taken away and he wondered if anything was left of the bodies and whether it was disposed of, but he noticed that they were markedly lighter but the liquid extracted from the dissolving agents from the bodies was heavier and in large quantity and needed to be borne by six men and it took a lot of effort to move the golden globe outside of the room.

After a moment of rest and conversation they are again instructed to come back up into the room above which for some reason they have to do again with the ladder, ropes and wings, while the virgins and attendants have their own special access which they are not allowed to use.

In this room the narrator now describes the golden globe in the middle of the room along with a series of polished mirrors and windows by which the sun shines onto the mirrors and thus onto the golden globe which created such a dazzle of light and heat that they could not look at it.

After the globe had cooled it was opened and inside was found a snow-white egg. This egg was then taken away. A little while later they were instructed to climb to the next level in the tower through a third hole to the fourth level of the tower, where they found the 'egg' being tended and a large copper kettle filled with yellow sand was being warmed over a fire and the egg placed in it.

It is well worth noting that the Red King and White Queen are alchemical terms and the 'chemical marriage' is the joining of these two disparate gendered compounds. The Red King is sulphur and the White Queen is mercury. The Moors head, is the third element 'negrido'

The egg hatches and a hungry bird emerges which they must feed on the blood of the beheaded kings and the 'bird' goes through several changes, turning black, then moulting all his 'feathers' which were replaced by white ones and the bird grew 'tamer' that is possibly, less chemically reactive. He was fed again and his feathers became all coloured. The water was evaporated off until a blue sediment or stone was left which was ground and painted onto the bird. After a break they were let into a fifth room where the bird was put into a milky looking bath and was covered with a fine white powder. The bath was heated slowly and they had to keep the bird from escaping from the hot bath. The bird lost all his feathers to the bath which appeared to be blue of colour.

The bird is a metaphor which represents both a chemical substance but also the alchemist involved in a transformative experience. The first stage observed was the black feathers, which is said by some traditions to represent the first stage of meditation when there is only darkness in the inner world. The next stage is the white bird, or white swan which is said to be the awakening of the etheric body of light. The next stage is the pelican, consciously being able to use the etheric body, followed by the Peacock which represents astral body consciousness and finally the phoenix which is the freeing of the spirit from the bounds of the physical.

Briefly, the alchemical transformation of the initiate is said to be a seven-stage process. The terms used to describe this transformation are also terms widely used in chemistry although a concept such a putrefaction, otherwise known as 'negrido' or blackening no longer has any particular scientific relevance, nor do the mediaeval chemical transformations of 'whitening' or 'reddening'.

If we look at the alchemical process psychologically then it is clear we are looking at a transformation of a person's character, behaviour and general outlook and from analysis the burning, melting and reconstitution terminology used it is clear that a very real ego-death is taking place. The question is how do you kill an ego and what does such a thing really mean or imply? Well, from examining the events of the Chymical Wedding we can see that confusion, foreboding, nervous tension, fear and terror, are all instilled in the….we might call him victim as much as initiate or candidate but I suppose like the term 'mystae' since this word represents he who undergoes the mysteries and fundamentally I believe all mysteries have had the same intention throughout the so-called religious cults of the ancient world, I say 'so called' because the beliefs of the Ancients cannot really be indulged with the term religion since its priests were knowingly using their secret knowledge of science to deliberately trick and mislead what we might call their flock of initiates. We have often heard how the priesthood exerted great power during the various periods of the roughly three-thousand-year period of generally acknowledged Ancient Egyptian history. Power is attained generally through knowledge though violence is another method though generally a much less reliable one, and even if violence is part of the acquisition of power, which in the case of the Arab conquests of the 7th Century, the acquisition of profound and deep knowledge following the violent conquest guaranteed the supremacy of the Arabs for several hundred years before the rise of the Turks who in their turn conquered through violence then knowledge.

To make things even stranger and more confusing, the experiment and the terminology used in the Chymical Wedding is strongly suggestive of the experiment described in the 16th Century alchemical treatise The Rosarium Philosophorum. The Name Rosarium or Rosary does not refer to the Catholic Rosary beads but to a 'rose garden' as a metaphor for wise-sayings but just as likely the Rosarium evokes the Rosicrucians since it is so close in its content to the Chymical Wedding.

The text is strongly suggestive of some kind of chemical experiment but with the suggestion of some kind of spiritual subtext, many commentors despair of making sense of the text and instead pay more attention to the series of twenty fascinating and strange woodcuts which accompanied the appearance of the text in 1550.

Some of the images are said to have antecedents in other alchemical work in particular the German Book of the Holy Trinity produced in the early 15th Century by a German Franciscian monk. The book gives a specifically Christian treatment to what was considered occult and impious magic and the specific Christian context of this, and of the Chymical Wedding provided a broad acceptance in society of what had hitherto been treat with suspicion by the church authorities.

Adam Mclean with his well-regarded analysis of the woodcuts writes of the work:

"In that it sought to unite these two alchemical realms, the Rosarium set a style for alchemical literature of the late sixteenth and early seventeenth centuries, in which the physical process became a mirror for soul development, and the inner content of soul experiences became projected upon outer processes in the laboratory or the natural world."

And this really is the accepted understanding of the significance of alchemical treatises, that they ostensibly describe a scientific process using contemporaneous scientific terms which also serve to simultaneously and obliquely describe spiritual, psychological and bio-chemical changes and transformations.

This may seem alien to us, this fusion of science and religion into an indivisible mass from which it is impossible to discern the glittering of spiritual truths from the solid lumps of science but as we have already discussed, in the ancient world science and religion were one and the same, because science was a jealously guarded secret and its mysteries were key tools for the priestly class to bamboozle, astound and enrapture their initiates.

The stages of the alchemical process of personal transformation are at the most basic, as follows: the first stage is calcination which is to subject something to extreme heat, so if we were to imagine how this metaphor might materialise within the context of some kind of initiatory mind-control programme then we would subject our mystae to extreme stresses and various other kind of pressures, in order to see which parts of him glow under the heat and which elements diminish and are burned off, figuratively speaking.

After this there is the sublimation or dissolution stage which is the chemical process by which a solid turns directly into a gas without passing through a liquid state. As this suggests, the calcination or burning causes extreme energetic changes in the person and they are entering a different stage of consciousness, one previously not experienced except during peak or extreme situations.

This is what is referred to by the bird losing its black feathers in the heat and turning to white as it is depicted in the Chymical Wedding. In the woodcuts which accompanied The Rosarium Philosophorum this stage is shown by the King and Queen sitting in a bath together, it is also represented by winged serpents and dark dragons. Another image which appears in the Rosarium Philisophorum is that of a Green Lion eating the sun. In parallel to the actual chemical experiments carried out by the alchemists the sun represents gold which could be dissolved by sulphuric acid, represented by the green Lion.

The Green Lion is the purified Vitriol, possibly hydrated iron sulphate or the aqua regia acid that can dissolve even the noble metal gold. In one of the woodcuts, we see the Green Lion devouring the Sun and releasing red blood, the 'blood' represents the red philosopher's stone being released from the reaction between aqua regia.

The next stage is separation and we can see that following the laboratory metaphor, impure elements are burned off or fused components separate into their respective elements. So, under the influence of what we can consider heat or agitation, the psyche in a sense, sees itself clearly for the first time. From this operation the 'quintessence' or 'fifth element' emerges, the hidden secret powerful depths of the mind and spirit. Something which historically had been described as 'the air of God' and even finer than light. Perhaps this is the stuff of the electromagnetic soul itself, or perhaps the soul is beyond even electromagnetism, the most powerful and fundamental force in the universe.

The next stage, Conjunction, is where we see the winged figure in the woodcut. This is the start of the reintegration of the psyche with all the impurities having been burned off. This is followed by Rectificando. This is the part referred to as the marriage of the sun and moon. It is a unification of the forces of the spirit, or quintessence with the material forces. This is symbolised by the woodcut of the king and queen in sexual congress.

Fermentation, also known as putrefaction is where the spirit trapped in the body sees the Earth around as something dead and that real life is beyond. The feeling of timelessness is often a symptom reported by those undergoing psychosis: they feel time is frozen or has vanished altogether and that what they are really experiencing is the frozen nature of our reality while their mind has been set to a different time-zone, namely of the eternity of the spirit. The pure quintessence from the previous alchemical stage has now realised it is here trapped on Earth, and though it has wings it cannot fly, please excuse the flowery metaphor but these are precisely the images which have been evoked and used to describe this particular stage in the ongoing mental process.

This alchemical process, can be applied to both the distillation and purification of a chemical substances like strong mineral acids from natural compounds, such as the elaborate distillation of sulphuric acid or what was known as oil of vitriol. Vitriol was so called because in nature it resembled glassy crystals usually found with gravel in mines where groundwater had drawn off iron-sulphate deposits. It was necessary to first calcify or burn the substance into ash, then dissolve or leech out the various compounds into water, then fermentation or putrefaction would have been the first stage of distillation which tended to create a highly malodorous substance as the organic compounds present in the sulphur for instance, would give the well-known smell of rotten eggs, which upon separation of the organic elements and distillation would produce the pure substance which could then be coagulated into a powder or 'stone' as it was then known. So, this alchemical process was basically a process of taking a natural impure compound, and through various treatments extracting the desired pure and rarefied compound, whether that be an acid, gas or crystal.

In the early 17th Century work The Azoth of the Philosophers we find what was later to become a Freemasonic moto which is often found inside the Masonic Chamber of Reflection, a small sombre room adjoining the main hall where the candidate awaiting initiation is placed. Along with the acronym there are several objects or representations of objects alluding to alchemical themes: "visita interiora terrae, rectificandoque, invenies occultum lapidem which means 'visit the interior of the Earth, rectify yourself and you will find the hidden stone' which in turn is a metaphor for some kind of inner alchemical transformation and spiritual realignment which will reveal the secret substance of the soul.

Things however do not quite seem to go well in the end for our RC, or at least that is how it is made to appear, it is likely that events unfolded precisely as they were planned. Despite the feeling of ultimately being honoured with celestial visions and the great pomp and ceremony of the King and Queen and the untold number of finely attired 'virgins' RC commits, or rather is induced to commit an act reprehensible in the eyes of the King. He sees Venus naked:

"Here (said he) if you please, we may go further down"; "I still follow you" (replied I) so I went down the steps, where it was exceeding dark, but the Page immediately opened a little Chest, wherein stood a small ever-burning Taper, at which he Kindled one of the many Torches which lay by. I was mightily terrified, and seriously asked how he durst do this? He gave me for answer. As long as the Royal Persons are still at rest, I have nothing to fear. Herewith I espied a rich Bed ready-made, hung about with curious Curtains, one of which he drew, where I saw the Lady Venus stark-naked for he heaved up the Coverlets too) lying there in such Beauty, and a fashion so surprizing, that I was almost beside myself, neither do I yet know whether it was a piece thus Carved, or an humane Corps that lay dead there; For she was altogether immoveable, and yet I durst not touch her. So she was again covered, and the Curtain drawn before her, yet she was still (as it were) in my Eye."

Throughout the 18th Century Isis veiled was a metaphor for modern science and unveiling Isis was a metaphor for making scientific discoveries. So here with the discoveries in chemistry of the alchemists the analogy of seeing Venus naked would be another allusion which only the initiate would understand the deeper meaning of.

Despite his page deliberately leading him to the chamber and even lifting up the covers so that he might specifically see Venus naked, he admits to his fault and as a punishment is told that he must take the place of the gate-porter. Indeed, the previous porter whom RC replaces is described as:

"Now in the first place I asked the King what the condition of this porter was. He friendlily answered me, that he was a very famous and rare astrologer, and always in high regard with the Lord his Father, but having once committed a fault against Venus, and seen her in her bed of rest, this punishment was therefore imposed upon him, that he should wait at the first gate for so long until someone should release him from it. I replied, 'May he then be released?' 'Yes,' said the King, 'if anyone can be found that has transgressed as highly as himself, he must take his place, and the other shall be free.' This went to my heart, for my conscience convinced me that I was the offender, yet I kept quiet, and herewith delivered the supplication."

We can infer that there is a feeling that after experiencing the unique initiation into the mysteries and to have the whole court apparently at your service in furthering your wisdom and spiritual knowledge you must again, take your place in the mundane world, now serving the order in a mundane fashion bereft and even excluded from the palace for ever more and only serving to allow entry to the next initiates into the mysteries:

"After me the rest were called for too, and came jocundly out again, which pained me still more, for I imagined nothing other than that I must finish my life under the gate. I also had many pensive thoughts running up and down in my head, what I should do, and how to spend the time. At length I considered that I was now old, and according to the course of nature, had few years more to live. And that this anguished and melancholy life would quickly send me from this world, and then my door-keeping would be at an end, and by a most happy sleep I might quickly bring myself to the grave. I had many of these thoughts. Sometimes it vexed me that I had seen such gallant things, and must be robbed of them."

The aim of the Illuminati is to create a psycho-chemical change in consciousness. The knowledge of this process has always resided within a secret repository of human knowledge in the possession of the priests and chosen adepts of the ancient mysteries. In Ancient Greece this transformation was called 'metanoia'. This information was used sparingly and then only ever employed with the availability of an antidote or ritual secret which could reverse the condition. And so, in the Bachic rites and the rites of Pan, we hear of the extraordinary states of temporary madness and frenzy which were felt to be a sign of the welcome possession of the God, yet which was always assumed to be only a temporary state. Socrates said: "the greatest blessing comes by way of mania, as long as mania is heaven-sent," and the word 'enthusiasm' comes from the Greek word 'en-theos' to be inspired or possessed by God. More sinisterly the word 'panic' means to be caused by the spirit of the Greek God Pan.

Many of the mystical rites of ancient Greece involved the use of psychedelic drugs and the rites of Bachus in particular used wine, presumably in great excess, along with other cues and auto-suggestions. Just to clarify what I mean by the term 'auto-suggestion' and this more than any drug, or external influence, has the power to affect the personal psychological transformation which is the purpose of the ritual. Without the auto-suggestion then the ritual would have no effect and the initiation would serve no purpose. This is why it was said that the mystae of the ancient mysteries of Eleusis were put to death if upon questioning after the unfolding of the mystery, they answered that they did not believe what they had seen to have been 'real', since, without the power of belief and auto-suggestion, there could be no hope of any of the desired transformative experience which has always been the key goal of any religious or spiritual ritual or ceremony.

Even religious rites and rituals, which are more properly termed 'liturgies' exist in our present age though are fast declining in the present secular age, such as the Christening of a child, where the belief that the ritual of a priest bathing the infants head with water while reading a blessing, will prepare that child's soul for acceptance into Christ's kingdom. The baptism liturgy only has any meaning or significance if the parents believe in it, and the child later believes that their Baptism has made them a Christian. Of course, in many instances Baptism is only a matter of form and social appearances, and the auto-suggestion or belief in the process itself is lacking and a mere formality of convention, but once the belief in the power of the ritual fades from the cultural identity this is then swiftly followed by the disappearance of the desire to even maintain the appearance of the belief in the process, at which point the ritual fades into obsolescence.

There are said to be two initiatory traditions: a Kabbalistic Jewish and a Greek tradition, and the events of the Chymical Wedding seem to indicate a fusion of both of these currents as we can attest from the presence of some of the key elements of the Greek mysteries such as the unveiling of Aphrodite/Venus and the death and rebirth of the Phoenix, which in this instance is clearly the culmination of some kind of chemical experiment. As we have seen previously, for the ancients the world of science and the spirit were wedded, no pun intended.

In Michael Laitman's commentary on the Zohar he decrypts the Kabbalah as being an attempt to systematically reverse the fall-of-man and return to a kind of spiritual Eden:

"The Creator's Light descended along these degrees, and at the lowest degree, created our world and man in it. Having realized his insignificance and wishing to ascend to the Creator, man (to the extent that he wishes to approach the Creator) ascends along the same degrees by which his initial descent took place."

The Chymical Wedding is the Kabbalistic marriage between the Bride (Malkuth) and the Bridegroom which is the Sefira of Tiferet and is connected to all the higher emanations but is the highest of the material world. It is the unification of Malkuth to Tiferet that begins the path of transcendence. The King is the bridegroom: Tiferet, and is represented by the sun. Therefore, unifying the material with the immaterial light: the work of the sun, so it could be that the chemical wedding is solar enlightenment, that is, becoming aware of the true nature of light. I have already written fairly extensively on this subject in my book Light in the Darkness which can be perused for further enlightenment on this subject.

The modern legacy of the alchemists is twofold. Firstly, the development of chemistry, which primarily revolved around agitating and separating volatile elements which in the instance of the modern petrochemical industry has hugely affected our lives in monumental ways yet based on fairly rudimentary, mediaeval experiments. The secondary legacy of the alchemical movement is much more subtle and has remained very much underground and forms the main thesis of this book, but what of the quest for the creation of gold? Was there ever anything in it?

Although it is obvious that no alchemist ever succeeded in creating gold their experiments must have been highly suggestive that such a thing might be possible. What they were able to do was break down and manipulate metals, liquids and gasses and change their states. Turning gold into a red liquid solution then precipitating it into powder and finally back into gold. They realised if they could somehow create this red powder or philosopher's stone via some other process, which they believed was the 'essence' of gold, then they would have the secret to the manufacture of gold. Even relatively early in the period of Alchemy and perhaps at its height, the 11th century Persian polymath 'Avicenna' Ibn Sina, way ahead of his time, cut to the very core of the matter when he declared:

"Those of the chemical craft know well that no change can be effected in the different species of substances, though they can produce the appearance of such change."

It is possible that something which superficially resembled gold was produced in some of the alchemical experiments, Thomas Sherwood in his book The Alchemists: Founders of Modern Chemistry reports that Albertus Magus, a Dominican friar and metallurgist had tested examples of so-called alchemical gold "but found that five or six treatments in the furnace reduced it to ashes." A similar story, by the way, is told of al-Razl, that some of his alchemical gold tarnished after many years, and that he took it back again. Doubtless many of these so-called golds were brassy alloys like the modern ormolu and pinchbeck, or possibly mixtures of these with some gold.

Interestingly on page 96 of the same book we find a statement about the origin of this influx of knowledge into the west:

"The men of the West knew neither Greek nor Arabic, the Arabs generally did not know Latin; but there were many learned Jews who knew some tongue that the "Franks" understood. By their aid, translations came to be made."

Here then we might understand the pivotal importance of the crusades in terms of forming a first meeting, though at times inauspicious with the butchering of the Jews of Jerusalem during the First Crusade, between the Christians of the West and the Jews of the East. It is likely that despite the bloody excesses of the First Crusade a quid pro quo was reached between the knights of the West and the Jews, and in particular of the Knights of the Temple or 'Templars', and it is seems that the Templars' knowledge in affairs of international banking, usury and compound interest can only really have come from one quarter.

Ibn Rushid, known in the west as Averroes, was a Berber polymath of 12th Century Muslim Spain who is better known in the West than in the Muslim world where he is largely forgotten. He is one of the key Muslims who could be said to have fed the intellectual revitalisation of the West after the fall of the Western Roman Empire, and while the Eastern Byzantine Empire continued for almost a thousand years after the fall of Rome, it was no longer a dominant force but only one which was continually trying to survive its own growing inability to compete with technological innovations from the East such as Turkish gunpowder and also riven from within by its own internecine conflicts which ultimately continually weakened it.

Averoes is known in the West for his commentaries of Aristotle and this work came, as we have previously observed, through translation into Latin from Arabic by Jewish intermediaries, at a time when no Westerner except perhaps a slave to the Moors would or could have learned Arabic.

Aristotle is variously known as the father of various things, from logic, to meteorology and scientific rationalism. Like Pythagoras he could be said to have been instrumental in forming a movement away from the Ancient Egyptian mystical conception of reality to a more materialistically bound cosmos: understanding things by their material phenomenon so when Pythagoras said "Man is the measure of all things" it was an early voice of materialistic scepticism in Greek thought, just as when he said: "As to the gods, I have no means of knowing either that they exist or do not exist."

Aristotle also rather presumptuously declared "Prayers and sacrifices to the gods are of no avail." Though his observation that: "Men create gods in their own image, not only with regard to their form but with regard to their mode of life" could be said to be demonstrably true with regard to the Greek and Roman pantheon.

In a strange way, showing us perhaps the cyclical nature of history, the Muslim world has pursued the very reverse course of the movements in thought and scientific progress which the West has pursued since the fall of Rome. The fall of Rome represented a massive cultural and technological reset with great cities of stone being progressively abandoned and a loss of several key technologies since the expertise in crafts and arts had become compartmentalised and specialised to particular regions in the Empire and these were the items these areas traded in. With the fall of the organising, commercial and logistical force of the Roman Empire the network which had brought technology, goods, food and ideas withered and died, leaving people suddenly destitute and bereft of things they had for so long taken for granted.

If our own 'world-empire' were to suddenly break down and the various items essential to our civilisation, such as Norwegian oil and gas, Chinese pharmaceutical ingredients and Egyptian tomatoes. It's not hard to imagine that were some kind of monumental disaster to befall our world infrastructure, paralysing the electronics and the transfer of data and information somehow, then we would probably find ourselves in a state somewhat akin to the European dark-ages. Crafts, skills and technology indigenous and innate to the particular geographic area would likely remain, provided they were not dependent on technologies and goods from elsewhere, but when this is precisely the case of so much of modern industry then our losses would be great, for even with the knowledge to maintain civilisation it would be useless without the actual tools, and so in time, with the loss of the tools necessary even the knowledge itself would become lost.

The Islamic conquest rose from the mutual exhaustion of two great empires, the Byzantine and Persian Empire, which had been locked in conflict for nearly a thousand years since the time of Cyrus the Great and were so set on destroying each other that they had no thought of what forces might rise against them in the absence of their might. It is strange that the Arab conquest began in the midst of what had been the Jewish Kingdom of Himayr in Arabia which had been taken by Ethiopian Christians in 525 AD.

Jews played an important if not pivotal role in the rise of Islam, Muhammed's first wife Khadija, the daughter of a leader of the Quraysh tribe, was a wealthy Jewish merchant in her own right and provided Mohammed with contacts and access to important and influential people as well as money which Mohammed used to free Muslim slaves and feed and maintain his army. Without Khadija there would be no Islam, but one has to wonder what motivated her? Clearly, she was part of an extended elite network of wealthy merchants but what if she were given a task: to foment a rebellion against the Christians by forming an army to drive them out of their own lands by the sword of conversion.

According to Alzog's Universal Church History published in 1902 "Mohammed was the only son of Abdullah, a pagan, and Amina, a Jewess, and was descended from the noble but impoverished family of Hashim, of the priestly tribe of Koreish, who were the chiefs and keepers of the Kaaba, and pretended to trace their origin to Ishmael, the son of Abraham and Hagar, was born at Mecca, August 20, AD 570..."

We cannot know what took place in the 'revelation of the cave' in which Mohammed was apparently visited by the Angel Gabriel and given the text of the Quran to recite and this is said to be a miracle since Mohammed was said to have been illiterate.

Since Mohammed was a merchant working for and raised by his uncle Abu Talib, who was the leader of the Banu Hashim clan, and as such part of the elite of Mecca, Mohammed being illiterate seems unlikely. For Mohammed to be raised as an illiterate makes no sense. Indeed, his uncle was a celebrated poet, and held a very important position in Meccan society as being responsible for feeding the Hajj pilgrims. Such a man was a figure of the Meccan elite and it would be a great shame to him to raise a child as an illiterate. In some Hadiths Mohammed is said to have written letters and also the marriage contract with Aisha.

Might it not be outside the realm of possibility that what took place in the cave was not a truly supernatural event but one stage-managed to appear so, just in the manner of the ancient mystery schools which eventually metamorphosised into Freemasonry and by these means managed to acquire an army of obedient servants willing to commit murder and crimes against the state and authority itself in the holy name of revolution?

The Jewish Rabbi Rabbi Mukhayriq, fought alongside Mohammed and bequeathed his entire fortune to him. It is possible that Mohammed himself was Jewish, since he belonged to the Banu Hashem, a clan of the Quraysh tribe, which originated from Hashim ibn Abd Manaf who was a Hanif, that is a follower of the religion of Abraham which could be taken to be ostensibly Jewish; the Hanifeya could be considered to be a kind of proto-Islam which maintained that Arabs are Abraham's descendants through the union of Hajar and Abraham. Mohammed even initially presented himself as the Messiah so long awaited by the Jews but being rejected by the them, led to a change in Mohammed's attitude toward the Jewish merchants leading to conflict when Mohammed successfully defended against a siege on Medina at the battle of the Trench.

Islam's early ruthless and bloodthirsty expansion at the expense of Christian lands and Kingdoms was fuelled with the money and contacts of influential elite mercantile bloodlines based in Arabia, a place where a Jewish kingdom had only recently itself been deposed by Christians, and it was this Himyarite Jewish Kingdom which had subsumed the city of Saba, home to the infamous Sabaeans.

Islam very quickly achieved its 'enlightenment' as it settled into ancient lands such as Egypt, ancient Babylon and Persia and the former Assyrian Empire. One can only dream of what these largely ignorant weaponised camel-traders could have discovered when they arrived; the wealth of the world's peak civilisations and their millennia of knowledge was it is said, generally imparted to them by those of the ancient priesthoods and scribes who had to quickly reach a quid pro quo and adapt to life under very new masters.

The Quran, being written in the post classical period, it is easy for the religion to easily co-exist with the paradigm of scientific exploration, contrary perhaps to the Old Testament which was written largely in the pre-scientific period, after the development of Greek and Latin science, and often appears to be specifically at-odds with the later scientific world which as we know led to conflict between the Church and hermeticists rediscovering ancient knowledge and building on it, but there was no such conflict between Islam and science since they were both happily contemporaneous and born within the same era. The Roman Church had inherited scriptures which were thousands of years old and not compatible with some of the implications which were emerging from the investigations of the mediaeval polymaths.

However, within Christianity it seemed only the weakening of the Roman Catholic church would permit the same development of the sciences which had taken place in the Islamic world, though it seemed just as the Christian world was emerging from the mediaeval dark ages the enlightenment of the Islamic world was starting to fade.

Eventually the Arabs were largely conquered by the Turks who adopted Islam and became the new flag-bearers of Islamic domination through the Ottoman Empire, but the Ottoman empire and the Muslims had run out of ancient records and seemed unable to develop from the stage of feudal theocracy to industrial society, the reasons for this are outside the scope of this work except perhaps, strangely, we find an inverse to the story of the Roman Church trying to model society based on the writings of a pre-scientific people we find with Islam that the world had outgrown its scriptures and the discoveries the Arabs had inherited when they first left Arabia. It seems that for whatever reason, they were unable to develop or build on what they had already acquired. And now we have a Muslim world which is effectively at the position the Roman Church had enforced in Europe, a retreat to fundamentalism in religion, where religion no longer serves man but man must serve religion, despite his empirical and logical senses telling him something is very wrong somewhere.

Not for nothing do we have the term 'ritual humiliation' in the standard cultural idiomatic lexicon of the English language: it has been part of mystery school initiations since the earliest moments of recorded history. A particular example of the Greco-Roman mystery school is outlined in The Metamorphoses of Apuleius; a picaresque novel which dates from the 2nd Century; also known as The Golden Ass, and the only ancient Roman novel to survive in a complete state. It depicts the adventures of Lucius, a curious young man who may be modelled on the author himself since the author is also known as Lucius, who dreams of great adventures and has "an overwhelming longing to experience magic at first hand". He travels to Thessaly, renowned as the centre of magic in the ancient world, spurred by a great curiosity of the magical arts which reaches a fever when he learns that Pamphile, the wife of his miserly host Milo is a witch and has been seen transforming herself into a bird. Here the magical agent is an ointment, which somewhat recalls the flying ointment of the European witches who were said to apply a balm of various herbs and plants which would be toxic were they to be ingested but applied to a sturdy stick, such as a broomstick, then the same moistened broomstick applied to the mucus membrane of the bare genital area and ridden vigorously, would allow the psychotropic alkalis to be harmlessly absorbed into the skin without the threat of poisoning. The 'flight' of the witches was thus more like the perceived flight of one under a heavy dose of psychotropics and not a literal flight, but the story here claims poetic license.

It was said that thus under this chemical influence the witches would then 'fly' to their sabbath, presumably taking place in the 'astral' plane, and would converse with each other. Despite the poetic license the writer of the Golden ass knows a great deal about the mystery-school and initiatory tradition of the ancient world, but then we are very much operating in a facts-vacuum when it comes to first, second or even third hand accounts of what might have taken place during the cult initiations of the ancient world.

But if we can separate the fact from the fancy, we are told several intriguing details which if you have read this far you may be willing to give a little more credence to as being an explanation of how these Gods and Goddess may have 'communicated' with those who were destined to be part of their cults.

First of all, Lucius is several times referred to as being of high-birth:

"Besides your sublime knowledge, and the nobility of your birth, you're an initiate of several cults and you know the value of silence on sacred matters."

Somewhat like the more familiar Canterbury Tales some thousand years later, the text takes the form of a compendium of tales broadly connected to the main themes and characters of the story though unlike the Canterbury Tales there is a singular lack of the relief of piety which the moral tales provide to counteract the bawdier elements. There is also a macabre and strange story which is told featuring a borderline case of necrophilia:

"...the paines of Child-birth, which went so hard with her that all thought she had been dead, so with much state, and great mourning she was interred. Now I thought with my self, during her Life thou couldst have no part in this Woman, but yet now dead as she is thou mayst embrace and Kiss her sufficiently; whereupon I took my Servant with me, who dug her up by Night; Now having opened the Coffin and locked her in my Arms, and feeling about her Heart, I found still some little motion in it, which increased more and more from my warmth, till at last I perceived that she was indeed still alive; wherefore I quietly bare her home, and after I had warmed her chilled Body with a costly Bath of Herbs, I committed her to my Mother."

Perhaps this is a window into the ancient world and its values. Lacking completely are any familiar Christian themes or any depiction of transcendental themes of righteousness, virtue and simple goodness, the tales and the narrative from the Golden Ass are at times, frankly a little hard to stomach since they revolve around the thousand cruel injustices of humans visited upon Lucius in his asinine form, and the tales, probably from a common repository of ancient tales, have no glimmer of moral goodness in them but revolve around sex, murder, human cruelty and avarice, many of which follow some of the ribald themes of the Canterbury Tales revolving around cuckoldry and devious tricks in order to sleep with another man's wife. But what interests us in particular is the tale from book 3 where Lucius, interested in becoming a witch, is informed by his aunt that Milo's wife is a witch. He goes over to her house and makes love to Photis (which is explicitly depicted in pornographic detail) a serving wench in their household and returning there the next day he is waylaid by three robbers whom he kills before going home to bed.

Witches are presented as a powerful and very real threat throughout the narrative and this gives us an insight into how a world would view witchcraft and witches if it was assumed that such things were real and perfectly possible within the understood laws of reality, which for thousands of years they were:

"'I don't think I've ever achieved a greater freedom, though I live in terror of the dark inescapable lairs of the magic arts. They say not even the sepulchres of the dead are safe, that the old witches hunt for relics and severed bits of corpses at gravesides and pyres, in order to work the living deadly harm..."

Some of the things the witches are accused of would be classed as Satanic ritual murder today; particularly noteworthy is the collecting of blood and a feature of some of the modern-day cases of Satanic ritual murder and ritual animal mutilation is the absence of blood in the body or at the scene, leading some commentators to be confused and assume a UFO or high-tech component to phenomena such as livestock mutilation:

"And with that she pushed Socrates' head to the side and buried her blade in the left of his neck all the way to the hilt. Then she held a flask of leather against the wound and carefully collected the spurt of blood so not a single drop was visible anywhere. I saw all this with my very own eyes. Next, so as not to deviate, I suppose, from the sacrificial rites, she stuck her right hand into the wound right down to his innards, felt for my poor comrade's heart, and plucked it out. At this a sort of cry rose from his windpipe slashed by the weapon's stroke, or at least an indistinct gurgle and he poured out his life's breath."

The following morning Lucius is awoken and arrested for having killed the three men, and he appears in court where inexplicably everything he attempts to say in his defence is met with laughter. He is about to be convicted and sentenced when the widow of one of the men calls out for the bodies of the slain men to be brought in order to confront Lucius with the severity of his crime. The bodies of the three men are revealed and shown to be nothing but three puffed-up wineskins. It transpires that the whole thing was just an elaborate and bizarre trick which the whole town played on Lucius as part of their annual festival of laughter.

One can see this story as part of an initiatory journey since Lucius is seeking the knowledge and practice of magic. The effects of this performance seemed to have been profound, not only the experience of the guilt for slaying the three men and the fear of impending capital punishment but then to find the whole thing a sham and that he was the centre of an elaborate joke. Such a scenario is something which has been played out in several Hollywood movies such as The Game and Anger Management, The Truman Show and Vanilla Sky, passing through the experience where one can hardly tell what is real with the final crisis of the mind becomes a transformative experience, the Golden Ass is the first time we see an account of what I consider a key part of the initiatory programme of the mystery schools of the ancient world which are now played out in our own world on a daily basis, completely unsuspected by most people. I know because I have experienced just such a programme:

"He urged me gently along and led me to his house by a winding route, careful to avoid the busy streets. I was still in a state of shock, and trembling with fear, and he could find no way to ease the indignation, at the treatment I'd endured, constricting my heart. Behold, clad in the full regalia of office, the magistrates themselves entered the house, and tried to calm me with these words: 'Master Lucius, we're not unaware of your dignity, and your ancestry. Indeed, the whole province knows your family's noble reputation. The experience you've undergone, that you're grieving over so deeply, was far from being intended as an insult. So banish the melancholy you feel, from your heart, and overcome your mental anguish, because you see our annual holiday in honour of Laughter, most delightful of the gods, always has to be embellished by some new jest."

However, this is just the start of Lucius trials and his curiosity to learn about magic and after Photis gives him the wrong ointment he is turned not into a bird but into an ass. A band of robbers then strike Milo's house and taking his horde of wealth they come upon Lucius the ass and loading him with some of the treasure they take him to their hideout. Eventually the robbers are discovered by the town's people and summarily killed and Lucius finds his way to a livestock auction where is purchased and serves a gang of castrated Gallus priests of Cybele whose description in the text gives us an interesting insight into how these strange people may have been viewed by society as a whole:

"Learn what he was: a eunuch, and an old one at that, bald on top but with ringlets of grey hair circling his scalp, the scum of society, one of the dregs who frequent the city streets sounding their cymbals and castanets, dragging the Syrian Great Goddess round with them, using her to beg."

In the mother goddess cult of Cybele, those who wished to join the priesthood had to undergo ritual castration. Despite this, it seemed part of the rites carried out at the Temple of Cybele were homosexual in nature were the Galli priests played the part of women and such activities were common in the time of King Asa of Judah who reigned in the 10th century BC as referenced in the Old Testament book of Kings:

"Asa did what was right in the eyes of the Lord, as his father David had done. He expelled the male

Shrine prostitutes from the land and got rid of all the idols his ancestors had made. He even deposed his grandmother Maakah from her position as queen mother, because she had made a repulsive image for the worship of Asherah. Asa cut it down and burned it in the Kidron Valley.

Yet it seemed that the cult persisted leading the 7th century BC king Josiah to take action:

"He took the Asherah pole from the temple of the Lord to the Kidron Valley outside Jerusalem and burned it there. He ground it to powder and scattered the dust over the graves of the common people. He also tore down the quarters of the male shrine prostitutes that were in the temple of the Lord, the quarters where women did weaving for Asherah."

The priests of Cybele are represented as effeminate to the point of parody with a sinister appetite for young-boys for upon returning home with Lucius the donkey:

"'Look what a pretty slave I've bought you, girls!' The 'girls' were his troop of eunuchs who began dancing in delight, raising a dissonant clamour with tuneless, shrill, effeminate cries, thinking no doubt his purchase was a slave-boy ready to do them service. But on seeing me, no doe replacing a sacrificial virgin, but an ass instead of a boy, they turned up their noses, and made caustic remarks to their leader. 'Here's no slave,' one cried, 'but a husband of your own.' And 'Oh,' called another, 'don't swallow that little morsel all by yourself, give your little doves the occasional bite.' Then amidst the banter they tied me to the manger."

Despite Lucius eventually being relieved of his ordeal by supplication to Isis and then joining her priesthood, the text is scathing in its subtle mockery of pagan idolatry by enumerating the many names of the goddess and representing her as all-powerful then fretting over the possibility that Lucius the donkey might drop her, it is pleasing little satirical moment, nicely crafted:

"'I call on the all-powerful, the all-creating goddess, Syrian Atagartis; and holy Sabazius too, and Ma of Commagene; on Idaean Mother Cybele and her consort Attis; on Lady Astarte and her consort Adonis; may they strike you blind as well for tormenting me with your scurrilous jests. Do you think I'd entrust the goddess, you fool, to some savage creature that might tumble her sacred image from its back, and be forced to run round like a servant-girl, hair streaming in the wind, to find a doctor for my goddess as she lay there on the ground?'"

The writer of the Golden Ass, Lucius Apuleius, himself was an initiate of several mysteries including the Dionysian mysteries and was a priest of Asclepius, despite this he was singularly critical and un-sparing in his contempt for the priesthood of Cybele, though this could be because the cult was seen as Anatolian in its origin and perhaps not entirely indigenous to Greece or Rome and the 'modern' ancient world and perhaps there was something about the cult of Cybele which was unmistakably primitive and disreputable, and also perhaps the cult offended Roman values of masculinity:

"The eunuchs stayed a few days, fattening themselves at public expense. Replete with the proceeds of their fortune-telling, those most holy of priests devised a novel variant on such ventures. They composed an all-purpose prophecy that would fit every situation, and fool the host of people who came to consult them on every sort of matter. The prophecy ran like this: 'Yoked together, those oxen plough the soil: To bring rich seed to future birth, they toil.' So, for example, if they chanced to be consulted on the suitability of a particular marriage, they'd say the oracle was favourable, and the 'yoke' of marriage would nurture 'seeds' of children. If instead it was a question of property, then' oxen', 'yokes', and flourishing fields of 'seed' were all involved. If someone sought divine auspices regarding a journey, they'd imply the tamest four-footed beasts were all but 'yoked together', and 'rich seed' foretold a profitable trip. If a man was off to fight a battle, or chase a band of thieves, and wanted to know if the outcome would be good, they'd argue that victory was guaranteed by that same blessed prophecy: the enemies' necks would go under the 'yoke', while a 'rich' and plentiful heap of spoils would be the clear result. With this cunning method of divination they raked in a pile of cash."

Lucius as a donkey carries the statue of Cybele on his back, but eventually gets free of them when the group of priests are discovered engaging in homosexual activity with a local boy, and Lucius, so disgusted by the homosexual antics, starts braying loudly, bringing a man who coincidentally thinking it was his own lost donkey, into the house and thus exposing all:

"On the back of a fictitious prophecy, they extracted a farmer's fattest ram for sacrifice, needing they said to appease the Goddess' hunger. Once the preparations were done, they paid a visit to the bath-house, returning afterwards with a guest, a strapping countryman, with strong limbs and thighs. They'd barely tasted their salad hors-d'oeuvres before those vile creatures were driven by their unspeakable urges to commit the vilest acts of perverse lust. They soon had the young man naked on his back, and crowding round him forced their foul caresses on him."

It is interesting that in the nihilistic pagan gloom of murder, cuckoldry, necrophilia and bestiality which fills the Golden Ass there is the gleam of some kind of wisdom and self-awareness almost worthy of the Christian mind:

"One in their midst began to rave more ecstatically than the rest, heaving breaths from deep in his chest, simulating a fit of divine madness, as if filled with inspiration from some god, though surely the presence of a deity should make men nobler than themselves, not disorder them or make them lose their senses."

A deity should indeed make one 'nobler than themselves' and to see this idea at work in the pagan mind gives one hope that perhaps the pagan Roman Empire was not quite as spiritually desolate and mired in demonically inspired depravity as one might infer from the same work. Though as he goes on, he might remind the Christian of the faults of their own church of Rome and of their Jesuits and other sundry Illuminated saints, who raved and chastised themselves and were beatified for it:

"But behold the benefit he won from these 'heavenly powers'. Raving like a prophet, he began to chastise himself with a concocted tale of some sin of his against the sacred laws of religion, and demanded self-punishment for his guilt. Then he snatched up the whip, the insignia of those emasculated creatures, with its long tufted strands of twisted sheep's hide strung with those animals' knuckle bones, and scourged himself savagely with strokes of its knotted lash, showing amazing fortitude given the pain from his gashes. The ground grew slippery with blood from the flashing blades and flailing whips, and I grew very uneasy at this gory flood from the countless wounds lest this Syrian goddess might have a stomach for ass's blood, yearning for it as some humans do for ass's milk."

At one point in the Lucius, being inwardly a human, becomes part of an 'entertaining' theatrical sideshow because of his human dining appetites such as the drinking of wine and eating of human food. A woman becomes attracted to him and pays his owner to take him to her bed. His resourceful and shrewd owner then decides to add this to the sideshow performance and we have a view of perhaps a peculiar fascination with sex between animals and humans which clearly was not a feature of the Christian world but is something which may have featured as part of some of the ancient rites, particularly of the rites of Pan where a sculpture discovered in the ruins of the ancient Roman city of Herculaneum shows a priest of Pan, dressed as a goat, having sex with a female goat.

Lucius calls for the intercession of the Queen of Heaven, the Goddess Isis to deliver him from being a donkey and after a ritual purification he is returned to human form during the Navigium Isidis, the annual Roman celebration of the Goddess Isis which is revealed to be part of his initiation into the rites of Isis whom he serves as one of her priests.

The 2nd Century AD Greek traveller and geographer Pausanias wrote how the only people who can enter the temple of Isis in Tithorea are those who are "invited in a dream" and we see this as the key motif in the communication between the Goddess, the initiate and her priests in the Golden Ass:

"And have faith in my power to oversee the execution of my orders, for at this very moment when I am here with you I am with my priest too telling him, in dream, what he must do. When I wish, the heaving crowd will part before you, and amidst the joyous rites and wild festivity no one will shrink from your unseemly shape, nor treat your sudden change of form as sinister and level charges at you out of spite."

Although the Golden Ass is indeed a burlesque, it is a moral tale in as much as it offers up the Goddess Isis as the redemptive transcendental figure who taking pity on Lucius and in exchange for his piety and adoration will confer his magical transformation back into a human, as a kind of act of salvation, and furthermore guide him to further success in life, but the price she exacts is a kind of quid-pro-quo of some kind of eternal adoration and servitude in the next world:

"Remember one thing clearly though, and keep it locked deep within your heart: the life that is left to you, to the final sigh of your last breath, is pledged to me. It is right that all your days be devoted to she whose grace returns you to the world of men. Under my wing, you will live in happiness and honour, and when your span of life is complete and you descend to the shades, even there, in the sphere beneath the earth, you will see me, who am now before you, gleaming amidst the darkness of Acheron, queen of the Stygian depths; and dwelling yourself in the Elysian fields, you will endlessly adore me and I will favour you."

The dreadful events of the Golden Ass and the meanness of the moral tone are perhaps only there to offer brighter relief of the final sense of peace and restoration which the Goddess can provide, and indeed, the story offers some satisfaction to some of our own mysteries that the ancients seemed to have established a line-of-communication with the citizens of the spirit world whom wished to be known as Gods and Goddesses and that this line of communication was said to most commonly occur through the dream-state. Also, in the dream state Lucius has premonitions of specific people and events which will take place during the initiation proper:

"....for the following night I had a vision in which an initiate dressed in white linen brought ivy-wreaths and thyrsi, with things that must be nameless, and placed these various objects on my household altar then, seated in my chair, ordered me to arrange a sacred feast. In order evidently to help me know him again by a sure sign of identity, his left ankle was slightly twisted, and he walked with a hesitant limp. My cloud of doubt was lifted by this clear manifestation of the god's own wishes, and after the morning prayers for the Goddess were complete, I at once began to ask about me, with utmost zeal, as to whether any there exactly resembled him of my dream. Confirmation came immediately, when I caught sight of one of the pastophori who not only limped like the man in my vision, but also was alike in his dress and appearance."

He is later urged by visions sent by 'the Gods' and undergoes more initiations including an initiation into the cult of Osiris where he has a vision of Osiris himself speaking to him in a dream:

"Finally, a few days later, Osiris, greatest of the gods, highest among the greatest, mightiest among the highest, lord of the mightiest, appeared to me in dream, and not in some semblance other than his own, but greeting me face to face, in sacred utterance urging me to win fame as now in the courts through my advocacy, without fear of the slanders provoked by my assiduous study of the laws of Rome. Furthermore, I was not to serve him as a minor member of the flock, but as one his college of pastophori, the shrine-bearers, and a member of the quinquennial council."

He reveals the apotheosis of the mysteries of Osiris being a singular vision, whether this vision was had in 'this word' or was achieved in an altered state of consciousness and was something seen 'in the next world' we can only surmise:

"So listen, and believe in what is true. I reached the very gates of death and, treading Proserpine's threshold, yet passed through all the elements and returned. I have seen the sun at midnight shining brightly. I have entered the presence of the gods below and the presence of the gods above, and I have paid due reverence before them."

The novel ends, rather prosaically, after all of the extraordinary adventures including discovering the truth of magic, being transformed into a donkey, and being rescued by the Queen of Heaven, Isis herself and being initiated into the highest 'night mysteries' of Osiris, to become a lawyer and the story ends with Lucius confident that the Gods will assure his success in his profession.

The Jewish Oral Tradition is the claim that after Moses met God on top of Mount Sinai and received the Ten Commandments and the dictation of the Torah he also received an oral explanation or analysis of the Torah from God which Moses did not write down but that which was transmitted to Joshua, then from Joshua to the Elders, then to the Prophets and then to the members of the Great Assembly.

Nowhere in the Torah are there any references to this. Neither Moses nor any of the subsequent Old Testament prophets make any mention of an Oral Tradition. Indeed, the Bible is more than clear and prescriptive about adopting any kind of supplementary material:

"See that you do everything I command you; do not add to it or subtract from it." Deuteronomy 12:32.

My belief regarding the Kabbalah is this and I will simply try to lay out my major thesis in all this:

How would you go about subverting something, a religion, system of morality, law and the worship of God: The Torah, committed to writing some three thousand years ago? You would do this by claiming some other 'secret' revelation which was not included in the original text.

The Kabbalah is not a mystical form of Judaism, it is a completely new gnostic religion which uses Judaism and specifically the Torah and the Hebrew alphabet of 22 letters, as its tenuous scaffolding upon which it creates a completely new imposter religion. The Zohar, using a literary device of a Rabbinical discussion plays semantic and gematria games with the words of the Torah in order to completely transform meaning in-line with the new gnostic theology of the Kabbalah.

The Bible is replete with repeated admonition of Israel and threats of imminent judgement and punishment from God precisely for rejecting the written law of Moses. For instance, the passage from 2 Kings 17 is typical and almost a trope or cliché of the angry God:

"They devoted themselves to doing evil in the sight of the LORD, provoking Him to anger. So the LORD was very angry with Israel, and he removed them from His presence. Only the tribe of Judah remained, and even Judah did not keep the commandments of the LORD their God, but lived according to the customs Israel had introduced."

Jesus in confronting the Pharisees is continuing this great prophetic tradition of accusing the Jews and Jewish priesthood of forsaking the law and "making void the word of God by your tradition that you have handed down."

Jesus refers to the 'oral tradition' as 'tradition of the elders' or the 'tradition of men'.

In Mark 7 he specifically refers to the Jews' Oral Tradition:

"And the Pharisees and the scribes asked him, 'Why do your disciples not walk according to the tradition of the elders, but eat with defiled hands?' And he said to them, 'Well did Isaiah prophesy of you hypocrites, as it is written,

'This people honours me with their lips,
but their heart is far from me;
in vain do they worship me,
teaching as doctrines the commandments of men.'

You leave the commandment of God and hold to the tradition of men.'"

So what is this oral tradition? The Talmud is fairly well known for some of its excesses in how to deal or interact with non-Jews but let us examine the Mishnah which is the proto-Talmud, the originator and a way-marker on the path to the full development of The Talmud of the 5th Century AD. In fact, to be more accurate, the Talmud is really two major separate works: The Mishnah, written in the 2nd Century AD as a commentary on the Torah and the Gemara written in the 5th Century AD as a commentary on the commentary of the Torah and this is what most people understand as the Talmud as it contains all of the most dubious and quotable material regarding the treatment of non-Jews.

The Perkei Avot or Ethics of the Fathers is a tractate of the Mishnah and outlines the key virtues required but some of the statements themselves are a little odd and one could well imagine that with further 'commentary' that is, subjected to the legalistic Rabbinical mindset, one could quite alienate anything good and true altogether and that is precisely what the Gemara achieves.

Take for instance the following advice from the Mishnah on the importance of study:

"Rabbi Yaakov would say: One who walks along a road and studies, and interrupts his studying to say, 'How beautiful is this tree!', 'How beautiful is this ploughed field!'---the Torah considers it as if he had forfeited his life."

See how profoundly this contrasts with CS Lewis' more Christian conception earlier in this work of drawing closer to God simply by doing something innocent which one enjoys. The Rabbinical idea that study alone can teach virtue and draw one close to God, and that expressing joy and sincere pleasure at creation, is somehow contrary to this and ought to cause one to forfeit one's life, makes one marvel at what kind of mind this would create were it to be taken seriously. And to think that this is taught to Jewish children; it seems like the perfect way to alienate the young from God, making them afraid to rejoice, wonder and marvel at the beauty of the world. The God of the Oral Tradition is so far contrary to the God which is often described in the Old Testament:

"Gracious and merciful, slow to anger and abounding in steadfast love" Psalm. 145:8.

Another strange comment from the Perkei Avot:

"Rabbi Shimon would say: 'Three who eat at one table and do not speak words of Torah, it is as if they have eaten of idolatrous sacrifices; as is stated, 'Indeed, all tables are filled with vomit and filth, devoid of the Omnipresent.'"

But the original phrase 'indeed, all tables' is from Isiah and is a reference to the 'drunkards of Ephraim' where Isiah is discussing what had become of all the lost tribes of Israel and had nothing to do with enforcing the Torah at the dinner table, but in the strange Rabbinical mind the original passage has been twisted to fit into a completely new context which was not the original Biblical intention. This is precisely the kind of thing Jesus was referring to when he said:

'You have a fine way of rejecting the commandment of God in order to establish your tradition!'

So what the Talmud (that is the Mishnah and the Gemara) does is create a rigid net loosely based on an original Biblical phrase taken out of context to construct an unreasonable and even contrary condition. Far from bringing one closer to God it alienates the mind since God is radically redefined. Notice how the Torah is used by the Mishnah as both the justification for their oppressive Rabbinical interpretation and the cause:

"Anyone who forgets even a single word of this learning, the Torah considers it as if he had forfeited his life. Rabbi Dusta'i the son of Rabbi Yannai would say in the name of Rabbi Meir: 'Anyone who forgets even a single word of this learning, the Torah considers it as if he had forfeited his life. As is stated, 'Just be careful, and verily guard your soul, lest you forget the things that your eyes have seen (Deuteronomy 4:9).'"

Some other strange pronouncements from the Mishah:

"One who is pleasing to his fellow men, is pleasing to G-d. But one who is not pleasing to his fellow men, is not pleasing to G-d."

"Rabbi Akiva would say: Jesting and frivolity accustom a person to promiscuity. Tradition is a safety fence to Torah, tithing a safety fence to wealth, vows a safety fence for abstinence; a safety fence for wisdom is silence."

So the Rabbis believe silent, sullen, obedient, mirthless and joyless people, enslaved by Rabbinical tradition under spiritual blackmail to tithe their wealth to the Rabbinical authorities are the kind which please God the most. I have to disagree and such an image conjures the kind of world of the Soviet or Communist system: grey, mirthless, and infinitely oppressed under a thousand rules controlling every moment of their lives. In this sense I would consider Stalinism to be a perfection of the Rabbinical system.

One can imagine what kind of people such strictures and impositions on the mind might be produced and Jesus was unequivocable in some of his choice epithets for the

Pharisees who with the destruction of the 2nd Temple in 70AD would go on to create Rabbinical Judaism in the power and religious vacuum which the Romans had created: 'hypocrites' 'children of Satan' 'child of Hell' 'full of greediness and wickedness'.

The Pirkei Avot contains the thoughts and maxims of the Jewish Rabbis and sometimes one is alarmed by the mentality which comes through and sometimes these saying raise a host of questions in themselves:

"Ten miracles were performed for our forefathers in the Holy Temple: No woman ever miscarried because of the smell of the holy meat. The holy meat never spoiled. Never was a fly seen in the slaughterhouse. Never did the High Priest have an accidental seminal discharge on Yom Kippur."

The Rabbinical conception of a miracle is a strange thing indeed and perhaps indicates that very little of the miraculous, which is usually associated with the presence and activity of God, occurred during the Rabbinical period.

Something which did occur however, and is very interesting in itself particular in light of the context of the ministry and murder of Jesus Christ by the proto-Rabbinical authority: the Pharisees, was a cessation of the miracle of the white thread. The chief priest had, apparently since the time of Aaron himself, as mentioned in Leviticus 16:7, traditionally drawn lots with his right hand to choose which of two goats would be sacrificed as a sin offering for the Lord and which would be released into the wilderness ritually imbued with the sins of Israel as a 'scapegoat'.

According to the Talmud:

"The Sages taught: During the tenure of Shimon HaTzaddi, the lot for God always arose in the High Priest's right hand; after his death, it occurred only occasionally; but during the forty years prior to the destruction of the Second Temple, the lot for God did not arise in the High Priest's right hand at all. So too, the strip of crimson wool that was tied to the head of the goat that was sent to Azazel did not turn white, and the westernmost lamp of the candelabrum did not burn continually." Talmud 39b Seder Mo'ed Yoma.

The Temple of Jerusalem was destroyed by the Romans in AD 70 response to the First Jewish Revolt but 40 years prior to this something monumental apparently transpired which severed God's favour from the Jews and led to the apparent rejection of their Temple sacrifices. If we consider that Jesus was said to have been born sometime between 6-4 BC (this date coincides with Herod's murder of the firstborn – though this event is slowly being written out of history if we look at the latest edits on the Wikipedia page which attempts to classify them even as a myth), was murdered by the Jews at 33 years old then we have the approximate year of Jesus' death at 30AD give or take a couple of years, precisely the time at which the miracles of the Temple ceased indicating that God no longer favoured the Jews and rejected their sin sacrifices.

Jesus knew that the Oral Torah had the precise effect of not only subverting the original Torah but as Jesus says, actually breaking the commandments and making this the official teaching:

"Whosoever therefore shall break one of these least commandments, and shall teach men so, he shall be called the least in the kingdom of heaven….For I say unto you, that except your righteousness shall exceed that of the scribes and Pharisees, ye shall in no case enter into the kingdom of heaven" Matthew 5:17-20.

Moshe ben Maimon born in 1138 or late 1137 known more commonly as Maimonides was heavily influenced by the Greek philosophers Aristotle and the Neoplatonist Plotinus. Neoplatonism emerged as a kind of cultural antidote to Christianity.

The trinity of the Kabbalah seems to be heavily influenced by Greek Gnosticism since it divides God's presence in creation into three parts represented by three mother letters, A (Aleph) which represents Air; M (Mem) which represents Water, and Sh (Shin) which represents fire. Just as Ain Soph where Soph is a Greek word for limitation.

The following from the book of the Lesser Holy Assembly which makes up part of the Kabbalah, makes a reference to a specifically Pythagorean concept which later became a Gnostic one, and subsequently informed the Kabbalistic idea of Ain Soph: The Monad.

"And thus all the other Lights are sanctified, are restricted, and are bound together in the Unity or Monad, and are One; and all things are HVA, *Hoa*, Himself."

Many heads of gnostic schools were identified as Jewish Christians by Church Fathers, and Hebrew words and names of God were applied in some gnostic systems and research into the origins of Gnosticism shows a strong Jewish influence traced to Alexandria and particularly from esoteric Hekhalot literature.

Maimonides was born in Islamic Spain and the rest of his life was spent living in different countries of the Islamic world. Maimonides was said to have outwardly practiced Islam during his life but secretly practised Judaism. He wrote the Yesodei haTorah where he used Rabbinical reasoning and a disingenuous appeal to the Torah to justify himself reframing the issue so that by denying his religion and becoming a Muslim, he was being righteous and to do the contrary would be breaking the commandments of the Torah, but in the typically Rabbinical reasoning by breaking the commandment he was following it:

"Should a gentile arise and force a Jew to violate one of the Torah's commandments at the pain of death, he should violate the commandment rather than be killed, because [Leviticus 18:5] states concerning the mitzvot: 'which a man will perform and live by them.' [They were given so that] one may live by them and not die because of them. If a person dies rather than transgress, he is held accountable for his life." Chapter 5 Hilchot Yesodei Hatorah.

It seems that Maimonides didn't quite have the courage of the convictions of his rabbi and mentor Yehuda Ibn Susan who accepted martyrdom or Kiddush Hashem rather than convert to Islam. Despite Maimonides choosing to quibble himself out of his integrity and devotion to his faith the precept of Kiddush Hashem or Sanctification of the Name had become the word for the martyrdom of Jews during the persecution of emperor Hadrian in the early 2nd Century AD.

He is also perhaps famously quoted by some critics of Rabbinical Judaism as being the author of the following from the Mishneh Torah of the 12th century:

"If a girl is older than three years and one day, she can be consecrated through sexual relations with her father's consent. Should she be below this age, if her father has her consecrated through sexual relations, the marriage bond is not established."

He also wrote, or perhaps merely codified what was already in the Rabbinical Oral Tradition, that a bonding marriage can be established by anal intercourse, this is commonly called 'sodomy' in the Torah and is expressly forbidden:

"When a person consecrates through sexual relations, one may assume that his intent is on the conclusion of the relations; when the relations are concluded, the marriage bond is established. Regardless of whether the couple engage in vaginal or anal intercourse, the marriage bond is established."

Some of the marriage regulations inscribed for glorious posterity by Maimonides boggle the mind at why such regulations had to be made in the first place:

"If, by contrast, [a man] consecrates [a woman] with the dung of an ox condemned to be stoned, the marriage is binding. Although it is forbidden to derive benefit from an ox condemned to be stoned, this prohibition does not apply to its dung. For the dung is considered of negligible importance when compared to the ox."

Such a paragraph raises so many questions. Who would an ox need to be stoned to death? Why would someone consider 'dung' to be a fitting inducement to marriage and how common were these strange 'dung' transactions relating to affairs of the heart.

Other strange stipulations, well not that the stipulations are strange, but that such stipulations had to be made in the first place, are strange and make one boggle at the moral framework within which the Jews operated at that time in history:

"If a man established a condition with a woman at the time of marriage or divorce requiring her to engage in sexual relations with her father, her brother, her son or the like, it is as if he made a stipulation that she ascend to the heavens or descend to the depths, and his condition is of no consequence. For it is not within the woman's capacity to cause others to transgress and to engage in a forbidden sexual relationship. Thus, he has made a stipulation that she is incapable of fulfilling. This complies with regard to all similar instances."

Also another of the moral codes of the Oral Tradition which Maimonides felt the need to record for posterity, the strange tale of the man who died from lack of sex, perhaps, who knows in this bizarre moral Twilight Zone we seem to have entered:

"When someone becomes attracted to a woman and is [love-]sick [to the extent that] he is in danger of dying, [although] the physicians say he has no remedy except engaging in sexual relations with her, he should be allowed to die rather than engage in sexual relations with her. [This applies] even if she is unmarried."

One wonders what kind of doctors they had in those days who prescribed sex. One can well imagine that such a thing must have happened, that some woman was being emotionally blackmailed by a man who was in league with a doctor who made a pact to enable him to have his wicked way with her, under doctor's orders.

All of this seems to hint at a dark sexual current which we will later see fully liberated in the books of the Kabbalah which is also considered to form part of the Oral Tradition and to have even been delivered by God to Adam himself. For instance Michael Laitman in his book explain the Zohar gives the following definition for the Hebrew term 'Zivug' which appears in the Zohar. Zivug means 'life partner' and is a curious term which comes from the Greek 'zogen' to join and it is curious how much Greek lexis and philosophy seems to have entered Jewish mysticism:

"The spiritual Zivug is an aspiration of the Upper One (ZA—male part) to pass the Light (pleasure) to the lower one (Malchut—female part). In doing so, both desires are completely selfless, as in the example of the guest and the host."

Maimonides himself considered the presence of God in the Old Testament, and even the famous vision of Jacob's ladder to be largely allegorical and not a representation of actual events. This is to cast aspersions of the integrity of the Bible itself and one can imagine that the only people who would want to do that did not themselves believe in the Bible but believed in something else. The ladder with the angels ascending and descending seen by Jacob in his vision, was according to Maimonides, only an allegory for the empires and their subjugation of his descendants. Maimonides states:

"Those who believe that God is One and that He has many attributes declare the Unity with their lips and assume the plurality in their thoughts."

From the 'My Jewish Learning' website:

"That also means that, in Aristotelian terms, one cannot actually say 'God is . . .' and proceed to enumerate God's attributes. To describe the Eternal One in such a sentence is to admit of a division between subject and predicate, in other words, a plurality.

Therefore, he concludes, one cannot discuss God in terms of positive attributes. On the other hand, one can describe what God is not. God is not corporeal, does not occupy space, experiences neither generation nor corruption (in the Aristotelian sense of birth, decay, and death.. Maimonides' conception of the Supreme Being is usually characterized as "negative theology," that is, defining by the accumulation of negatives."

For a so-called Jewish scholar and father of Rabbinical thought, to say that God cannot be discussed 'in terms of positive attributes' is a fundamental change in position. Radically different from the Old Testament theology and completely contrary to what Jesus taught. What benefit is it to teach God as an aloof force with no positive attributes, relegating right and wrong, good and evil, morality and immorality, piety and wickedness, to mere frames of reference unsupported by any larger deistic reality. It can only benefit those who wish to do evil and get away with it.

Even more strangely, the Zohar takes the imagery of the story of Jacob's Ladder and turns it into a mystery pantomime. The 'Initiation of Rabbi Hiya' from the Zohar clearly indicates some kind of ongoing initiatory cult, initiatory cults have nothing to do with the history of the Israelites and their God who was always opposed to such activities:

"Then Rabbi Hiya saw his fellow students standing around the, masters and they wended their way to the celestial school. Some were ascending and others descending thither, and at their head was the great winged angel of the presence (Metatron), who was saying he had heard in the palace on high that the king, visits everyday and does not forget his lone and loved ones who are struggling towards the higher life unnoticed and unregarded by the world. At that moment three hundred and ninety worlds trembled and shook as with an earthquake. Stars as of fire descended from on high and fell into the great sea, whose ruler then stood up and swore by him that lives forever, that he would dry up all the waters of creation if ever the world and its powers should gather themselves against the children of light to destroy them.

As he ceased speaking, Rabbi Hiya heard a voice from heaven exclaiming: 'Fall back! make room for the King Messiah coming to the school of Rabbi Simeon, whose students are all initiates and master teachers of the secret doctrine.' Then came Messiah and visited all the celestial schools and confirmed the teachings and expositions of the mysteries given by their appointed instructors. As he entered the great assembly crowned with many crowns, all the great masters rose up and saluted. Turning to Rabbi Simeon, the emanation of whose light reached up to heaven, Messiah spake and said: "Blessed art thou, Rabbi Simeon, for thy mystic teachings are of the highest worth and valued and cherished by all. They only, along with those of Hesekiah, King of Judah, and Achiya, the Solonite, are marked and sealed with the approval of the holy one. I have come hither because I know that the angel of the presence visits no other school save yours."

What appears in the Mishah, and this together with the Gemara is quite different from the Old Testament and seems to inject a note of moral license and relativity. Such might be the recourse of a band of rogues who wished to continue their roguish ways despite clear instructions to the contrary. Moses is not here to testify and God appears unwilling to make a physical appearance and either countenance or deny this claim, though the last time he did and spoke through Jesus, things didn't go well so understandably God has said his piece and will probably only remain as a curious on-looker to the tragedy of the human race. So in the absence of denials the Rabbinical authority seems to be accepted and much of modern Judaism is not in the Torah or the first five books of the Old Testament which most of us can read and readily understand and even sometimes accept the validity of some of the proscriptions made against such things as child sacrifice, commandments against practising homosexuality and the interdiction of murder, adultery and other such things which are generally understood to be useful laws for the benefit of civilised human society.

In the absence of Temple sacrifice (which we saw were no longer accepted by God in the 40 years subsequent to the murder of Jesus and the destruction of the Second Temple) the Sukkah Talmud seems to show how in the subsequent spiritual power-vacuum, divine authority has become a free-for-all with Rabbis' vying for spiritual supremacy and appointing themselves, or being appointed 'messiah' level powers:

"And Ḥizkiya said that Rabbi Yirmeya said in the name of Rabbi Shimon ben Yoḥai: I am able to absolve the entire world from judgment for sins committed from the day I was created until now. The merit that he accrued through his righteousness and the suffering that he endured atone for the sins of the entire world. And were the merit accrued by Eliezer, my son, calculated along with my own, we would absolve the world from judgment for sins committed from the day that the world was created until now. And were the merit accrued by the righteous king, Jotham ben Uzziah, calculated with our own, we would absolve the world from judgment for sins committed from the day that the world was created until its end. The righteousness of these three serves as a counterbalance to all the evil deeds committed throughout the generations, and it validates the ongoing existence of the world."

But to finish this strange chapter on some further strangeness, among the 'classic texts' of Jewish law and includes a chapter on how to go to the toilet. Since we're here I might as well share those edifying joys with you. The 16th Century Shulchan Aruch, the last 'great' codification of Jewish Law has a chapter entitled Lavatory Conduct:

"One should also conduct himself modestly when entering a lavatory, uncovering himself only to the extent required and not even a moment before the time required. This should be done only when he is seated, and only a handbreadth from behind and — to allow for urination — two handbreadths in front…A woman should uncover nothing in front, and either a handbreadth or two handbreadths behind herself…In practice, one should uncover as little as possible.

If a person relieves himself in an open place that is not surrounded by partitions, he should face the south with his back to the north, or vice versa. He should not have his back to the west or to the east, out of reverence for the Divine Presence, which abides in the west, facing east. This is why the east is referred to as 'the front' and the west, 'the back,' as reflected in the verse, 'You have hedged me behind and in front.' The south is thus called the right, or teiman.

If there is a [private] corner one should relieve oneself there, provided no one else is present. If, however, there is another person there, even a non-Jew, it is forbidden to relieve oneself in his presence — i.e., if he is close enough to be observed, even if his uncovered body cannot be seen — for it is considered immodest to be observed from nearby.

Where possible, it is preferable to make a point of facing south with one's back to the north, and not the opposite, so that one will not be easing oneself in the direction of Jerusalem and the site of the Beis HaMikdash. This applies in most of these countries that are located more to the north of Jerusalem than to the west, and even more so in those countries which are located directly to the north of Jerusalem.

When one urinates while standing, and many drops of urine will fall on his feet if he does not lift his organ, he is permitted to raise it by lifting his testicles. If the drops fall on his feet, he should clean them off immediately with his hands and not walk among people in this manner. He should not hold the organ itself to raise it, for 'he who holds his organ is considered as if he brought a flood upon the world,' lest he become aroused and emit seed wastefully. [This stringency applies] unless he holds the organ from the corona downward, i.e., towards the ground, for this will not arouse him. Alternatively, he may hold [the organ] with a thick cloth, for this too will not arouse him.

When a person is married, and his wife is in the same city as he is, and she is ritually pure, the letter of the law permits him to hold the organ even above the corona. Since he 'has a loaf in his basket,' he will not be stimulated to improper thoughts or to arousal. Nevertheless, pious behaviour dictates stringency."

My final thoughts in this chapter are that when a people becomes so totally dominated by laws and rules in every little aspect of their life, they literally reach such a point of mental impotence that they need instructions on how to go to the lavatory.

The Kabbalah is commonly referred to as a collection of works which comprise a form of Jewish mysticism. QBLH meaning 'tradition' as in 'Oral Tradition' is principally comprised of three books: The Sefir Yetsira (Book of Formation), the Sefir ha-Bahir (Book of Illumination) and The Zohar (Splendour); the earliest of these - the Sefir Yetsira is attributed to Rabbi Akiva Ben Joseph who died, probably murdered by the Romans during the Third Jewish Revolt lead by the self-styled Messiah: Bar Kokhba. Although these key texts of the Kabbalah generally appeared in the 12th century onwards the attribution of these texts is much earlier, generally to the historically critical post Second Temple period though such attribution may be an artifice of mediaeval writers seeking perhaps a false authority for their writings and there is much ongoing debate among Jewish and mainstream scholars as to who really wrote these texts and when.

Interestingly we can observe at least two major breaks from Jewish orthodoxy in the Sefir ha-Bahir and this will very much become a theme I wish to focus on since this attempt to subvert Judaism from within by a secondary force which seems antagonistic to the Torah and wishing to destroy it despite claiming the contrary, is a key part of my thesis. The following excerpt shows the promulgation of a belief in reincarnation, an idea alien to conventional Judaism but which was a fundamental belief of the Pharisees who would later become the core of Rabbinical Judaism after the fall of the Second Temple and it is worth noting that the majority of Pharisees themselves were not of the lineage of Israel but were actually Edomites. Reincarnation has historically been more commonly associated with Hinduism, Buddhism, and probably more pertinently here, the mystery religions of Ancient Greece:

"Why is there a righteous person who has good, and [another] righteous person who has evil? This is because the [second] righteous person was wicked previously, and is now being punished. Is one then punished for his childhood deeds? Did not Rabbi Simon say that in the Tribunal on high, no punishment is meted out until one is twenty years or older. He said: I am not speaking of his present lifetime. I am speaking about what he has already been, previously."

This isn't to dismiss reincarnation as a concept, merely to point out that it is inconsistent with Jewish religious tradition and to see that it is adapted by the key writers or compilers of the Kabbalah, shows that something which is alien to the Jewish tradition entered their religion and transformed it, I would say a whole package of alien traditions entered Judaism and turned it into something infinitely dangerous: a religion with an acquired arsenal of techniques from the Greek mystery religion to transform consciousness; if such techniques are used, out of context or within a framework which is not properly adapted to them, then the consequences can be extremely grave and such techniques can become extremely destructive to the people undergoing them and to the society as a whole which also becomes transformed. If additionally, these techniques are used as a weapon to actually subjugate and conquer a perceived enemy, which I believe to ultimately be the case, then whoever holds the key to these transformative techniques can dictate not only the physical reality which is experienced by those who are dominated by the secret esoteric machinery of the secret society's mystery religion but can also dictate their spiritual reality, which is infinitely more insidious.

It would seem therefore that the doctrines of the Eleusinian mystery school, which taught reincarnation within the context of the Orphic religion, spread throughout Greek society and the ancient world of the Gentiles and was promulgated by luminaries such as Pythagoras and Socrates. The Orphic religion teaches that in order to achieve salvation or detachment from the wheel of birth and rebirth it is necessary to undergo a ritual purification called 'telete' while the uninitiated 'amuetos' must reincarnate indefinitely.

We can only guess what might have transpired during these ancient rites suffice it to say that with a combination of psychoactive compounds, extreme emotions and a sense of fear for one's life, combined with witnessing extraordinary events being manifested with a variety of special effects and scientific knowledge known to the priesthood but not the initiate, then all sorts of illusions can be drawn on to strongly influence the mind of the initiate and no doubt, some real kind of revelation truly brought to bear.

An example from the Christian era of the priesthood having special knowledge which gave them power over people would be the case of the monks of the 11th Century order of Saint Anthony. They were primarily based in France and would treat those who were suffering from Saint Anthony's Fire or ergotism, that is the presumably accidental ingestion of the highly toxic ergot fungus as a result of its contamination with the local grain crop from which ergotised bread was made. It is surmised that the efficacy of the Order of Saint Anthony lay solely in their knowledge of what caused ergotism and that they simply cured their patients by removing them from the source of ergot in their diet by giving them bread which either grew in areas without an ergot infestation of by using grain which had been previously screened. The knowledge of ergot was something we have conjectured may have been known to the priesthood of the Eleusinian mysteries who may have deliberately used this agent as a psychoticant. Additionally, knowledge of the effects of ergot must have been known to early Iron Age societies in Europe since it has been found in the stomachs of those ritually murdered and placed in bogs. Drugging prior to ritual death was also common in South America where coca leaves and alcohol were used as a sedative in the transition of life to death, the purpose of their death being that they would then become 'ancestors' to spiritually watch over their people.

Another unusual and one might say heretical extract from the Sefer ha-Bahir, relates to the Biblical fall of man and this material has actually become somewhat accepted amongst certain circles of esoteric Christianity:

"The soul of the female comes from the Female, and the soul of the male comes from the Male. This is the reason why the Serpent followed Eve. He said, "Her soul comes from the north, and I will therefore quickly seduce her." And how did he seduce her? He had intercourse with her."

It is probably a stretch to consider the story of the Garden of Eden as anything more than an allegory for some other key events which may have taken place in the remote history of mankind in the area in which he seems to have developed all of the arts and from where human civilisation emerged. It is in the Middle-East and the area specifically between the Euphrates and Tigris which is where Eden was said to have been situated. But why the keenness to sexualise this story and introduce an element which had not previously been suspected? And why the need to claim that gender is something which also exists in the spiritual realm? What need would spirits have of being gendered since they presumably do not reproduce. This is a theme we will also see develop greatly: the overt sexualisation of the Torah and of spiritual matters in general.

Founder of the international Kabbalah foundation: Bnei Baruch, Michael Laitman claims that Rabbi Shimon bar Yochai wrote the Zohar in the 2nd century. Known as Rashbi, he was the most eminent disciple of Rabbi Akiva and was said to have compiled 3,000 years of Kabbalah and many of his sayings are found in the Talmud, although modern scholars doubt this.

Rabbi Akiva is renowned as one of the great Jewish sages or 'tanna' and the Sefir Yetsira is attributed to him although there are scholastic doubts as to this, although it is more plausible that he was the creator of the early divisions of the Mishnah. It was Akiva who gave the ill-fated Jewish military leader of the third and final Jewish revolt against the Romans Simon ben Kosevah the sobriquet Simon bar Kokhba, (son of the star: a reference to the messianic prophecy of an Israelite military leader referred to in Numbers 24:17) and considered him to be the long-awaited Messiah.

The revolt ended in 135AD with the wholesale slaughter of the Jews (with as many as half a million killed) and the razing of their towns and villages. It is probable that this event became the catalyst for their long-term programme of world domination and total subjugation of gentiles. Subsequent Talmudic opinion of Simon bar Kokhba considers him to be a 'false-messiah'.

The Zohar appeared in 13ᵗʰ century Spain and was published by Moses de Leon who ascribed it to Rashbi in mythical and unlikely terms. It is Rashbi who is credited with saying:

"The best of the gentiles merit death; the best of serpents should have its head crushed; and the most pious of women is prone to sorcery."

There is also criticism of the Kabbalah, specifically the Zohar as being evidently written from a post Talmudic perspective and also some of the references in the text firmly place it in a 13ᵗʰ century context.

For instance, the Zohar predicted the arrival of the Jewish Messiah in the 70th year of the 6th millennium: the 14th Century, and that he would be caught up in the wars between the Muslims and Christians. But since there were no Muslims in the 2ⁿᵈ century it cannot have been written by Rashbi but clearly by someone contemporaneous with the activities of the crusading Christians. The crusader wars between Christians and Muslims had been waged for 200 years and were ongoing during the lifetime of Moses de Leon so it might have seemed a safe bet that they would continue into the future.

Unfortunately for the writer of the Zohar, whoever he was, but it was probably de Leon, the Crusader presence in the Holy Land effectively ended in 1291 with the Fall of Acre, so this constitutes a failed prediction and rebuffs any suggestion of the text being divinely inspired. These passages are generally not included with published versions of the Zohar (for obvious reasons) but they do make up the corpus of the written texts, but such failed predictions serve both to date the writing of the Zohar to sometime in the 13ᵗʰ century prior to 1291 and also to discredit it as having any prophetic or revelatory value.

William Wynn Westcott co-founder of The Hermetic Order of the Golden Dawn, celebrated Freemason and 'ceremonial magician' authored a translation and commentary on the Sefir Yetsira for members of the Theosophical Society, The Golden Dawn and the Rosicrucians and it would become a major source for the Golden Dawn's initiation ceremonies. Westcott encapsulates the Sefir Yetsira as: "..a most curious philosophical scheme of creation, drawing a parallel between the origin of the world, the sun, the planets, the elements, seasons, man and the twenty two letters of the Hebrew alphabet." Eliphas Levi, the man who popularised the inverted Satanic pentagram, said of it: "The Sepher Jezirah and the Apocalypse are the masterpieces of Occultism".

From Schuchard:

"This mystical capacity to visualize the architectural and pictorial expression of complex mathematical and geometrical speculation became associated with the practical expertise of the architect and master mason. In the schools of Merkabah mysticism, Jewish adepts increasingly portrayed Solomon as an architectural magus and his master mason Bezalel as a craftsman magus, initiated in the secrets of the Sepher Yetzirah. Thus, 'Bezalel knew how to combine the letters by which heavens and earth were formed," while he and his Merkabah heirs could visualize and manipulate the 'measure of the body' of God (called the Shi'ur Komah).'

The Sefir Yetsira is perhaps *the* foundation text of the Kabbalah where many of the key concepts such as the ten Sefirot and the 32 paths to God are first elucidated although at this early stage in the mythos of Kabbalah no names have yet been attributed to the Sefirot, only that there are ten of them: "Ten is the number of the ineffable Sefirot, ten and not nine, ten and not eleven" just to be sure. In terms of historical critical textual analysis this very much creates the impression that the Kabbalah was something which aggregated and not something which emerged as a complete and self-contained work. The 32 paths of wisdom, according to Jewish tradition, are apparently derived from the 32 times the name 'Elohim' is mentioned in Genesis. This in addition to the 22 letters of the Hebrew alphabet being added to the 10 Sefirot to make 32 combinations.

The 10 Sefirot are first named in the Sefir ha-Bahir and the names of the first seven are taken from the Old Testament book of Chronicles (although there are technically 11 Sefirot on the Kabbalistic Tree of Life including Da'at but this is seen as all the Sefirot simultaneously so it can be viewed as a state rather than a distinct Sefirot):

"Yours, O Lord, is the greatness (chesed/gedullah), power (gevurah), the glory (tiferet), the victory (netzach), the splendour (hod) for everything in heaven and earth is yours. Yours is the kingdom (malchut) and you are exalted as head over all." Chronicles 29:11.

The idea became developed in the Talmud that God created the universe specifically using these attributes which would later become the stations or the Sefirot of the Kabbalistic Tree of Life:

"By ten things was the world created, by wisdom and by understanding, and by reason and by strength by rebuke and by might, by righteousness and by judgment, by loving kindness and compassion." Talmud, Tractata Hagiga 12a.

The ten Sefirot in descending order are: Crown (Keter), Wisdom (Chokmah), Understanding (Binah), Kindness (Chesed), Discipline (Gevurah), Glory (Tiferet), Victory (Netzach), Splendour (Hod), Foundation (Yesod) and Kingdom (Malkuth).

The logic of the ten Sefirot and even of the Ain Soph is an internal one which has no observable independent reality, even in metaphysical terms and cannot really be validated. It seems to be and perhaps it might be more useful and charitable to see this system as an idealised from of spiritual self-discipline but the very fact that the Kabbalah was built on such shifting sands and from the very beginning seemed to be more a series of word and number games being stacked up on top of each other through the centuries by successive Rabbis, might lead one to the conclusion that any deeper meaning and spiritual insight which can be derived from the Kabbalah might be entirely accidental.

It is worth noting that according to William Westcot:

"Many Kabalists have shown how the Ten Sefirot are symbolised by the zig-zag lightning flash."

This could perhaps be the reason for David Bowie's, and later Lady Gaga's adoption of this style motif. Bowie's interest in the Kabbalah and Crowley are generally well-known by now.

On the subject of Crowley, this evidently opportunistic approach to Jewish mysticism led to people like Aleister Crowley, who himself probably knew full well what a sham the Kabbalah was, adopting the terminology and structures to suit his own nefarious purposes. So while Da'at supposedly represents the idealised state of all 10 Sefirot acting in perfection, for Crowley it represents 'The Night of Pan'. No doubt some kind of unsavoury experiment in frenzy and practised abominations, and as expected Crowley writes:

"The truly magical operations of Love are therefore the Trances, more especially those of Understanding; as will readily have been appreciated by those who have made a careful Qabalistic study of the nature of Binah. For she is omniform as Love and as Death, the Great Sea whence all Life springs, and whose black womb reabsorbs all. She thus resumes in herself the duplex process of the Formula of Love under Will; for is not Pan the All-Begetter in the heart of the Groves at high noon, and is not Her 'hair the trees of Eternity' the filaments of All-Devouring Godhead 'under the Night of Pan?'"

He furthermore adds that:

"Night is that time of symbolic death where the adept experiences unification with the All through the ecstatic destruction of the ego-self."

Such things are not made quite so plain in the texts of the Kabbalah though they are hinted at in the metaphor of the Alchemical 'Great Work' (which is incidentally a term used by the Freemasons) and the psychological transformations and how they might be achieved are fleshed out in the Rosicrucian Chymical Wedding text.

Beyond Crowley's sordid self-serving sexual agenda, he reveals the same hidden purpose which we have seen exposed time and time again in this work, through the centuries, whether of the UFO contact cults, or Revolutionary agents and assassins or mystical Scientific societies of the middle-ages, Crowley writes:

"There are many magical teachers but in recorded history we have scarcely had a dozen Magi in the technical sense of the word. They may be recognized by the fact that their message may be formulated as a single word, which word must be such that it overturns all existing beliefs and codes."

Crowley, the Rosicrucians, the Italian bankers and their change agents, the French and the Russian revolutionaries, the UFO cults, all controlled by the same force throughout time and space all dedicated to one theme: 'overturning all existing beliefs'. We now live in the world where their programme is about to achieve its final goals bereft of the idealism which would have sustained those meddling and wrong-headed do-gooders of the past.

I found this quote during my research though I have forgotten the attribution and the internet search results being now so strictly filtered it is presently impossible for me to find out, but it perfectly encapsulates what has happened to the world and how everything has been subverted from within by the secret societies enacting this millennial old agenda, emerging slowly in the mediaeval period, informed by and secretly perpetuating Jewish mysticism amongst the elite of the West:

"To destroy Western society it is not necessary to teach evil in place of Christianity, it is just necessary to teach Judaism."

Although Crowley was no doubt a most unpleasant man obsessed with his own pleasure at any cost, even to the lives and sanity of others, by sexualising the Kabbalah he was only exaggerating what was already implicit in the original texts. The fundamental problem with the Kabbalah is that it is obsessed with male and female forces and sees these as spiritual forces rather than merely physical ones. I suppose it is a matter of opinion but I do not see the spiritual world as having any gender. It ought to be evident that gender is a requirement of physical procreation in the physical world and can serve no purpose once physicality ends in the spiritual world. But according to the Kabbalah it persists and is primordial, emerging from the very point of contact from the great Ain Soph to the Kether. With the third Sefira Binah as being the 'reflection' of God, that is God seeing itself, then Binah is receptive and hence a feminine principle and is known in Kabbalah as the 'mother' archetype. Confusingly however each successive Sefira has an androgynous nature of both receiving and transmitting, receiving being a supposedly feminine principle and transmitting being a masculine one.

The opening tractate of the Zohar is entitled The Rose and it could possibly be the true origin of the term Rosicrucian. In the Zohar the rose is revealed to be a symbol for Israel, would this make Rosicrucianism, that is, the rose and cross the first society of Christian Zionism? This analysis would make perfect sense.

"Rabbi Hizkiyah opened, 'It is written, as a rose among thorns.' That a rose is the Assembly of Israel. Because there is a rose and there is a rose, just as a rose among thorns is tinged with red and white, the Assembly of Israel consists of judgment and mercy. Just as a rose has thirteen petals, the Assembly of Israel is surrounded on all sides by the thirteen attributes of mercy."

In the Zohar the masculine energies Chokmah (wisdom) impregnated Binah (understanding) with light to produce Tiferet or Beauty. To the Kabbalist the spiritual realm seems to be held together with constant repetitions of sexual energies, it is hardly any wonder then that we hear rumours of Freemasonry being little more than a cleverly disguised cult of the phallus in the style of the ancient Egyptian fertility mystery schools such as the allegory of the search for the poor Osiris' lost penis.

In his 2008 book Essential Judaism, George Robinson writes:

"Hokhmah is the "sperm" that will impregnate Binah (Understanding) as the first step in the Creative process."

"..it is the means by which Tiferet, the male principle of the Divine, impregnates Shekhinah or Malkhut, the female embodiment of the Divine. Yesod is the way in which Divine Creativity and Fertility are visited upon all creation. Yesod is associated with the phallus..."

The other danger is the insistence of the Zohar of literally embodying the fundamental spiritual powers of God in the human body. In the Zohar this is called the Microprospus or Damuth Adam, the primordial man, and might be more familiar as the pentagram which in reality is a stylised representation of the human body. So the various Sefirot are said to manifest at different points in or near the human body. I wonder if you can see where this is heading? The problem is that again, sex does not seem to be something merely physical but also primordial, in this belief system then, one can justify all kinds of sexual rites in the delusion that these are spiritual forces and therefore they escape any kind of ideas of modesty or morality, and these are precisely the errors the Ancient World fell into. Where the Gods of the Ancient World were merely expressions of man's own nature, it was at least to Judaism's credit that they insisted that God created Man in his own image and not the other way around. But the Kabbalah precisely does that, it takes the physical world and all its desires, emotions and polarities and thrusts them into the spiritual domain, up to the very highest levels until it reaches Ain Soph and ends in nothingness.

Master Mason and Rosicrucian, Samuel Liddell MacGregor Mathers who co-founded the Golden Dawn along with William Westcott also authored a translation of some of the tracts of the Zohar which he translated from the Latin version of Christian Knorr von Rosenroth.

In his 'Confessions' Aleister Crowley wrote of the decline of the Golden Dawn and of Mathers himself and makes an intriguing allusion:

"...Mathers, of course, carried on; but he had fallen. The Secret Chiefs cast him off; he fell into deplorable abjection; even his scholarship deserted him. He published nothing new and lived in sodden intoxication till death put an end to his long misery."

According to one-time personal secretary to Aleister Crowley and populariser of the occult in the 1960's Israel Regardie, the Kabbalah was handed down to Adam after the fall of Man and the expulsion from the Garden of Eden.

Regardie is particularly scathing of religions, however he claims that Kabbalah does not belong to any religious traditions, and also has a soft-spot for Witchcraft. In his book he mentions Crowley, for whom he has 'a tremendous respect' unfortunately this respect would not last once Crowley accused Regardie of 'pure theft' when he edited a 4 volume work on The Golden Dawn and in a bitter feud revealed to the world that Regardie had once visited a prostitute in France and contracted gonorrhoea, neglecting to mention that it was Crowley who had ordered him to visit the prostitute in order to lose his virginity and overcome his inhibitions.

Although Crowley in his *Confessions* depicts Mathers as the true source of spiritual contact between Crowley and the entities he served:

"As far as I was concerned, Mathers was my only link with the Secret Chiefs to whom I was pledged. I wrote to him offering to place myself and my fortune unreservedly at his disposal; if that meant giving up the Abra-Melin Operation for the present, all right."

Mathers it seemed was in full psychic contact with various spiritual entities; Crowley reports how he would play chess against pagan Gods, the moves apparently being communicated to him and the opponents' pieces he would move on their behalf. One could still ascribe this to an over-active imagination I suppose, but is it likely that merely an overactive imagination is enough to influence the world on such a phenomenal cross-cultural and global scale, taking control of the highest echelons of the ruling secret societies and being the hidden hand behind the façade of our society?

A similar end awaited Crowley himself whose last words were reported to have been either: "I am perplexed, Satan get out!" or "Sometimes I hate myself" but Crowley's reference to 'Secret Chiefs' having deserted Mathers is intriguing and possibly hints at some kind of ongoing psychic contact with a disembodied spiritual force.

In her book about occult societies Talking to Gods Susan Johnston Graf states that The Golden Dawn was: "...the most important and influential Western organisation of its kind". She gives a good summary of the general purpose and aim of the group:

"For a Golden Dawn initiate the work at hand was to make contact with the divine spark that was thought to reside in all humans...The Golden Dawn initiate was wanted to raise his or her consciousness to attain what is termed *conversation* with the Holy Guardian Angel. The practise of ritual magic in the Order of the Golden Dawn was an attempt to change consciousness and to control the imagination by active participation in psychic events.'

If the aim of the Golden Dawn is to establish contact or 'conversation' with a so-called Holy Guardian Angel then in theory, the whole human initiatory apparatus might be wholly unnecessary. It might therefore be possible to directly contact this force using only a pro-forma set of directions to express intent and the sense of required ceremony. Such an approach was attempted by a blogger at the following website: https://www.llewellyn.com/journal/article/365

"You might think that having achieved my goal I would stop, but just the opposite was true. After all, the word "initiate" means "to begin," not end. <u>Self-Initiation into the Golden Dawn Tradition</u> continued with what I need to learn to go into the next degree of the tradition, and even included a self-test to make sure I knew the material and was ready to go on. I'm working on that now.

Holy art Thou, Lord of the Universe!
Holy art Thou, Whom Nature hath not Formed!
Holy art Thou, the Vast and the Mighty One!
Lord of the Light and of the Darkness!

I felt like I was in a trance as I continued with the initiation:

I am the inheritor of a dying world, arisen and entered into Darkness. The Mother of Darkness hath blinded me with her hair. The Father of Darkness hath hidden me under his wings. My limbs are still weary from the wars which were in Heaven.

Unpurified and unconsecrated, thou canst not enter our Sacred Hall.

And I was purified with water and consecrated with fire and finally, kneeling, I was ready to take the oath.

...in the Presence of the Lord of the Universe, who works in silence and whom naught but silence can express, and in this Hall of the Neophytes of the current of the Golden Dawn, do, of my own free will, hereby and hereon, most solemnly promise...to dedicate my life to the pursuit of the mysteries of the Golden Dawn tradition of magic and to the completion of the Great Work. I solemnly promise to persevere with courage and determination in the labors of the Divine Science, even as I shall persevere with courage and determination through this ceremony which is their image...

I was trembling as I said the next words:

Rise Neophyte of the 0 = 0 grade of the Golden Dawn. (p. 31)

Before anybody asks, I don't think I'm a member of the Golden Dawn group, but I know that I am initiated as a true neophyte into the tradition of the Golden Dawn."

Intriguingly the next part reminds us of the experience of Barbara O'Brien communicating with that 'something' in the casino:

"In Atlantic City, for the first time ever, I went to the casinos came back a winner. I would move from one slot machine to another just in time to get another big reward."

He also mentions several other apparent benefits which although we may surmise the cause we cannot be sure except perhaps that he had connected with that 'something' which has a remarkable power to provide beneficial coincidences. As to what that 'something' is, that is perhaps the life-work of the reader to discover it for themselves and decide whether this is a positive or negative force:

"I drive to various locations, I end up with parking places very close to the entrances. The pain in my knee has vanished. I need sixty–ninety minutes less sleep nightly than before. I no longer have a need for coffee in the morning in order to get going. My minimal artistic skills have improved. My reading speed and retention of what I read has vastly improved."

But according to Susan Johnston Graf being a member of the Golden Dawn, was apparently not without a certain danger and she and hints about the reasons for the group's secretive nature:

'The beliefs are hidden or secret because of the perceived danger to the practitioners... the danger from within comes in the form of psychic disintegration'

The Golden Dawn has 10 grades which correspond to the ten Sefirot of the Kabbalah as first outlines in the Sefir Yetsira and Golden Dawn member WB Yeats wrote on these degrees and their attainment:

"It matters nothing whether the Degrees about us are in the body or out of the body.

In 1901 Yeats wrote to a fellow Golden Dawn member hinting at some kind if implicit social-change agenda involving the organisation:

"We have set before us a certain work that may be of incalculable importance in the change of thought that is coming upon the world."

A super elect group was formed within the Golden Dawn which claimed to have even more advanced secrets, the group was called The Red Rose and the Cross of Gold.

Dion Fortune, an occultist who established psychic contacts with 'Ascended Masters' and "the Shemesh of the Aquarian Age" describes the character of the initiate in the following, alchemical terms:

"He is tried in the furnace of sorrow and suffering until his nature undergoes the flux of the soul and can be remade. Then he is forged on the anvil of discipline by the hammer of danger."

Susan Johnston Graf states:

"Yeats, Fortune and Blackwood all believed that humans possessed latent power which resided in the subconscious mind, and each of them spent their lives trying to tap that reservoir for the good of the human race."

Christian Knorr von Rosenroth was a very early 17th Century Theosophist who mistakenly believed he might find some insight into Christianity in the Kabbalah and ultimately, he gave a somewhat balanced view of the Kabbalah which confirms some of my own criticisms:

"I entered the path, worn by few, traversed by no one I knew, and, furthermore, filled with so many hard stones, uneven places, chasms, precipices, and such mud that it is not surprising that so many, filled with dread abandoned it with disgust.. I shall sketch for you in a few words what gold and whatever gems I have thus far dug out of this dirt and what hope leads me further."

I can readily agree with the feelings of disgust with the constant sexualising of the finer things of the spirit world and of the nature of God, along with the chasms of meaningless gematria drivel which shrivel the mind. The feeling of studying the Zohar is thinking you may have stumbled on something valuable, something shines and sparkles because it is a phrase which actually makes sense, perhaps a phrase like:

"Tepheret is the path to beauty.." you read on and it continues: "which equals the letter V" then talk about Queens and things flowing, and then Hebrew consonants and silly gematria conceits and more numbers and then a snatch of the Torah and a reference to Jacob. This is the sum total of the Zohar, an endless permutation of meaninglessness, almost fractal in its complexity reaching out deeply into precisely nowhere. A kind of procedurally generated cerebral noise from minds perhaps, estranged from God and so far from understanding that they had to invent a whole bizarre theosophy of their own in order to populate their minds with something they think resembles spirituality.

But the overt repeated sexual imagery used in the Zohar leads me to the strong suspicion that this is the origin of the Satanic themed sex cults which occasionally make the news or more frequently, are exposed by former insiders and victims of the cult, communicating through the alternative media. Groups such as Crowley's Order of the Oriental Temple were a surface resurgence of this ancient current which had previously surfaced in the form of the Duke of Wharton's and later Sir Frances Dashwood's Hellfire Club of the 18th Century. The Duke of Wharton was hugely indebted to banking interests as a result of the collapse in the share price of the South Sea company in which he had heavily invested. In 1723 after the dissolution of the Hellfire Club he became the Grand Master of the first Freemasonic Grand Lodge of England. One wonders, like so many other pawns of the manipulators whether Wharton's debts forced him to act for that financial power which sought to use him to exercise its covert social agenda which we have seen either hinted at or historically emerge from cover and unleash its furious agenda usually ending in the destruction of Christian institutions and mass bloodshed and butchery.

Intriguingly Sir Frances Dashwood served, for a short time at least, as Chancellor of the Exchequer, despite, like Winston Churchill, being dubiously qualified:

"Of financial knowledge he did not possess the rudiments, and his ignorance was all the more conspicuous from the great financial ability of his predecessor Legge. His budget speech was so confused and incapable that it was received with shouts of laughter." Pollard, (1901) 'Dashwood, Francis'.

From the Lesser Holy Assembly, a book of the Zohah, we find references which recall the lexicon and iconography of the Rosicrucian 'Alchemical' process: the talk of 'brides' and the union of Kings and Queen, not to mention references which are markedly less guarded and ambiguous than the ostensibly Christian Rosicrucian literature:

"The second association of Yesod with the genitals arises from the union of the Microprosopus and his Bride…When the male is joined with the female, they both constitute one complete body, and all the universe is in a state of happiness because all things receive blessings from their perfect body. And this is an arcanum (secret)."

And a strangely profane, almost sacrilegious reference to the Bride:

"And she is mitigated, and receiveth blessing in that place which is called the holy of holies below." Referring to the female genitals in terms of the holy sanctuary of the great Temple of Jerusalem would certainly not meet with approval with what one conceives as the Torah studying conservative Jewish mind and one cannot help but feel that such sexual rites and imagery was the very thing the Levite priests were so critical of in Leviticus.

So too the masculine sexual energies are unambiguously referred to and put in spiritual terms and given a specific Sefira in the Tree of Life and the male member too as Yesod is referred to as 'most holy'. One can just imagine what kind of excesses and perversions of spirituality could emerge from a cult which reveres sexuality and specifically the sex organs as holy objects worthy of reverence:

"And that which floweth down into that place where it is congregated, and which is emitted through that most holy Yesod, foundation is entirely white, and therefore is it called Chesed."

And how "Chesed entereth into the Holy of Holies".

Yesod is mirrored on the Tree of Death by the Qlippoth Gamaliel, or the 'obscene one', this is when the sexual energy is repressed and builds up in the conscious mind leading to more and more obscene sexual visions and the demon Lilith is the ruler of this domain. The problem is if a mythology is created then invariably cults and worshippers will arise who will choose to follow this 'path'. So by creating the mythos of a 'Tree of Death' ruled over by various evil spirits and entities, they also invariably unleash these forces into the world as a kind of contrary 'spiritual' tradition, it is all the more tragic that such followers commit real evil acts and atrocities which daily degrade life on Earth and whatever forces of chaos are unleashed by wanton evil, are all based on nothing but the most irrational and very silliest form of absolute nonsense.

For instance, it is rather a sad and awful satire to hear genitals and semen referred to as holy, and the genitals as 'they holy of holies' and surely must constitute sure and certain direct evidence of the inner corruption of the Judaism of the patriarchs. So much of the Zohar follows this template. A Sefira is referenced, then a quote from the Torah, then something sexually suggestive about mothers, queens or brides. Then a suggestive remark like 'the holiness of the male enters' or 'beautiful path into the queen' or 'the influx of pleasure' or 'marital conjunction'; make a reference to Hebrew consonants then refer to a Biblical patriarch and you have your Kabbalah mysticism. This is the seed in order to procedurally generate the Kabbalah.

Something like the following is typical:

"The husband hath dominion over the wife.. combination with the female, the letter I or Yod is the fundamental member by which the world is preserved.. The father illuminating the mother."

In fact, some passages were considered so 'off colour' that Samuel Mathers did not translate them into English but kept the original Latin of Christian Knorr von Rosenroth. We can't be sure about what is being discussed but there seems to be a reference to semen and fertility:

"For everything that is the oil, and the declaration of, and in the power of these men also, is gathered together out of the whole body; for they are all of the army, which is produced from them, and come forth, and all pour in the openings of the genital organs."

This next excerpt refers to the action of the penis entering inside the uterus of a woman:

"Through the Yesod, he goes into the woman in a place called Zion and Jerusalem. For here is the wife's secret feminine place and it is called the uterus."

It is possible that the Zohar is partially a kind of text based marital aid for inexperienced couples, or a form of sex education. In the Lesser Holy Assembly, the so-called Star of David or Seal of Solomon, according to the Zohar, is a symbol of sexual congress:

"Chokmah is the fire: I, and Binah is the water: H, the Father and Mother who, conjoined, produce the Son. Now the fire is symbolized by a triangle with the apex

uppermost △ , and water by ▽ , these two together united form  the sign of the Macrocosm, the external symbol of Vau: V, Microprosopus."

Judaism is pretty clear when it comes to sexual license and such things, all though not strictly considered shameful are certainly not considered holy, they are most assuredly 'things of the flesh that perisheth," though notably this is a New Testament reference. In fact I had assumed that the Bible was globally censorious regarding 'the sins of the flesh' but to my surprise I found that it was largely the New Testament, not the Old Testament, which exhorts the mind to think on spiritual things.

This distinction is hardly made in the Old Testament and leads one to the suspicion of a certain unreformed carnality in the Jewish mind which the Christian mind rejects and sets itself with a view on higher and better things. The Old Testament however is full of sexual immorality, often committed by the Israelites themselves. King David having sex with Bathsheba, then murdering her husband to cover up his immorality for example. The major sexual crimes in the Old Testament tend to refer to homosexuality or of Israelite women sleeping with non-Israelite men. Gross sexual license and carnality seems to be common in the Old Testament and indeed is most often the behaviour of Israel's Kings for which they are chastised by the prophets and punished by God.

The book of Deuteronomy warns the children of Israel:

"Do not set up any wooden Asherah pole beside the altar you build to the LORD your God, and do not erect a sacred stone, for these the LORD your God hates."

Ahab King of Judea set up an altar to Baal and an Asherah pole. It is possible that The Tree of Life comes from a time predating monotheism in Judaism, when Jahweh was said to have had a wife: Asherah, who was represented by a stylised tree or wooden pole. Asherah was an Ugaritic mother Goddess and the role of Asherah was said to be the mediation of opposites, which is exactly what we see with the Kabbalistic Tree of Life and is said to be part of the alchemical process. The result of mediation of the opposites which we have seen has been such a key theme of the so called Western mystical current since the middle-ages is quite startling.

According to the Jewish Encyclopaedia:

"... the "Sefer Yeẓirah" draws the important conclusion that "good and evil" have no real existence, for since everything in nature can exist only by means of its contrast, a thing may be called good or evil according to its influence over man by the natural course of the contrast."

What's more it is my belief that the Biblical Tree of Knowledge in the garden of Eden from which God commanded Adam not to eat, was a reference to the Kabbalistic Tree of Life and was an injunction not to follow Asherah worship and the associated rites. This also makes sense of the word for serpent which supposedly tempted Eve to eat of the fruit. The Hebrew word for serpent is Nachash which also means the occult.

Mexican occultist and creator of the Universal Christian Gnostic Movement: Samael Aun Weor followed in Aleister Crowley's footsteps in capitalising on the sexual nature of the Zohar by deconstructing the whole Zohar and the Torah in sexual terms and then creating his own bizarre cult on the back of it which judging by several accounts on the internet, was quite good at destroying people's lives:

"During my near decade going through the various gnostic movements, I watched as people wept while they gave up their assets and hobbies (even their jobs) in order to 'sacrifice themselves for humanity.' I myself wept as I did things like destroy my video game consoles and movies (or give them away) and even destroyed a huge collection of books I had because they didn't fit in with the ideas of the Samael gnostic movements. I stopped in the middle of my bachelor's degree program because I was persuaded by gnostic leaders to not 'damage my intellect.' I was lucky to be welcomed back to the program by my professors after years of abandonment. I was lucky to have a lot of support after I left the movements."

Despite this there are clues that Weor's dubious movement had discovered, or had access, to some fundamentally ancient, quasi magical knowledge, the kind of knowledge such groups can use to manipulate and control society around them and allow them to operate way beyond the understanding and envisioning of normal people:

"As I understood it, the Astral is this sort of 'place' that is actually inside you, and all your demons live there. It's where you go when you dream. It's very hard for a beginner to navigate because you have to learn to 'see through' your dreams: the complexes/demons/egos (whatever you call them) which have a pretty large amount of control over you in waking life have pretty much total control over you in the astral realm, hence the typical total inability to control ourselves in dreams and the instability of the environment and instability of logic in dreams.

According to the teaching as I understand it, you are supposed to get more and more conscious in your waking life, then more and more conscious in your dream life. As all your dreams become lucid, you will start to 'see through' them, in the sense of having greater insight into what they mean. This gives you a huge edge in battling your egos. In waking life you are just meditating and trying not to let your desires, etc. get the best of you. But in the astral (dream) realm, you can actually see your egos at work weaving the dream picture, and see your egos in personified form interacting with you in the dreams.

Eventually, as you become an adept at this work, you see through the egos at work in your dreams so well that your dreams start to actually stabilize. This is really where the phrase 'astral realm' comes into play. The dream world now becomes this sort of other world that you can explore in a more or less rational fashion. You learn to enter and exit the astral realm at will, meaning you don't have to be tired and fall asleep per se, you can just lie down and whisk yourself off whenever you want to.

Although it is 'internal', since we are all connected you can actually meet and work with other adepts in the astral realm. It really starts to become this other world. You can visit the 'Great White Lodge' (or something like that) where all the best saints working for the salvation of humanity are hard at work.

The goal is to destroy the egos to achieve complete and total consciousness. The whole reason you play around in the astral realm is to take the fight to them. Apparently it gets perilous as you start to clear up the astral realm: your demons see the threat and work extra hard to destroy you. There are all kinds of defensive prayers and mantras and stuff you are supposed to be prepared with before you start doing this stuff in earnest.

Some of the guys at the retreat were talking about being in the astral together. It made me a little envious and wanting to strive to reach that point. From personal experience I can attest to meditation and waking awareness exercises contributing to an increase in lucid dreams. So there is at least something to that part, that much I can say for sure.."

There seems to be some ambiguity about the Weor's cult. Outer members are apparently told to abstain from ejaculation, smoking, drinking alcohol and indeed, most kinds of physical pleasure. No doubt however the 'inner circle' have a very different experience.

Initially Weor had planned to die and reincarnate in his own body but a few years before his eventual death he prepared an Egyptian mummy in which to physically return. The man could have been an honest lunatic but I suspect the truth is that he, like Crowley, had manufactured his very own cult with him as the high priest. Such high-office demands the promise of miracles and Weor was merely playing along with his part, while no doubt enjoying it immensely. I can only hope that such an impious old fraud is now enjoying his just rewards for those who waylay and betray other people's credulity. Though it has to be said, that without the mass of simple-minded sheep souls so ready and willing to be waylaid by these predatory and evilly inclined people, they would not be able to profit quite so well here on Earth as they seem to do and it does seem to be something of a dance of the polarities: the timeless partnership of eternal limitless stupidity with eternal limitless evil.

Without stupidity, evil would not be able to manifest long on Earth and attain its goals, but the fact that it has done so for so long is a testimony to the presence of that silent dance-partner, the dim-witted, brainless victim who always seems to be so plentiful here, like fields of wheat waiting to be reaped. I don't want to waste any more time on this unpleasant charlatan, I will just let his analyses speak for themselves and move on, but the following passage culminates in a direct Rabbinical-style reversal of the Biblical injunction from Genesis 2:17 'you must not eat from the tree of the knowledge of good and evil' here we will see the 'Gnostic' Samael Aun Weor in the role of a literal Satan:

"And when the woman [sexual organ] saw that the tree was good for food she took of the fruit of it and did eat." – Genesis 3: 6.

This indicate that hitherto their love had been angelic and pure, but was now changed into sexual desire first arising in [their physicality made of bones and flesh] the woman [Malkuth] and leading them to conjugal relationship, for a woman [Eve, symbol of the sexual organ] is the inspirer of love whilst man [Adam, symbol of the brain] is the receptacle of it and in this resembles angelic beings whose actions are determined by pure love unblended and unmingled with sexual desire.

"And the serpent was wiser than any animal of the field which Jehovah Elohim had made." – Genesis 3: 7

In the moment that Adam and Eve became thus associated, the lower soul [נפש Nephesh] became excited and aroused by sexual desire in which it delights, as scripture said: 'mayest freely eat' to the prohibition from ejaculating the living manna [semen].

Thus, in saying, 'Of every tree of the garden thou mayest freely eat' indicates that Adam is permitted to eat even from the tree of knowledge, but together with God [Shaddai-El-Chai]."

Samael Aun Weor was a member of the Fraternitas Rosicruciana Antiqua (F.R.A.) and apparently learned the 'Great Arcanum' or white 'sexual magic'. In 1964 he published a book called Cosmic Ships in which he promulgates the doctrine that alien spaceships from other planets are present on Earth. He mentions that sometimes these vessels crash or explode in flight (funny that they travelled all that distance through space only to arrive here and explode) In the book he states that he doesn't seek to check the authenticity of these alien spaceships because for him it is beyond all doubt. He claims these cosmic vessels were created by the angels, archangels, and seraphim, all flesh and blood being apparently, including a flesh and blood angel called Saint Venon from the planet Soort. Saint Vernon's spaceships are apparently powered by gravity, but Weor writes that he doesn't want to tire the reader with technical details. When humanity arrives at its maturity it will have the right to access and use these spaceships and we will receive education from superior humans from space. Some people from Mexico were apparently taken to Venus and one person from Brazil was taken to Mars and he mentions that we are on the verge of a cosmic cataclysm but our space brothers will try to help us.

It is worth noting that a group of Tibetan Lamas possess several spaceships hidden deep under the Himalayas and the inhabitants from other planets walk in our towns and cities unnoticed. Mars, Venus and Mercury are all inhabited by these aliens and Venus has a fantastic civilisation where there is no money and everyone works only two hours per day and receives everything they want. Weor reveals that we can all share in this utopia if we can learn to get rid of our ego, then we will be able to psychically communicate with these benevolent space-brothers.

It all seems like tragic nonsense of course but a lot of people take this stuff very seriously, but beyond all of the nonsense is something real. Namely that there are processes which can destroy the individual sense of self and 'ego' which then does indeed lead to the possibility of telepathic communication with some kind of discarnate beings. We have seen some examples of these beings and their interactions in the story of Barbara O'Brien. I suggest this is not something which we ought to encourage but this seems to be part of the worldwide Rosicrucian agenda, and hopefully by now we can start to see what the agenda, its aims and the final result might be.

The Jewish Old Testament conception of God may seem strange to us now, since Jesus has introduced a new conception of God as a fully transcendent being whose presence was manifest in goodness and love and who had no need of rituals or a tent to live in, nor of vociferous liturgical prayers, nor animal sacrifice. We may assume that despite appearances to the contrary, humanity is gaining in awareness of the metaphysical and transcendent realm and so the modern mind has no need of a God which demands of Moses that the sons of Aaron barbecue meat for him because the burnt offering is 'an aroma pleasing to the LORD'; though it seems that the best part of the offering always ended up in the hands of the priests while God had to make do with a barbecued head and the rest of the bits nobody else wanted.

But reading those passages in Leviticus may make us wonder who or what it was that Moses was communicating with. It seemed God was manifested to Moses as a voice in the Temple of Meeting which gave Moses clear instructions regarding the sacrifice of animals and specific cooking instructions. In fact, apparently anyone who wished to speak to God could go to the Tent of Meeting which was just outside the main camp and God would speak and appear in a pillar of cloud. On Mount Sinai, God was even able to manifest to Moses physically, and had a face, a hand and a back, and could 'pass by' as if it were something which was localised and not, as we might assume of God, omnipresent. We can only guess what any of that really means or whether it even happened at all.

We cannot say whether this was a real historical occurrence or not. We just have to trust the narrative, but if we do that, then it suggests at least some kind of spiritual being which is able to manifest in a limited but significant way and communicate with people. But how do we know this is God? This could be one of the beings which communicates directly with the manipulators: some kind of astral intelligence which when animals have their life sacrificed to it, gains some kind of energy or strength.

The strange thing is that this is precisely the kind of activity which is reputed in Witchcraft and Satanism, where animals are routinely sacrificed, and if the rumours and insider accounts are to be believed, fellow humans as well. In fact, history is replete with examples of ritual human sacrifice. The mercy of the Old Testament and Israelite conception of God is that human sacrifice was not required and this was one of the specific crimes of the Canaanites which were said to include child sacrifice, bestiality and homosexual religious rites which kindled God's wrath, although those that had so far escaped Joshua's God driven genocide of the Canaanites were apparently allowed to remain:

"I also will no longer drive out before them any of the nations which Joshua left when he died, so that through them I may test Israel, whether they will keep the ways of the Lord, to walk in them as their fathers kept them, or not." Judges 2:21.

Could this be the ongoing project for humanity to this day? Are we all being tested on a daily basis by some kind of elite secret priesthood using a three-thousand-year-old blueprint? In order to corrupt a population, the population has to willingly choose to be corrupted. It might seem hugely counter-productive to corrupt countries and societies and drive them into confusion and degeneracy, but one country and one people in particular benefit from the disarray of their perceived ancient enemies. These people have long memories and they have been operating as a people with a particular continuous cultural identity for at least 3,000 years. No other people, ethnic or religious group, can compete with that level of cultural organisation which will always be one-step ahead of any attempts to thwart their plans. Unfortunately, anyone who are not of their tribe is an enemy and their specific God given scriptures specifically instruct them to show no mercy to their enemies.

I contend then that the Kabbalah and by extension the so called 'Oral Tradition' of the Rabbis passed on to generation from generation from the time of Moses is nothing more than the same ancient evil of Asherah and Baal worship, albeit cleverly camouflaged to hide within Judaism and claim a kind of inner-logic to make it seem to fit within Torah Judaism when it is the very force which the Torah was written specifically to oppose all those thousands of years ago. This is why the Kabbalah is so keen to introduce feminine aspects of God, even though as we have discussed, it makes no logical sense to bring gender into spiritual concerns but IF what you are secretly worshiping is an ancient Goddess cult, in fact THE ancient Goddess cult, then this is how you slowly rehabilitate the Goddess. The Kabbalah, although it talks of the Ain Soph as being the ultimate image of God this is cleverly dismissed as 'nothing'. It cannot be worshipped because it has no attributes, it is everything and nothing. It is only at the point at which this force can become personalised as the Shekinah, a feminine force, a Goddess, that God becomes something which can be acknowledged, worshipped and which will respond and interact with humanity.

Shekinah is the Hebrew word for the 'dwelling' or 'settling' and describes the manifest divine presence of the Lord. Neither this term, nor anything which can be associated with it, appears in the Bible. Nor was it found in any of the texts of the Dead Sea scrolls associated with the Essenes. It is solely a product of Pharisaic Rabbinical literature and appears as a feminine form in the Talmud and the Zohar. The Shekinah is also described as the Sabbath Bride:

"One must prepare a comfortable seat with several cushions and embroidered covers, from all that is found in the house, like one who prepares a canopy for a bride. For the Shabbat is a queen and a bride. This is why the masters of the Mishna used to go out on the eve of Shabbat to receive her on the road, and used to say: 'Come, O bride, come, O bride!' And one must sing and rejoice at the table in her honor … one must receive the Lady with many lighted candles, many enjoyments, beautiful clothes, and a house embellished with many fine appointments…"

The bridegroom of the Shekinah is sometimes the name for the Sefira of Tiferet, but there is so little consistency of terms or even of their meanings with the Kabbalah that none of these concepts or definitions can be said to have any fixed meaning. Tiferet is in the middle of the Tree of Life and is connected to all the other Sefirot except Malkuth which, within the logic of the Zohar, it interacts with through the phallic Yesod. Within the abstract realm of the Kabbalah the Shekinah is considered to be spirit where 'God' interacts with the physical world and is represented by Malkuth. 'She' is often referred to as 'the daughter of God' and reflects the divine light the way the Moon reflects light upon Earth. The idea of Shekinah was a relatively recent addition in Rabbinical literature particularly in the work of Isaac Luria and his Aader Bishvachin song which is sung at the Sabbath evening meal:

"Let us invite the Shechinah with a newly-laid table
and with a well-lit menorah that casts light on all heads.

Three preceding days to the right, three succeeding days to the left,
and amid them the Sabbath bride with adornments she goes, vessels and robes.

May the Shechinah become a crown through the six loaves on each side through the doubled-six may our table be bound with the profound Temple services."

Shekinah also appears in the gnostic texts of the Mandaeans and Manichaeans; 'Manda' is the Aramaic word for 'knowledge' and hence 'gnosis' but those among them who have attained the true secrets of their religion they call Nasoraeans, and this word has been used to describe 1st Century Jewish Christians including Jesus himself and to this day the Arabic word 'Nasrani' is a word used to denote a Christian.

Despite this the Mandaeans consider Jesus to be an 'apostate Mandaean' and refer to him as the 'False Messiah' and believe him to be doomed to 'Matarata' or purgatory. According to their text Haran Gawaita, the advent of Jesus was something which should not have happened and disrupted the order of the House of Israel:

"… something was placed in the womb of Mary, a daughter of Moses, and for nine months this 'thing' bewitched her."

"..And he took to himself a people and was called by the name of the False Messiah. And he perverted them all and made them like himself who perverted words of life and changed them into darkness and even perverted those accounted Mine. And he overturned all the rites. And he and his brother dwell on Mount Sinai, and he joineth all races to him, and perverteth and joineth to himself a people, and they are called Christians."

They called Mohammed the 'Son-of-Slaughter' and believe the evil Archon Mars worked through him and say that "he prophesises as a prophet and performed circumcision like Jews, but he changed sayings and he is the most degraded of false prophets'. According to the Haran Gawaita, once the Arab rule of 4,000 years comes to an end, Jesus will return:

"..the false messiah, son of Miriam, will succeed him, and that he will come and will show forth signs (wonders) in the world until the birds and the fish from sea and rivers open their mouths and bless him and give testimony, until (even) the clay and mudbrick in a building bear witness to him, and until four-legged creatures open their mouths and testify to him "

Though the Mandaeans are still warned:

"Nasoraeans, and righteous elect men, testify not to him, for he is a fake Messiah that walketh by fraud and sorcery. He is Mercury, who attracteth attention and doth whatsoever he wisheth and his mind is filled with sorcery and frauds."

But confusingly it then says:

"When the Messiah hath returned, ascending to the sky - and his reign will last six thousand years - he will ascend and assume his first body. From that epoch until world's end, wickedness will depart from the world; that which issued from the earth will enter the earth and that which descended from the sky will return and enter the sky. And there will be righteous people in the world, and no man will covet his neighbour's goods. And people's senses will return to them and they will not perform circumcision; they will be converted and Nasoraeans will increase in the world. The eye of envy will be lifted from them and the sword will depart from the world."

It is not clear if this is referring to Jesus, but it could possibly be John the Baptist who would be the closest thing they have to a messianic figure.

In any case the Mandaeans fled to Babylon in the 1st century AD either after being persecuted by the Jewish authorities or because of Jesus' prophetic warnings of the events of 70AD.

The Mandaeans claim to be from a monotheistic tradition which predates Islam, Christianity and Judaism. The Mandaeans believe the world is created by a synergy of the holy spirit 'Ruha' which is similar to the concept of Shekinah, which the Mandaeans view as a negative force as the lower distinctly feminine, emotional nature of the human mind. They believe that Adam was created by an evil demiurge Ptahil, which used a spirit from the underworld: Ruha, to animate Adam but that his soul is from the light world. The light world soul apparently then reveals Nasiruta (the Nasoraean religion) to him and his wife Hawwa (Eve) and the Mandaean gnosis which involved him freeing his soul and spirit to return to the light world. Ruha as a spirit, uses the planetary spirits to infect Adam's mind to prevent him hearing the voice of his soul.

The Mandaeans have a ritual handshake: the Kushta, or handshake of truth, and it resembles a Masonic handshake in that the thumb is pressed to the knuckle of the other person's hand. The thing which makes me consider whether somehow, part of the Mandaean cult cross-pollinated with the Kabbalah to become what we know of as the Freemasons is the fact that the Knights of Saint John, who along with the Knights Templar, brought the Eastern esoteric tradition to the West, are named after John the Baptist, whom the Mandaeans hold in special reverence and it is even said that both orders placed Saint John higher even than Jesus.

The Templars were even said to have been in possession of the head of John the Baptist to which they offered prayers. Furthermore, the feast day of John the Baptist is the 24th June, a day which is also celebrated by the Freemasons and Freemasonry actively acknowledges John the Baptist as one of its patron saints. It is also possible that the Freemasons have adopted elements of Sabaeanism; if we look at the clue of the Masonic tracing board which shows seven 'stars' which are the seven planets which were worshipped by the Sabaeans, and the sun and moon have prominent place on the Masonic tracing board and it was these two principal bodies which the Sabaeans worshipped in particular. Much of the ritual behaviour of the Sabaeans became later subsumed into Islam but their worship of heavenly bodies ended under the monotheism of Islam. The Mandaeans still exist to this day as the longest surviving gnostic sect in the world, however since they are based mostly in Iraq they have suffered from persecution at the hands of Islamic extremists.

The Nag Hamadi texts discovered in Egypt in 1945 revealed to the world the Gnostic 'Christian' tradition. Those texts discovered at Nag Hamadi had presumably been the few to have avoided the fires of the church. The Sethian Gnostic tradition along with the Valentinianism and Basilideanism comprise the three currents of 2nd and 3rd century Gnosticism. Basilides was a second century teacher of gnostic mysteries in Alexandria Egypt and he was said to have been taught by the Samaritan Gnostic, Menander who became the leader of the School of Simonians after the death of Simon Magus.

According to the entry on Simon Magus in the 1911 Encyclopaedia Britannica:

"...Epiphanius .... tells us also that he gave barbaric names to the 'principalities and powers,' and that he was the beginning of the Gnostics. The Law, according to him, was not of God, but of 'the sinister power.' The same was the case with the prophets, and it was death to believe in the Old Testament."

The Greek 2nd century Christian bishop and dogged opponent of heresies, Irenaeus says of him:

"Samaritan Simon, from whom all the heresies took their origin."

It would seem that Simon Magus is not only the origin of Gnosticism but potentially of the Kabbalah as well, or at least, the earliest known emergence of its 'secret doctrine'. Hippolytus reports that Simon Magus taught a doctrine of 'free love' and gave interpretation of the Old Testament (much in the manner of the Rabbinical tradition one suspects). In his scholarly book length essay on Simon Magus G.R.S. Mead writes how Simon was adept at 'reinterpreting' the texts of the ancients and by doing so dramatically altering their meaning, much in the style of what would later become the main currency of the Jewish Oral Tradition and the Kabbalah:

"So then Simon by such inventions got what interpretation he pleased, not only out of the writings of Moses, but also out of those of the (pagan) poets, by falsifying them. For he gives an allegorical interpretation of the wooden horse, and Helen with the torch, and a number of other things, which he metamorphoses and weaves into fictions concerning himself and his Thought."

Interestingly, Menander also believed, like the Mandaeans in the importance of a ritual water baptism. He taught that the God of the Jews was a demiurge and had 365 Archons above him with Abrasax ruling over the Archons then above him, Dynamis (power) and Sophia, Phronesis, Logos, Nous (mind), and finally the Unbegotten Father as supreme God. The seven letters of Abraxas' name represent the 7 archon heavenly bodies and in Greek isopsephy the Greek letters of the name add up to 365. Here we see a clear influence for Jewish gematria and since the Greek alphabet has a similar source in Semitic Phoenician which is an offshoot of the Hebrew alphabet both systems could have this already encoded in them from the earliest days of the development of writing. Many heads of gnostic schools were identified as Jewish Christians by Church Fathers, and Hebrew words and names of God were applied in some gnostic systems.

The other major Gnostic school was that developed by Valentinus. Like Augustine of Hippo who abandoned Manichaesm and became a Christian because he found better career opportunities within the church, Valentinus abandoned the church after being overlooked for a bishop's position to invent his own heresy, at least according to Tertullian. Valentinus was born in Alexandria and was connected to a group Alexandrian Jews. In common with other Gnostic movements, he also associated the God of the Old Testament with the demiurge. In the Gospel of Philip, a Valentinian gnostic, we find the same strange sexual innuendoes we previously saw in the Zohar and the references to a bridal-chamber which are also commonly found in Rosicrucian materials:

"There were three buildings specifically for sacrifice in Jerusalem. The one facing the west was called 'The Holy'. Another, facing south, was called 'The Holy of the Hoin ly'. The third, facing east, was called 'The Holy of the Holies', the place where only the high priest enters. Baptism is 'the Holy' building. Redemption is the 'Holy of the Holy'. 'The Holy of the Holies' is the bridal chamber. Baptism includes the resurrection and the redemption; the redemption (takes place) in the bridal chamber."

Irenaeus writes:

"A few of them prepare a bridal chamber and in it go through a form of consecration, employing certain fixed formulae, which are repeated over the person to be initiated, and stating that a spiritual marriage is to be performed after the pattern of the higher Syzygia."

The Gnostics used the word Syzygy (as in Ziggy Stardust) to describe a concept which is the same as the Kabbalistic concept zivug, or 'coupling' which means 'male-female pair' and Sophia is apparently the counterpart of Jesus Christ and considered 'the Bride'.

A passage from a gnostic ritual detailing this strange and pointedly euphemistically sexual union unfolds in this manner:

"I will confer my favor upon thee, for the father of all sees thine angel ever before his face ... we must now become as one; receive now this grace from me and through me; deck thyself as a bride who awaits her bridegroom, that thou mayest become as I am, and I as thou art. Let the seed of light descend into thy bridal chamber; receive the bridegroom and give place to him, and open thine arms to embrace him. Behold, grace has descended upon thee."

I think we can very safely establish a strong commonality here between gnostic so-called Christianity and the strongly sexualised metaphors of the Kabbalah. Church father Irenaeus in his Adversus Haereses of 185 AD considered these Gnostic texts in general to be part of:

"..an indescribable number of secret and illegitimate writings, which they themselves have forged, to bewilder the minds of foolish people, who are ignorant of the true scriptures."

Further similarities with the Kabbalah are found in Sethian Gnosticism and the Apocryphon of John. Sethian Gnosticism is said to have Jewish roots and one of the reasons for the apparent similarity between Gnosticism and the Kabbalah is because the Jewish progenitors of Christian Gnosticism are precisely imbuing their understanding of Christianity with the Jewish Oral Tradition.

The Monad of the Gnostics is the same principle as the Ain Soph and is described in the same terms. It is infinite, ineffable, and it is not quantifiable, nor can its qualities be expressed, just as the Ain Soph has no positive attributes since to give it positive attributes would be to create a duality. The Monad, just like the Ain Soph, must exist beyond opposites. From the Monad comes a feminine divine entity called Barbello. This is similar indeed to the Shekinah principle. It is 'the first thought' and 'image' of the Monad. She is also described as the 'first man', again a principle present in the Zohar the 'Adam Kadmon' or primordial man, the first spiritual 'world' after the contraction of God's infinite light.

She is the first of a class of beings referred to as the Aeons and an exchange between herself and the Monad brings the other Aeons into being. Additionally, the properties of Light and Mind are born from the Monad's reflection on Barbelo. The Barbelo is the first of the Aeons but the Aeon Sophia apparently disrupts the harmony and creates demonic archon called Yaltabaoth who has the head of a lion and the tail of a serpent and represents the planet Saturn. The other heavenly bodies are present and possessed of their Archon including the Sun whose Archon is named the familiar Biblical Adonaios. Mercury represents Elohim and Jupiter is Jahweh.

In the Apocryphal Gospel of John, the God of the Old Testament is called Yaltabaoth, also called Samael. The Archons imprison Adam in the Garden of Eden, a false paradise. The concealment of the Tree of the Knowledge of Good and Evil represents the Archons denying knowledge and freedom to Adam. And the tree actually represents Sophia trying to access Yaltabaoth's realm. Yaltabaoth also sent a flood over the Earth to destroy his creation.

The text also rather presumptuously states that Moses got it wrong and that Noah didn't hide in an Ark but in a cloud of light. Additionally, Christ tells John that it was his presence that caused Adam to eat the fruit from the forbidden Tree and Eve and he was sent to help to free the trapped light soul in Adam.

The 18th Century book Geheime Figuren or Secret Symbols published in Germany has an illustration entitled …"The heavenly and Earthly Eve, the mother of all creatures in heaven and Earth… the star of the East." This is clearly a reference to some kind of mother Goddess, and Eve is not referred to in any such terms in the Bible, in fact Eve is seen as instrumental in the tragedy of the fall of mankind, so it would appear that the Rosicrucians worship something else, something clearly non-Biblical, and they merely call it Eve, perhaps to escape any charges of pagan occult goddess worship. The figure is a stylised female form with a sun in place of the head and has the title Virgin Sophia.

There are seven Archons which we are told in the Apocryphon of Saint John correspond to the seven planets of the ancient world and thus to the seven days of the week. The Gnostics believed that the pagan Gods worshipped by the ancients were in reality the Archons and that they were able to control the thoughts and feelings of human beings.

Many of the texts of the Old Testament take on a new reading with the Gnostic analysis, for instance the plurality of the Gods:

"Let us make mankind in our image, in our likeness." Or Ephesians 6:12 "For our struggle is not against flesh and blood, but against the rulers, against the authorities, against the powers of this world's darkness, and against the spiritual forces of evil in the heavenly realms."

They believe that the seven planets (in antiquity this referred to the Sun, Mercury, Venus, The Moon, Mars, Jupiter and Saturn) were ruled by seven Archons and each heavenly body gives its name to a day of the week. In Arabic and Hebrew, the days of the week do not have their own names and are called, day one, day two, day three, with the exception of Shabbat, or Saturday in English: Saturn's Day.

There is a curious and undeniable etymological and linguistic equivalency between the Hebrew word Shabbat and the Latin word Saturn. According to a derivation by Cicero in De Nature Deorum:

"The Latin designation 'Saturnus' on the other hand is due to the fact that he is 'saturated' or 'satiated with years' (anni); the fable is that he was in the habit of devouring his sons - meaning that Time devours the ages and gorges himself insatiably with the years that are past."

While the Hebrew שָׂבֵעַ: śâbaʻ and śâbêaʻ mean to be sated, fulfilled, in the same sense as the Latin 'satur'. The English word 'seven' has its origins in the word Sabbat, although this is more apparent if we look at the French word 'sept' which is clearly a form of the word sabbat. In Arabic the number seven is called 'Saba'. If we consider that Saturday was considered the seventh day of the week before Constantine made 'Sunday' the Sabbath day, arguably because Constantine was an unreformed sun worshipper, but this effectively ended millennia of continuity and made the 7th day the 6th day and the 1st day the 7th day. Such a description has been said to fulfil the prophetic Daniel and the fourth beast commonly considered by some Christians to be a foretelling of the Antichrist:

"And he shall speak great words against the most High, and shall wear out the saints of the most High, and think to change times and laws: and they shall be given into his hand until a time and times and the dividing of time." Daniel 7:25.

If such an analysis is correct it would appear that the Constantine's Church of Rome was the Antichrist, or at least, one of the beasts which comprise this force which has always sought to destroy the Christian message.

Tacitus writes: "We are told that the seventh day was set aside for rest because this marked the end of their toils...Others say that this is a mark of respect to Saturn."

However, for all of this interesting historical exploration there in no reason to believe anything about the existence of these Archons is real. Especially as they are presented to us in such ridiculous terms and the fact that their names and attributes vary depending on the Gnostic tradition. Athoth the Archon, apparently has a sheep's face, the second, Eloaios has a donkey's face while the seventh Archon representing the planet Saturn they call Sabbataios, has a face of flame and fire. It's all a little silly and is probably best not taken particularly seriously and indeed my thoughts of Gnosticism are that although it might be of some comfort to believe that the world is created by evil Gods with animal faces, it isn't necessarily true and it really doesn't do much for one's quality of life. It's all just a fancy and abstraction. No different from the Kabbalah. The question is why do people invent these fancies and who are they? The origin of these Archon fantasies and much of Gnosticism seems to centre on one place in particular: Alexandria in Egypt. This place became the centre of Gnosticism and is home to all of the major currents of Gnosticism.

The Kabbalistic Tree of life seems as much as anything else to be a framework of different aspects of the psyche and the conditions therein. There is perhaps a reason why psychiatry is such an eminently Jewish science and also perhaps again an example of the practitioner imposing his view on a phenomenon for reasons known only to himself. Just as the psychiatrist imposes his own definitions so too, the Kabbalist impose his own definitions on God.

The Zohar is the central and most important book of the Kabbalah. Much of its discourse is based on secret interpretations of the Torah in such a way to bend, change or even contradict the original meaning. It does this by creating a whole secondary study on the meaning of the words used in the Torah by interpreting and ascribing some kind of mystical interpretation to the Hebrew letters themselves.

I have previously written on the fascinating origin of the alphabet as pictographic symbols, a fact many people are completely unaware of today except for students of linguistics; this fascinating study opens up vistas into our most remote past and confronts us with some intriguing mysteries. For instance, learning that the letter C represent a 'Gamal' or 'throwing stick' we might wonder how this ancient Egyptian hunting tool found its way to the Australian Aborigines. The word 'Gamal' is the Arabic word for camel and it is possibly the distinctive bent, or arched shape of the throwing stick and also the word for 'bridge' in Aramaic is 'Gamla', no doubt the distinctive 'arched' shape of the camel back being the inspiration but all of these words have their origins with the Ancient Egyptian word for a 'throwing stick' and the verb QMR or 'qamar' which meant 'to throw'. We can see how with the passage of years consonantal shift may slightly obscure the origins. So 'q' and 'g' and 'r' and 'l' are largely equivalent and phonetically very close when it comes to the movements of the tongue and the mouth for their articulation.

The Study of the letters of our own alphabet also betray the Middle-Eastern, ancient Semitic origins of our letters. The alphabet we may consider to be Greek since the letters of 'Alpha' and 'Beta' are known, but the 'Aleph' and 'Beet' of the Hebrews may be less widely known. The Semitic 'Beet' represents the floor plan of a house and our letter B still shows us the two rooms of this house. Every letter in fact is a picture of something and often correlates with words which use that letter to convey that meaning.

Over the years the letters may have transformed somewhat by flipping either to the left or right or upside down. So the letter A, known in Greek as 'Alpha' and in Hebrew as 'Aleph', was originally a pictogram of an ox's head. If you turn the letter upside-down and return it to its original orientation as an Egyptian hieroglyph and the two horns and face of an ox appear. In the Hebrew alphabet 'Aleph', like all of the letters of the Hebrew alphabet, is supposed to have mystical significance. 'Aleph' is composed of two yods with a diagonal letter waw (or f) connecting the upper, hidden qualities of God and the lower visible presence of God in the visible world.

In some instances, some of these symbolic interpretations may actually contain something genuinely insightful or even revelatory. The letter 'Yod' for instance or 'Iota' in Greek, as in 'not one iota' or 'not one jot' as the smallest letter represents the immense power of God and the single, smallest point of the microcosm from which all creation emanates; it is also significantly, the first letter of the 'tetragrammaton' YHWH or 'Jahweh'.

In his book The Palm Tree of Deborah, Shelomo Alfassa describes the attainment of the highest level of the tree of life, Kether or Crown, though like so much of the Kabbalah this in itself is an inconsistent claim since it was said that in the Zohar that Moses himself had only perceived as high as Tiferet and the Patriarchs Malchut, so from this we are to assume that the higher Sefirot are probably off limits to humanity, yet Shelomo apparently is able to explain the attainment of Kether, the highest emanation closest to the infinite and unknowable Ain Soph.

"It does not raise nor exalt itself upwards; on the contrary, it descends to look downwards at all times. For this there are two reasons. The first is that it ashamed to gaze at its Source, but the Cause of its emanation looks continually into it to give goodness to it while it looks down to those beneath."

The suggestion of being 'ashamed' to look at the source which is Ain Soph or the unknowable God suggests estrangement from God and evokes the fall of man in the Garden of Eden being where the first sign to God that Adam had disobeyed his commandment not to eat from the Tree of Knowledge was his shame and the fact that he hid himself when God came to look for him. It can be no coincidence that the serpent is a stylistic representation of the journey up the Kabbalistic tree of life, and we may recall that the word snake in the Hebrew Old Testament is Nachash which also means occult.

According to The Kabbalah Experience by Michael Laitman, "a great part of the Kabbalist's journey is spent in the worlds of ABYA (Atzilut, Beria, Yetzira, Assiya), where the Kabbalist gradually turns intended and unintended sins into virtues, and thus justifies the works of the creator and His guidance."

We find what might be an interesting oblique reference to one of the key doctrines of the Kabbalah in the Chymical Wedding of Christian Rosenkreutz, that of turning vices into virtues, and although nothing is made explicit in the text, it ought to be understood that he who is not initiated into the Kabbalistic secrets of the Rosicrucians is unlikely to make any sense of events which might only stoke his curiosity and induce him to join the group but the real intention is to convey meaning to those who already understand what is being alluded to:

"Meantime the King and Queen, for recreation's sake, began to play together, at something which looked not unlike chess, only it had different rules; for it was the Virtues and Vices one against another, and it might ingeniously be observed with what plots the Vices lay in wait for the Virtues, and how to re-encounter them again. This was so properly and cleverly performed, that it is to be wished that we had the same game too."

The Kabbalist pursues mystical insight rather than intellectual beliefs or moral action though it seems to me to be a trick to escape the reality of moral judgement of the kind outlined in the Torah. The Kabbalah has many such semantic and legalistic tricks in order to redefine moral absolutes and continue to live a life which we might say, pleases man more than it might please God. This is best exemplified or instance in the Kabbalistic doctrine of what we might call 'holy sin' and is explained clearly by Laitman:

"..In the Almighty's sight the repentant sinner has a higher status than the man who has never sinned. This is the meaning of the rabbinic teaching that in the place where the penitent stands the perfectly righteous cannot stand (Ber. 34b). The reason for this has been expounded by the Rabbis in the chapter 'He Who Builds,' where it is stated that the letter He is shaped like an exedra (Is a Greek word for exedra was a covered place in front of a house but open to the outside) so that whomsoever wishes to go astray may do so. That is to say, the world was created by means of the letter He and the Holy One, Blessed is He, created the world wide open in the direction of sin and evil. As the exedra, the world is not fully enclosed but is broken open towards the direction of evil (Sabbath)."

Reading from the Kabbalah Experience, where The Kabbalah is explained in a series of question and answers, we find the following passage about the cessation of perception of time experienced by the initiate into the Kabbalah mysteries:

"What about the lack of perception of time? It's hard to understand the lack of sensation of time. But 'time' in spirituality is no more than the changing of emotions."

The distortion of the perception, or even as Laitman suggests, the cessation altogether, is a classic symptom of some kind of neuropsychiatric and neurological disorder and in present in many mental impairment disorders ranging from Parkinson's disease through to bipolar disorder and schizophrenia. It is my contention that this is the goal of working with the Kabbalah and the results of travelling through the stations of the Tree of Life are tantamount to developing psychosis. Indeed, I maintain that this is the apotheosis and pinnacle of the mystery initiatory tradition and always has been, even more so to this day.

It is interesting to note that the Tree of Life bears no reference to anything taught or mentioned in the Jewish Torah and it ought to be evident that the two systems are not mutually inclusive: there is no mention of Jahweh in the Tree of Life, the Ain Soph is an impersonal definition for 'eternity' which is the closest thing to God in the Kabbalistic system. Kabbalah doesn't really deal with a moral universe in the sense of right and wrong, and actively opposing duality, merely extols relative levels of awareness and has much more in common with gnostic systems revealed from the synthesis of Greek and Jewish thought in the centuries after the ministry of Jesus.

The Kabbalah then is the attempt to justify the backsliding of Israel through semantic tricks and word-play in order to justify many of the things which were specifically forbidden by the Torah, above all of them being initiation into the occult mysteries which the Kabbalah specifically exalts.

There are many chapters of the Zohar which relate the supposed secret initiations of the Hebrew patriarchs, again as we have seen, using the selective use of passages from the Torah to give false justification for the exegesis.

"It is stated, 'He went on his journeys from the south even into Bethel, the place where he had pitched his tent at the beginning'; he progressed and advanced in the divine life so that by the mental and spiritual illumination which he ultimately attained, he became fully initiated into the comprehension and understanding of the mysteries of the Hidden Wisdom and graduated to that degree termed 'teleiaor,' perfection, when it is written, 'And there Abraham called on the name of the Lord' (Gen. XIII. 4) and became a just man made perfect. Blessed are they who attain unto this degree of righteousness, for they become invested with an aureole of light and are jewels in the crown of the Holy One. Blessed are they in this world and in. the world to come. Of these it is written, 'The path of the just is as the shining light that shineth more and more unto the perfect day' (Prov. IV. 18)."

"On observing this general depravation of manners and modes of living, it is written, 'And Abraham went down into Egypt to sojourn there.' Here the question may arise, what was the reason and object of his going down into Egypt? It was because at that time Egypt was a great center of learning, of Theosophy and the science of the Divine Mysteries, and therefore referred to in scripture as 'the garden of the Lord like the land of Egypt.' In it, as in the garden of Eden, of which it is stated, 'From the right of it went forth a river called Pison that encompassed the whole land of Havilah, where there is gold,' flowed a great mystical river of divine knowledge, very precious and unobtainable elsewhere. Abraham having entered into the garden of Eden and become an adept in the secret doctrine, desirous of passing through all its grades on two the higher mysteries in order to become 'teloios' or perfect, went down into Egypt where there was gold, or the Hidden Wisdom."

So, the implication is clear that the prohibition of initiatory or transformative rites of the pagans which are continually rebuked in the Torah are now reversed and such rites are specifically encouraged, indeed, such is the whole purpose of the Kabbalah.

The very fact of initiation is something forbidden in the earliest Greek translation of the Hebrew Bible the Septuagint. The name Septuagint comes from the story that Ptolemy II the Greek Pharoah of Egypt of the 3rd century BC, asked for a translation of the Torah from Hebrew to Greek to be included in the Library of Alexandria by 72 Jewish Elders.

"There shall not be a harlot of the daughters of Israel, and there shall not be a fornicator of the sons of Israel; there shall not be an idolatress of the daughters of Israel, and there shall not be an initiated person of the sons of Israel." Deuteronomy 23:17

'Initiated' person is usually translated as 'ritual homosexual prostitution' and this line was added by the 70 Jewish scholars to further clarify the following verse.

"Thou shalt not bring the hire of a harlot, or the wages of a dog, into the house of Jehovah thy God for any vow: for even both these are an abomination unto Jehovah thy God."

The wages of a dog is also translated as "male prostitute's payment" and this is because this was associated with the mysteries of Anubis, hence the Septuagint's reference to 'initiation'.

With this in mind are we to assume that the biggest secret of secret society initiation is the homosexual sex act?

It is this force which now rules the world today through the proxy of Freemasonry which it infiltrated via Rosicrucianism and the general Alchemical sciences transmitted by those Kabbalistic Jews to the idealistic and perhaps well-meaning Christians to infect the West.

The Kabbalah uses the interpretation of letters to imbue new meanings in order to completely rewrite the fundamental parts of the Torah and it does this in order to justify its own initiatory system of mysticism. In the Zohar the Biblical phrase "Let us make man" is taken and the word Man or 'Adam' is analysed thus:

"...known to the angels the mystery and occult signification of the word Adam (man), the letters of which indicate his relation to both worlds, the seen and unseen, the known and unknown. By the letter M which is written as a final or closed mem, is found thus contrary to rule in the word *lemarbeh*, occuring in the verse, 'Of the increase of his government' (Is. ix. 7). Man is connected with the higher world, whilst daleth or the letter D, closed on the west side, indicates his relation to the lower and sensible world. The principles of which these letters are the symbols ultimated in their manifestation on the phenomenal plane of existence and the production of a blended and harmonious whole, viz., of man in the form of male and female until the Lord God caused a deep sleep to fall upon him (Gen. ii. 21). The Holy One then separated them and having clothed the latter in a form most fair and beautiful brought her to man, as a bride is adorned and led to the bridegroom. Scripture states that He took one of the sides or parts (of the androgynous form) and filled up the place with flesh in its stead. In a very ancient occult book we have found it stated that what God took from the side of Adam was not a rib but Lilith, who had cohabited with him and given birth to offspring. She was however an unsuitable helpmeet for Adam and therefore Scripture states, 'But for Adam there was not found a helpmeet for him' (Gen. ii. 20). After the disappearance of Lilith and Adam's descent into the world plane of existence, then it was, as stated, 'The Lord God said, It is not good that man should be alone, I will make him a helpmeet for him.'"

So here the Kabbalah is saying that Adam, or Man originally cohabited with Lilith and the Lilith was Adam's first wife and she subsequently became a demon which persecutes children:

"She dwelled there until Adam and his wife sinned. Then the blessed Holy One plucked her form there, and she rules over all those children – small faces of humanity – who deserve to be punished for the sins of their fathers....She toys with them and kills them. This happens in the waning of the moon, whose light diminishes; this is me'orot (lights) deficient."

According to Kabbalistic analysis of the passage above this means that God released the spirit of Lilith specifically to punish and murder children.

From this belief one can see how ritual child sacrifice has come into being and we can see how the Zohar has given rise to modern Satanic 'theology' and practice and I wonder whether child sacrifices are carried out to this day when the moon's light wanes. If so they would be being carried out according to Jewish scripture. According to the Zohar Lilith was created by mixing the perfect light of Jahweh with the imperfect light of Samael.

Israel is often described as a prostitute in the Old Testament, an epithet God applies to Israel more than any other in the whole of the Old Testament. God also accuses Israel of adultery 40 times in scripture. The children of Israel frequently departed from the worship of the one God and into Ba'al worship, trafficking with demons and all kinds of immorality. Nothing has changed.

From the Zohar, in a chapter concerning the union of the higher and lower self which beguilingly begins with an excerpt from Genesis:

"Said Rabbi Eleazar: 'It is written, "But with thee will I establish my covenant" (Gen. vi. 18): as the continuity of the covenant or good law on earth is the same as in the higher spheres, we infer from these words that when men become just and upright in this world they contribute to the stability of the good law in both worlds.'

Said Rabbi Simeon: 'The words just cited have an occult meaning. The love of the male for the female is based upon jealous desire. Observe, when there is a just man in the world, or one whose higher and lower self have become harmonized and unified, the divine spirit or Shekinah is ever with him and abides in him, causing a feeling of affectionate attachment towards the Holy One to arise similar to that between the male and female. Therefore the words, 'I will establish my covenant with thee' may be rendered thus, 'Because of the union between thy higher and lower natures giving rise to a yet diviner life, I will abide with thee forever. I will never leave nor forsake thee. Come thou therefore into the ark into which no one unless he is just can enter.'"

The mystical union of the higher and lower self, or of the bride with the Bridegroom within the context of the Rosicrucian mysteries, is the key goal of any continuous initiatory programme. This mystical union involves process which eventually lead to a change in brain chemistry such that the right and left hemispheres of the brain are in continually equal activity and that the right brain, that is the subconscious mind which is the residence of the higher self, is brought into day-to-day awareness and not merely relegated to explicit activity during our sleeping hours. This essentially means that what is termed the astral aspect of consciousness, which the right brain specifically interacts with, is brought down to Earth. This leads to the classic symptoms of schizophrenia which include auditory and visual hallucinations; feelings of unreality, dream-like states, feelings of impending death or even of actually being dead and in some kind of limbo state. The reason for this is because the right brain, the dormant part of our consciousness is in full operation and reality has indeed become partially dreamlike because we have brought that part of ourselves, that ability to access the astral dream realm, into our day to day lives. In addition to the negative effects there are some secondary effects which are prized in the occult community such as the ability to contact spirits and even the performance of feats of precognition and premonition since there are feats which our mind is capable of in the dream-state where there is no sense of time and all events past and present can be accessed by the astral consciousness.

This unification of both hemispheres of the brain leads to the state of primordial being or Adam Kadmon, or Adam Auilah in Hebrew, where man supposedly has his fully divine spark awakened and is one with the creator and all ten Sefirot are manifested. It is arguable that Jesus Christ underwent a similar experience to achieve his miracles but most people who undergo this experience probably become schizophrenic but for the Kabbalist and the Gnostic, the primordial man is the image of the perfect man as he was before the fall and the fragmentation of his mind into two distinct parts.

The right brain element to our mind is referenced in the Siphra Dtzenioutha or the Book of Concealed Mystery and makes it clear that this aspect of ourselves is ordinarily hidden from our normal perception:

"THE Ancient One is hidden and concealed; the Microprosopus is manifested, and is not manifested. When the inferior man descendeth (into this world), like unto the supernal form (in himself), there are found two spirits. (So that) man is formed from two sides--from the right and from the left."

We can readily understand that this explanation that man has 'two spirits' and 'two sides' to himself refer to the left and right hemisphere of the brain which are indeed two spirits in the sense that the two parts of our consciousness are usually more or less very tightly sealed or insulated the one from the other.

For instance, we may remember snatches of key moments from our dreams which we have managed to bring into remembrance in waking left brain consciousness, but we never remember the whole varied dreamscape and the events which played out in our minds during the night. Similarly, when asleep we tend to have a very reduced awareness of our everyday life, perhaps the odd few people from our physical lives appear from time to time, but it is also true that we may also see people whom we have not seen for many years.

While asleep we tend to forget about the many details of who we are while awake, and so when asleep we can suddenly find ourselves in situations that are entirely at odds with our personal situation in real life.

The Arikh Anpin, meaning: the Vast Countenance, otherwise known as 'The Ancient One' or Macroprosopus, is a term used to describe the attainment of Kether, the first and highest Sefira closest to the divine emanation of the Ain Soph.

The Macroprosopus and the Microprosopus or the Microcosm and the Macrocosm, are the meaning of the well-known hermetic principle from the so-called Emerald Tablet of Thoth which first appeared in Arabic in the late 8th Century, and is the foundational text of European Alchemy:

"That which is below is as that which is above, and that which is above is as that which is below, to perform the miracles of the one thing."

This is encoded in Eliphas' Levi's drawing of Baphomet with two fingers pointing upwards and two downwards while a caduceus of serpents, one black and one white are entwined around the middle. This is also represented by the two triangles of the Jewish hexagram, or Seal of Solomon, with the upper triangle representing spirit coming into matter while the lower triangle represents matter being elevated into the spirit world.

Incidentally Eliphas Levi, described the Sepher Yetzirah in his Histoire de la Magie as: "a Genesis of illumination, the Sepher Jezirah is a ladder formed of truths," and that "The Zohar represents absolute truth, and the Sepher Jezirah provides the means by which we may seize, appropriate and make use of it."

There is an interesting commentary by Samael Aun Peor, founder of Universal Gnosticism who was also a member of the Fraternitas Rosicruciana Antiqua movement:

"Binah is ruled by Shabbatai שבתאי, Saturn, we have an atom of Binah in the pineal gland, the door of heaven, which in the Male Goat of Mendes is represented with a torch upon a horned goat head (letter Shin ש). The two horns of the goat (as well as those of Moses) relates to Binah בינה and Chokmah חכמה. Binah relates to the left hemisphere of the brain and Chokmah-Uranos to Aquarius, the right hemisphere of the brain. They form the Tetragrammaton of Esh אש ('fire') in our Rosh ראש 'head.' This is why the name Iod-Hei-Vav-Hei יהוה, the Tetragrammaton, relates to Chokmah and Binah in the world of Atziluth. Above them in the torch or pineal gland is Kether, the crown, ruled by Neptune, the superior waters of Chaos; in other words, Pisces, the fluid emanations of the Theomertmalogos, the Christonic substance of the Solar Logos."

Rav Kook, the first Chief Rabbi of Israel, writes intriguingly about the Zohar:

"This composition, called The Book of Zohar, is like Noah's Ark, where there were many kinds, but those kinds and families could not exist unless by entering the ark. …Thus the righteous will enter the secret of the Light of this composition to persist, and thus is the virtue of the composition, that immediately when engaging, with his desire for the love of God, it will draw him as a magnet draws the iron. And he will enter it to save his soul and spirit and his correction. And even if he is wicked, there is no fear should he enter."

This is a symbolic representation of the attainment of the Philosopher's Stone, that is the unification of right and left hemispheres of the brain and the co-operation of the Microprosopus or the left brain rational logical physically oriented mind with the Macroprosopus of the right brain, the astral or spirit element of our mind.

The right brain as we know is concealed from our awareness except during sleep or as a result of the culmination of successful rituals and secret society initiations. In his introduction of his English translation of Knorr Von Rosenroth's Latin translation of some of the books of the Kabbalah, Macgregor Mathers writes:

"Of Him it is said that He is partly concealed (in the sense of His connection with the negative existence) and partly manifest (as a positive Sefira). Hence the symbolism of the Vast Countenance is that of a profile wherein one side only of the countenance is seen; or, as it is said in the Qabalah, 'in Him all is right side.'"

In the Siphra Dtzenioutha or The Book of Concealed Mystery, another of the texts which make up the Zohar we find further clearer references to the distinction between the left physical brain hemisphere of the physical world and the right, astral or spiritual realm aspect of our consciousness and this is also something encoded in the left and right pillars of the Kabbalah, like the symbolic left and right pillars of Freemasonry Boaz and Jachin as well as the three principle degrees of Freemasonry which are also referenced in the Zohar:

"There are three degrees, yet each is independent even though they are one, connected into one and do not separate one from the other."

"With respect unto the right side he had, Neschamotha Qadisha, the holy intelligences; with respect unto the left side, Nephesh Chiah, the animal soul. Man sinned and was expanded on the left side; and then they who are formless were expanded also. When both were at once joined together generations took place, like as from some animal which generateth many lives in one connexion."

In the book of the Greater Holy Assembly of the Zohar we find a reference to what could be an allusion to some kind of chemical agent being pivotal to this transformation which could accord with the Hoffer Adrenochrome Hypothesis already outlined in this book. Perhaps this too gives the hidden meaning behind the title 'Chymical Wedding' where the chemical transformation is within the initiate, incidentally the website for Phoenix Masonry have seen fit to publish Mather's translation of The Kabbalah Unveiled on their website, proving I think, the suspected link between Kabbalism and Freemasonry.

"And from that skull distilleth a dew upon Him which is external, and filleth His head daily. And from that dew which floweth down from His head, that which is external, the dead are raised up in the world to come. Concerning which it is written, Cant. v. 2: 'My head is filled with dew.' It is not written 'It is full with dew;' but NMLA, Nimla, 'it is filled.' And it is written, Isa. xxvi. 19: 'The dew of the lights is Thy dew.' Of the lights-- that is, from the brightness of the Ancient One. And by that dew are nourished the holy supernal ones. And this is that manna which is prepared for the just in the world to come. And that dew distilleth upon the ground of the holy apple trees. This is that which is written, Exod. xvi. 14: 'And when the dew was gone up, behold upon the face of the desert a small round thing.' And the appearance of this dew is white, like unto the colour of the crystal stone, whose appearance hath all colours in itself. This is that which is written, Num. xi. 7: 'And its varieties as the varieties of crystal.'"

"And that membrane hath an outlet towards Microprosopus, and on that account is His brain extended, and goeth forth by thirty and two paths.

This is that same thing which is written: 'And a river went forth out of Eden' (Gen. ii. 7). But for what reason? Because the membrane is (then) opened, neither doth it (completely) enshroud the brain.

Nevertheless the membrane is opened from below. And this is that which we have said: Among the signatures of the letters (is) ThV, Tau, Th; nevertheless He impresseth it as the sign of the Ancient of Days, from Whom dependeth the perfection of knowledge, because He is perfect on every side, and hidden, and tranquil, and silent, like as good wine upon its lees."

The results of involvement in the programme of the Kabbalah are usually confined within the context of the Freemasonic and Illuminati organisations but there is a semi-public Kabbalah organisation founded in 1922 by Rabbi Yehuda Ashlag called The Kabbalah Centre which has offices throughout the world but mostly in the United States, South America and Europe.

In the 5th October 2015 online edition of The London Evening Standard there is an article detailing some specific complaints about activities taking place at the London centre:

"The London Kabbalah Centre used by Madonna has been infuriating its neighbours who say they were disturbed by a 36-hour chanting session in the building's car park.

Residents near the Kabbalah Centre in Stratford Place W1, which also counts Gwyneth Paltrow among regulars, say loud prayers, clapping and chanting had kept them awake for an entire weekend.

Westminster City Council's noise team launched an investigation after being contacted over the weekend, with officers 'issuing advice' to the centre.

Katherine Corbett, who lives in a flat overlooking the car park, said the building held mass open-air religious services between Friday evening and the middle of Sunday morning.

'I was sitting listening to my own music and I still couldn't hear for the noise,' she said. 'They were screaming and shouting. When I heard them on Friday night I took the video, shut my windows and slept in great heat, but I didn't think it would go on all night.'

The centre is understood to have erected a temporary shelter in the grounds as part of its Sukkot celebrations, a week-long Jewish festival that marks the end of harvest and the Exodus of the Jews from slavery in Egypt."

The BBC reported on 9th January 2005 how a:

"..senior figure in the controversial Kabbalah Centre - the sect championed by stars including Madonna and Demi Moore - seems likely to spark a storm of protest by saying Jews killed in the Holocaust brought their downfall upon themselves.

Eliyahu Yardeni, of the London Kabbalah Centre, made the astonishing claim to an undercover reporter investigating high-pressure sales techniques employed by the group, which promotes its own brand of beliefs, part ancient Jewish mysticism and part pseudo-science.

Talking about the wartime massacre of the Jews, Mr Yardeni said: 'Just to tell you another thing about the six million Jews that were killed in the Holocaust: the question was that the Light was blocked. They didn't use Kabbalah.'

The same article also details cynically fraudulent claims about the Kabbalah Centre's own brand of 'healing water':

"The probe also revealed how Kabbalah Centre representatives claimed bottles of 'healing' spring water sold by the group could help cure cancer - and how they sold a batch to a sufferer for hundreds of pounds.

A second investigator, who worked undercover as a Kabbalah Centre volunteer for four months, was told how the Kabbalah water worked, with a devotee explaining: 'We start with the purest artesian water and then we do the various meditations, injecting energy into it.'

The Kabbalah Centre website explained that a process called Quantum Resonance Technology 'restructures the intermolecular binding of spring water'.

The investigation discovered the water actually comes from CJC Bottling, a bottling plant in Ontario, Canada, which was the subject of a public health investigation in 2002 into how its water was tested.

CJC was ordered to improve manufacturing techniques, though there was no suggestion that they ever sold polluted water.

Regarding fundraising, the statement went on: 'As a registered charity, the centre has to fund raise to cover administrative costs and outreach work, the effects of which are felt across the world on a daily basis.'

The centre has launched a US$1m campaign asking followers to donate money so it can send its own brand of Zohar books and water to the victims of the Asian tsunami.

In Israel, the authorities have refused to give the charity a certificate of proper management for three years running because of accounting inadequacies, and in Britain the Charity Commissioners have criticised the centre's accounts for 'significant shortcomings in transparency'."

A final article reported on the Judiaciaryreport.com website regarding the London Kabbalah centre is of a much more serious tenor. The article reports how Phiona Davis, apparently became a victim of mental abuse after becoming involved in Madonna's Kabbalah centre in London. The website claims that Davis was conned out of 2 million pounds and was spied upon in her home with hidden cameras and illegal telephone wire-tapping. They then made it known to Phiona Davis at meetings what they knew about her. This is the key focus of the phenomenon known as 'Gang Stalking', to drive the victim to madness and despair, which, in their system, is the initiation to Kether and so called 'union' with God. The website doesn't quite understand why they did this and is under the belief this was all in order to obtain money from Ms Davis, in fact the whole experience led to Phiona Davis becoming psychotic and this led to her murdering two people:

"Fashion student Phiona Davis reportedly confirmed to police that she had been attending Madonna's Kabbalah centre in London and told police she was being 'controlled' and people from the Kabbalah centre were walking around her flat. A few months later she killed telephone salesman Keith Fernandez by stabbing him 58 times at her home in Green Lanes North London reportedly saying 'God done good, for this is done through God.'

The next day she killed her grandmother Mary Skerritt by stabbing her 130 times. She then tried to set fire to the flat. She then went outside the flat in Stoke Newington saying 'I am God, I am the benevolent one, burn the demons inside her.' 'You can arrest me but you can't punish me. Only God can punish me.' She was also seen holding her arms out saying 'I am the Messiah.'

Later at Stoke Newington police station she attempted to strangle herself and smeared crosses on the wall in blood and excrement. She shouted at the police, 'I am the messiah and the King of Kings. I will forgive you all.'

She reportedly told the police she thought her former boyfriend Keith Fernandez was a robot and her grandmother was the devil. She was sent to Broadmoor and can be released only with the express consent of the home secretary."

The purpose of Kabbalah is precisely to induce schizophrenic illness. This is the attainment of Kether and 'union' with God. Hence when Phiona Davis reportedly commented to police and firefighters that she was God/the Messiah in her delusion. As reported by Phiona Davis some month prior to her murdering two people, she was being covertly monitored, followed, spied on and harassed. This was the programme of the Kabbalah, to induce a change in brain chemistry through various personally and psychologically invasive means which can lead to entirely unpredictable consequences.

Kabbalah is a transformative process which acts upon the human energy centres through the 'the Tree of Life' as they term it, to radically create a transformation in consciousness. The Tree of Life can also serve as a metaphor for the human vertebrae. The human spine is made of 32, 33 or even 34 bones and the Kabbalah has 32 paths which approximate to the average number of human vertebrae in the human spinal column. This immediately gives the meaning of the 33 degrees of Freemasonry; each degree symbolically advances through each stage in The Tree of Life, advancing the energies through the whole of the spinal column in order to arrive finally, at the crown.

There are 32 paths, which as we know, are formed of the 22 letters of the Hebrew alphabet with the 10 Sefirot and the modern hermetic tradition has made these paths into mini courses of study, and one rises in descending order with the 32nd path being the first and the 1st path being the last. The initial paths involve studying astrology and understanding the effect the heavenly bodies have on the human personality and the destiny of one's life. Such a thing might be learned and understood more or less directly with a little work, reading and application, not to mention belief; the final paths in the Kabbalah however are much more radical and suggest something less about study and more about a programme of psychological transformation.

From the Zohar, Acharei Mot, with commentary in capitals:

"This river is called the mother of the Garden of Eden, DENOTING MALCHUT, AS BINAH IS REFERRED TO AS MOTHER (HEBREW. EM, ALEPH MEM), AS IT IS WRITTEN, "IF (HEBREW. IM, ALEPH, MEM) YOU CRY AFTER BINAH" (MISHLEI 2:3), being higher than the Garden. IT IS CALLED MOTHER, because EDEN, DENOTING CHOCHMAH, joins with it and does not leave it. For this reason, all the springs OF MOCHIN come out, draw FROM IT and water all sides, BOTH TO THE RIGHT OR TO THE LEFT, and open doors within it. Hence, there is Mercy coming from it, DENOTING THE CENTRAL COLUMN and Mercy opened in it AS THE BEGINNING OF THE OPENING OF THE CENTRAL COLUMN, WHICH RECONCILES AND JOINS RIGHT WITH LEFT BEING THE PERFECTION OF EVERYTHING, STARTS AT BINAH."

The central column of the Tree of Life is the human spinal column and the reference to the right and the left refer to the hemispheres of the brain. We have seen in previous chapters how a transformation can be wrought by repeated fear and prolonged anxiety as in the case of Barbara O'Brien. However, there are references to fear, not only Kabbalah but we can also observe a similar theme in the Jesuit's training techniques, and we shall do just that later in this chapter.

Moses de Leon, previous to writing or at least redacting the Zohar wrote the Sefer ha-Rimon or The Book of the Pomegranate which must be symbolic of the forbidden fruit of the Garden of Eden since he also refers to the Tree of Life in the same context:

"See the pomegranate in the garden of delight." He also calls this pomegranate 'image of the precious stone' which could potentially be the origin of the concept of the Philosopher's Stone, and since so much of the lore and imagery of Alchemy seems to originate in the Kabbalah and specifically the presumed work of de Leon: The Zohar, this could be a reasonable conclusion. In the area of research of Jewish mysticism we have seen that there seems to be something of a 'snowball effect' where terms in previous works which may be loosely defined or somewhat only half-formed ideas, are latched onto by successive Kabbalists and given fuller definitions and the ideas fully fleshed out, by writers eager to add to and expand on the mythos and somewhat 'make it up as they go along' but drawing on previous writers and even the Torah to justify their innovations and conceits. I suspect the idea of a pomegranate having some mystical significance is just another example of this kind of continuous scaffolding of ideas until something sticks and a whole edifice of mystical significance can be built using the most tenuous support structures:

"Thus it is called pomegranate, and it is filled with the secrets of God and the commandments of One who dwells in habitations," habitations is a reference to the Shekinah spirit, so there is an allusion to the pomegranate as the forbidden fruit of the Garden of Eden, the (Philosopher's) Stone, all in one relatively modest work. These ideas of course have long since broken out beyond their original fragile beginnings to become ideas which have taken on a life and huge cultural significance of their own.

In the Book of the Pomegranate, Moses de Leon writes:

"Worship through fear is the beginning [through which] to enter into the cleaving of the Creator. It is the opening to enter upward so that the upper attributes will rest upon him and he will be complete...for if fear does not rest upon his head...he is not worthy to cleave to the Torah and the commandments."

Scholar of Jewish mysticism Elliot R. Wolfson writes in his commentary on the Book of the Pomegranate:

"The commandment to fear God can be said to comprise all the commandments, for without fear one cannot begin to cleave to God or the Torah. That is to say, the fear of God is the one commandment that holds the key to all the other commandments and, as such, contains the others within itself.... Devotional life is thus centered about this one commandment and the divine emanation which it symbolizes. The overriding purpose of the commandments, for de León, is to cleave to the Shekhinah in order to facilitate both the possibility of the individual's ascending upward on the Sefirotic ladder and of creating a downward flow of energy from the uppermost source to the other divine gradations and the cosmos. In emulation of Moses, the one who truly fears God is united to the level of the fear of God and, consequently, merits the whole range of commandments contained therein."

Wolfson further elaborates:

"Naḥmanides interpreted R. Ezra's passage in his commentary to Ex. 20:8 with a slightly different emphasis... Shekhinah, which emerges out of the potency of fear, the fifth emanation."

The Kabbalah emerged from 12th Century Spain with some possible origins in the 1st and 2nd century. Something else to emerge from Spain, another arguably transformative movement was that of the Jesuits. The Jesuits almost certainly emerged from the Alumbrados of Castile of the 15th and 16th centuries, who were said to have been mostly conversos, that is Jewish converts to Christianity; quoting Britannica.com:

"While they counted some of the high aristocracy among their number, most of the Illuminists seem to have been *conversos*."

In the Alumbrados we find a development of the broad themes of the Kabbalah and the beliefs of the Alumbrados are a good snapshot of the kind of spirit of sensuality and sexual license which would later intwine itself into Freemasonry, the various Hellfire clubs and the Bavarian Illuminati which all seemed to present themselves on the scene within a close time-frame and as we have seen, many of the members were intricately connected to each society.

The Alumbrados believed that it was possible to reach a state of union with God whereby one could freely indulge in sinful acts and express sexual desires freely. They too believed in a kind of direct revelation of God, whereby they could actually obtain direct communication with him. This is enough to give pause and make one question just what it was that these people thought they were actually contacting. What voices and delusions overthrew them and led them to believe it was God itself that they were trafficking with. We cannot know how exactly the Alumbrados pursued this path to 'contact' but we can examine the work of Ignacio de Loyola for a clue since the Jesuits were the inheritors of this subversive heretical tradition which managed to find a home within the Catholic church and Loyola was even summoned to stand before an ecclesiastic commission while he was studying in Salamanca in 1527 on a charge of being in league with the Alumbrados.

The book The Jesuit Order as a Synagogue of Jews by Robert Aleksander Maryks goes into extensive detail exploring the particular ethno-religious conflicts of the period during the early years of the Jesuits and the ongoing attempts of various groups to wrest control of the direction of the order. It seemed largely to be a contest between

Jews who had apparently converted to Christianity and non-Jewish Christians. It is revealed that most of the original directors of the organisation were Jews, although there are rumours and suspicions that Loyola himself was a Converso this is not made explicit in the book.

It is worth nothing that Philip II of Spain observed that "all the heresies in Germany, France, and Spain have been sown by descendants of Jews" and the Inquisition was formed precisely to root out the heretical corruptions of 'converso' Jews, or Jews who now professed to be Christian but who may secretly still have practised their former faith and who may indeed have a particular interest in attacking Christianity from within.

It is difficult to find hard and reliable information about the Alumbrados outside of the archives of the inquisition but one particular area of research where information about the Alumbrados can be found is, somewhat perversely, the area of gender studies with a specifically feminist narrative. The reason for this is that the movement of the Alumbrados were apparently inspired by, and largely promulgated by women.

A lady called Marina Lee-Anne Stuparyk for her MA thesis for the University of Northern British Columbia, wrote a paper entitled The Case Against Maria de Cazalla. Although her article is dreadful feminist nonsense which entirely misses the point of what she has discovered, she does unearth several interesting facts about the mysterious Alumbrados movement.

For a start she observes:

"Alumbradismo in Toledo during the early sixteenth century is an important area of study given that it developed under a female leader: Isabel de la Cruz. Many of the core members, María included, were also female."

Isabella de la Cruz she describes as a 'beata' as in a blessed-saint, who became "the true mother and teacher of all the Alumbrados."

Maria herself is described in the paper as "a middle-aged woman, around fifty years of age. Married to Lope de Rueda with six children, María descended from a family of conversos, meaning that her ancestors were Jewish and converted to the Catholic faith." Incidentally presumed co-leader of the Alumbrados, Pedro Ruiz de Alcarez was also a born from a family of conversos."

It is discussed in the paper whether the early 16th century's Sister Maria de Santo Domingo, known as the Holy Woman of Piedrahita, was a kind of proto-Alumbrado, or was secretly a member of the then secret group or directly inspired their formation. Maria was said to have conversations with the Virgin Mary and Jesus Christ himself, not only that but she actually also told people that Christ was with her and that she was

Christ. This is eerily familiar to the strange ravings of the unfortunate victim of the Kabbalah's 'personal development' techniques Phiona Davis.

Maria de Santo Domingo had many high-profile supporters like the later Alumbrados and Maria de Cazalla who was supported by the Duke of Alba though her behaviour was described as 'lascivious' and the Dominican Order's Master General, Thomas Cajetan suspected the devil was inspiring Maria's mania and she has been cited, according to The Catholic Encyclopaedia as 'an early adherent' of the Alumbrados but notes "it is not certain that she was guilty of heresy".

She was illiterate, the daughter of a simple labourer, and her words were recorded and published in The Book of Prayer of Maria of Santo Domingo and although there is little which is outright subversive of Christianity, except perhaps that she channels 'God' at one point, there is little that is especially destructive in her ministry or whatever it might be called and the Inquisition found: "her life and doctrine exemplary".

However, the Alumbrados were most assuredly not found 'exemplary' by the Inquisition and there can be few doubts that not only were they antagonistic to the institution of the church but also of the Christian religion itself.

For instance, if we cite the example of Maria de Cazalla as presented by Ms Stuparyk, who was considered to be the de-facto leader of the Alumbrados:

"María's case was troubling because she taught publicly and presented other Alumbrados in her circle like Isabel de la Cruz and Pedro Ruiz de Alcaraz as greater than the saints, including Saint Paul."

This might not be surprising if we consider that these Jewish 'conversos' never really abandoned their Jewish culture and traditions and became Christian largely because it allowed them to continue to live and if we recall Maimonedes statement in the Yesodei haTorah "Should a gentile arise and force a Jew to violate one of the Torah's commandments at the pain of death, he should violate the commandment rather than be killed." It is rumoured that the great Maimonedes himself became a Muslim and dissimulated his own Jewish faith, Jewish scholar Alan Nadler writes:

"Maimonides practiced the time-honored medieval Islamic tradition of Taqiyya, or prudent dissimulation, by dressing and behaving like a Muslim publicly, perhaps occasionally presenting himself at a mosque, while remaining an observant Jew during the darkest period of Almohad persecution..."

So according to the feminist analysis provided by Ms Stuparyk in her research paper: ".. María subverts sexual expectations and church teachings regarding chastity, marriage, and virginity through various claims made against her. The most prominent being that she lifted the status of marriage over that of virginity and that she believed she was closest to God during carnal acts than if she "was praying the loftiest prayer in the world."

In A History of the Inquisition in Spain, Henry Charles Lea cites the example of Fernando Mendez a priest from Seville but secretly a member of the Alumbrados:

"He taught his disciples to invoke his intercession, as though he were already a saint in heaven; fragments of his garments were treasured as relics; he gathered a congregation of beatas and, after mass in his oratory, they would strip off their garments and dance with indecent vigor — drunk with the love of God — and, on some of his female penitents, he would impose the penance of lifting their skirts and exposing themselves before him."

Born late in 15th Century Spain, there is no doubt that Loyola would have been familiar with Kabbalistic treatments and was perhaps an associate of the Alumbrados. Ignacio de Loyola was born Inigo Lopez, Lopez, although a Spanish surname meaning 'son of the wolf' is also considered a Shephardic Jewish surname. It is thought that Inigo Lopez changed his name to Ignacio de Loyola to allay any suspicions about possible Marrano origins and place him within the context of indigenous Spanish nobility.

As a young man he became a servant of the Spanish nobleman Juan Velázquez de Cuéllar, who was treasurer to the Spanish King, King Ferdinand. He was said to have had a carousing and dissolute life of a knight until he suffered a bad leg wound fighting the French in the battle of Pamplona. The sudden reversal in his fortunes, the terrible pain of his shattered leg and the ongoing torture as the doctors continuously tried to set and reset it must have inspired some of the dark rhetoric which inspires his Spiritual Exercises which are a mental conditioning manual for the infamous Jesuit Order.

Once when Inigo was preaching in the street, three women who had been investigated by the Inquisition for being members of the Alumbrados started experiencing suspicious ecstatic states:

"One fell senseless, another sometimes rolled about on the ground, another had been seen in the grip of convulsions or shuddering and sweating in anguish." Inigo himself had been imprisoned on being suspected of being Alumbrado but was eventually released without charge.

It is suspicious since such activity has historically been considered to be a sign of demonic possession. That fact that Inigo was able to elicit a kind of resonant demonic possession in these three Alumbrado women indicates that he himself was possibly operating under the impulse and control of the demonic realm.

The Spiritual Exercises form the key element of preparing the mind for acceptance into the Jesuit mental framework though I would say that the key aim is the auto-induction into psychosis through the deliberate and continual contemplation, in the words of Loyola: "to see with the sight of the imagination" of hell and rumination of one's own evil nature. The fifth exercise for example, is a meditation on Hell. The novitiate is required by stages, or degrees you might say, to visualise Hell, to place himself there with his mind.

"The first Point will be to see with the sight of the imagination the great fires, and the souls as in bodies of fire. Second Point. The second, to hear with the ears wailings, howlings, cries, blasphemies against Christ our Lord and against all His Saints."

In general, the system of the Jesuits is as I have stated, a fast track to auto-initiated psychosis. As we have heard the Rosicrucians have a psychic initiatory framework whereby degrees and information are revealed psychically to particular favoured people. It is my contention that the Jesuit system is the same and it does this by establishing contact with some kind of 'astral agency' which can only approach the human psyche once it is sufficiently weakened and unable to resist. Of course, the Jesuits think this is God because their system tells them that it is, and that they are suitably humbling themselves by wallowing in their sins, in order to apparently make them fully repentant enough to be worthy of God's favour. Repeatedly the Jesuit Spiritual Exercises make plain their aim to invoke confusion and shame in the novitiate.

"The first Point will be to bring the memory on the First Sin, which was that of the Angels, and then to bring the intellect on the same, discussing it; then the will, wanting to recall and understand all this in order to make me more ashamed and confound me more, bringing into comparison with the one sin of the Angels my so many sins, and reflecting, while they for one sin were cast into Hell, how often I have deserved it for so many..."

"..it will be to ask shame and confusion at myself, seeing how many have been damned for only one mortal sin, and how many times I deserved to be condemned forever for my so many sins."

Thus, he is specifically instructed to pray for pain, torment, shame and confusion and to see himself in the lowest terms:

"..to see all my bodily corruption and foulness; to look at myself as a sore and ulcer, from which have sprung so many sins and so many iniquities and so very vile poison."

It goes without saying that the most obvious fallacy here is that he is appealing to God, the presumed creator of humanity and all life on Earth, either directly or indirectly, while presenting himself as an example of God's creation in the lowest and foulest possible terms. Such self-abasement has nothing appealing in spiritual terms and if anything might only possibly appeal to a being who has a great hatred of humanity, such a well-known adversary we do not need to name here for fear of labouring a point.

Additionally, these 'prayers' or 'invocations' or whatever one might call them, are often under instruction to take place just after midnight or in total darkness:

"..to deprive myself of all light, closing the blinds and doors while I am in the room, if it be not to recite prayers, to read and eat."

"at midnight, bringing myself to confusion for my so many sins, setting examples, as, for instance, if a knight found himself before his king and all his court, ashamed and confused at having much offended him, from whom he had first received many gifts and many favors: in the same way, in the second Exercise, making myself a great sinner and in chains; that is to say going to appear bound as in chains before the Supreme Eternal Judge; taking for an example how prisoners in chains and already deserving death, appear before their temporal judge."

It is evident to most according to millennia of religious and metaphysical literature that God and the angels are usually associated with light while other types of beings and unwholesome spirits are generally, in the folklore, said to be most active and abroad at night and in conditions of darkness.

The gist of the Spiritual Exercises seems to be instead of drawing closer to God and achieving a more positive relationship with the divine creative principle, the contrary seems to be the logical outcome. The repeated invocation of shame, of one's loathsome sinful nature and finally the:

"...understanding how in sinning and acting against the Infinite Goodness, he has been justly condemned forever."

In fact, the Spiritual Exercises specifically deny contemplation on the positive aspects of the Christian message and of Jesus' ministry, but instead to continually ruminate on death and judgement exclusively:

"Not to want to think on things of pleasure or joy, such as heavenly glory, the Resurrection, etc. Because whatever consideration of joy and gladness hinders our feeling pain and grief and shedding tears for our sins: but to keep before me that I want to grieve and feel pain, bringing to memory rather Death and Judgment."

Nor indeed to think of the Good News Jesus brought, of our salvation through his sacrifice/murder by the proto-Rabbinical authorities following their own traditions alien to Torah Judaism but instead:

"...force myself to grieve, be sad and weep."

Furthermore Jesuits are taught:

"Not to laugh nor say a thing provocative of laughter...(and) restrain my sight, except in receiving or dismissing the person with whom I have spoken."

This leads to the creation of a peculiarly unappealing personality. One who does not laugh or enjoy humour and is not interested in encouraging humour or laughter in others; not only that but a man who will only make eye contact twice, upon receiving and dismissing someone. Such rules are designed to further alienate such a person from other people and the simple human pleasures of human fellowship. This could only be forbidden by someone wanting to make someone estranged from goodness and languishing only as we have seen, in pain and torment. If we recall the words of C.S. Lewis from his Screwtape Letters, God wants only the best for us and certainly would not have created the majesty and wonder of the world in order for us to be self-flagellating slaves crippling ourselves and renouncing even the good things about the human experience.

The Jesuits are even encouraged not to take any simple pleasure in the eating of food:

"Another time, while he is eating, he can take another consideration, either on the life of Saints, or on some pious Contemplation, or on some spiritual affair which he has to do, because, being intent on such thing, he will take less delight and feeling in the corporal food."

Focussing on the bad and renouncing the good can only have the effect of making a man become what he focusses on: evil. And this I have no doubt was the devious aim of the Jesuit organisation: the inculcation of a militant band of priests languishing in evil, cutting themselves off from humanity, goodness and becoming brooding beings of pestilence, death and sin. Nothing good can come from such auto-suggestion because as Proverbs remind us:

"For as he thinketh in his heart, so is he."

Not only were the Jesuits told to take no pleasure from life and " to leave off the superfluous of delicate or soft things" but indeed to actually provoke pain and damage to their own bodies:

"..to chastise the flesh, that is, giving it sensible pain, which is given by wearing haircloth or cords or iron chains next to the flesh, by scourging or wounding oneself, and by other kinds of austerity."

Loyola also praises fear, servile fear no less, as a way, if not the best way, to serve God, but this directly contradicts Biblical teaching which tells us:

"God hath not given us the spirit of fear; but of power, and of love, and of a sound mind," (2 Timothy 1:7).

"Although serving God our Lord much out of pure love is to be esteemed above all; we ought to praise much the fear of His Divine Majesty, because not only filial fear is a thing pious and most holy, but even servile fear -- when the man reaches nothing else better or more useful -- helps much to get out of mortal sin. And when he is out, he easily comes to filial fear, which is all acceptable and grateful to God our Lord: as being at one with the Divine Love."

This focusing on fear, doom, terror and all such negative qualities seems to be the key focus of the Jesuit system and it is ironic that we find a similar mental framework being evoked in the 1st degree initiation into the arch-enemy of the Catholic church, the Royal Black Lodge, a high level sub-group of the protestant Orange Order of Northern Ireland said to have taken its rites and history from the Knights Templar. The following extract is from evangelicaltruth.com:

"In this interview the Black Grand Registrar reveals much about the actual nature of the Royal Black and its very reason for existence. In essence, he admits that it is a secret Order that is immersed in the accoutrements of death. He admits that it is a society that is in a continual state of mourning. Take away the mourning and the Black loses its identity. It is an Order that proudly parades the symbols of death as an outward representation of its inward beliefs and spiritual psyche.

The skull and cross-bones is not merely a Black emblem but is an important exhibit used in its ritual initiations and in certain secret formal gatherings to lay stress upon, or represent secret esoteric teaching. In probably one of the most shocking practices existing within the Loyal Orders, the candidate entering the first degree of the Black – the Royal Black degree – is met with a display of human remains. There, before him, sits an actual human skull and bones amidst a gathering of sober Black brethren. As the entrant views the human skull he is solemnly instructed on the teaching of the Black on death, the resurrection and eternity."

Interestingly the same website gives details of the sequence of events in the initiation and we find the interesting detail:

"Something on a table under a white cloth being uncovered, was perceived to be a human skull, which the witness was desired to take up, and view it, and was told it was a real skull of a brother called Simon Magus. Porter was poured into the skull, which the witness was desired to drink; he did so, and it was handed round the whole Knights."

Simon Magus, "from whom all the heresies took their origin," according to the words of Irenaeus.

So here we have a recipe for the auto-induction of psychosis, schizophrenia and demonic possession, and it is clear at times that Loyola himself was in a state of deep spiritual confusion and trapped at times in just the kind of manic-uncertainty that can lead to the development of chronic conditions of psychosis. The following example, where Loyola must have stepped on the cracks in the pavement, visualising them as a Christian cross, might lead the disinterested reader, if he or she has any knowledge of the kind of manias and inescapable double-binds that many suffering from severe mental illness report, to the conclusion that the Loyola was not quite in a condition of full mental-health:

"After I have stepped on that cross, or after I have thought or said or done some other thing, there comes to me a thought from without that I have sinned, and on the other hand it appears to me that I have not sinned; still I feel disturbance in this; that is to say, in as much as I doubt and in as much as I do not doubt. That is a real scruple and temptation which the enemy sets."

Strangely, Loyola seemed to have had an inkling of what he was doing and perhaps he was in some doubts as to whether his Spiritual Exercises were not in fact demonically inspired and that reading the following extracts and then comparing it to the broader work in general we may see that he had unwittingly given the key and explanation to the creation of not only his own work, but the Jesuit order and their operations in the world to this present day:

"The enemy looks much if a soul is gross or delicate, and if it is delicate, he tries to make it more delicate in the extreme, to disturb and embarrass it more. For instance, if he sees that a soul does not consent to either mortal sin or venial or any appearance of deliberate sin, then the enemy, when he cannot make it fall into a thing that appears sin, aims at making it make out sin where there is not sin, as in a word or very small thought."

The thirteenth rule of Loyola's Jesuits as outlined in his Spiritual Exercises is as follows and must surely be the most damning especially if we consider that Jesus said of himself: "I am the way, the truth and the life." For the Jesuits, the 'truth' is whatever the institution of the Roman Church says it is:

"Thirteenth Rule. To be right in everything, we ought always to hold that the white which I see, is black, if the Hierarchical Church so decides it.."

An interesting historical character to emerge from the gloom of the Jesuits is Miguel de Molinos. As a youth he was educated by the Jesuits and ordained as a Jesuit priest in 1652, joined the brotherhood of the School of Christ. He was sent to Rome where he became very influential and soon developed a powerful network of patrons including the exiled Queen of Sweden.

While in Rome he developed the 'philosophy' or perhaps more accurately, the heresy for which he has become recorded in history: 'Quietism', the details of which he thoroughly outlined in his book 'The Spiritual Guide which Disentangles the Soul'.

The key point of the book is Miguel's advocacy for what he terms 'contemplation' over the 'meditation' of the Jesuits. Meditation in his terms refers to the Jesuit techniques of visualising key scenes from the Bible, specifically the Passion of Christ and also visualising hell itself as we have just read in the Spiritual Exercises of Ignacio Loyola. The ostensible purpose of Molino's Spiritual Guide was to teach man a method of drawing closer and knowing God by curtailing the activity of the mind and the personal will.

After a hitherto successful career in the church and Molinos' doctrine of Quietism having become broadly accepted and not then considered heretical, something changed. Jesuits felt they needed to rebut the specific attacks made in the book about their methods of 'meditation' and there was a lively back and forth between Quietists and Jesuits as to which method was the best, whether the 'meditation' (which is more like a form of contemplation) of the Jesuits or 'contemplation' (which is really a form of meditation) of the Quietists. The Inquisition took an interest and investigating in 1681 declared the Spiritual Guide of Miguel de Molinos orthodox and compatible with the teachings of the Church. However, in 1685 the tide turned against him and he was arrested under instruction from French authorities and while many in Rome were sympathetic to Molinos in 1687 he confessed his errors to the Inquisition and died after spending nine years in prison. At his trial according to Britannica.com:

"Molinos defended sexual aberrations committed by himself and his followers as sinless, purifying acts caused by the Devil. He claimed they were passively allowed in order to deepen a quiet repose in God."

Pope Innocent XI wrote of Molinos:

"....these doctrines were leading the faithful from true religion and from the purity of Christian piety into terrible errors and every indecency."

The Catholic Herald online summarises thus:

"In that same year, however, he published his Spiritual Guide, which purported to lead the reader through the various stages of the spiritual life to perfection in this world, whereby one would remain perfectly passive before God as the highest state. Once there, a person need not fear sins committed under the temptations of the Devil, but should remain at peace, even after committing the vilest acts."

This 'doctrine' if we can call it that, ought to recall what we have seen of the Kabbalah and the idea of 'holy sin' or sin even serving a useful purpose in making a person more righteous before God.

We even find this very dangerous idea had crept into the theology of Pope Gregory I to whom Molinos refers:

"That we may not make Poison of Physick, and Vices of Vertues, by becoming vain by 'em; God would have us make Vertues of Vices, healing us by that very thing which would hurt us: So says St. Gregory."

And Pope Gregory reaches this conclusion by some highly Kabbalistic logic worthy of Simon Magus himself:

"I'd like to look inside the fortified bosom of grace with how much God keeps us by the favor of mercy. Behold, he who exalts himself about virtue returns through vice to humility. But he who is extolled for his virtues, is wounded, not by the sword, but, so to speak, by medicine. For what is virtue but medicine? and what is vice but wound? Because, therefore, we treat the wound as a medicine, he makes the medicine of the wound, so that we who are smitten by virtue may be cured by vice."

It is all rather unfortunate because most of the early elements of the Spiritual Guide and the core of Quietism is basically a form of Zen meditation which is an extremely useful spiritual and psychological tool which can be used to experience other states of being once the mental chatter of the brain has been quietened, however this is not an idea original to Molinos and it is likely he learned about it in his studies and decided to adopt it as a plausible cover for his true aims which may have been deliberate subversion or at least, an excessive enjoyment of physical pleasures. The Catholic Herald reports how:

"Cardinal Benedetto Odescalchi and the exiled Queen Christina of Sweden became admirers (although the Queen regarded Fr de Molinos's huge appetite for food with sceptical amusement)."

The true origins of Molino's 'Quietism', or at least those to emerge in the West, are to be found in the works of a late 5th Century Greek philosopher using the pseudonym of a 1st Century Greek convert to Christianity by Saint Paul known as 'Dionysius the Areopagite'. Pseudo-Dionysus the Areopagite as he is known was a philosopher who apparently was both a Christian and conversely, a Neo-Platonist. He expounded proto-

Kabbalistic ideas which we can derive from the following from Corrigan & Harrington (2014):

"According to pseudo-Dionysius, God is better characterized and approached by negations than by affirmations. All names and theological representations must be negated. According to pseudo-Dionysius, when all names are negated, 'divine silence, darkness, and unknowing' will follow."

A PHD thesis by R. A. Agnew for the University of Edinburgh comments on Pseudo-Dionysus linking his philosophy to the 'Illuminati':

"He, further, explains that Quietude and Silence are necessary, since 'only like can know like'; and 'God is peace' and 'Repose', 'the One all perfect source ... of the Peace of all'; and He is Silence 'the angels are, as it were, the heralds of the Divine Silence'.

In silence then 'let the intelligent soul transcend intelligence and it forgets itself ... Closed, ... mute and silent ... and sheltered, not only from exterior but also from interior impulses; he is made God.' This is deification, the principle of Eckhart, the doctrine of the Brethren of the Free Spirit, and the teaching of the Illuminati."

Agnew in his PHD paper writes, citing Pseudo-Dionysius:

"We find in Dionysius the doctrine of the three ways: the Purgative; the Illuminative; and the Unitive. Through him this division has become the standard for all later exponents of mysticism. To explain it, he writes Moses was enjoined first to purify himself, then he saw the light from the smoking mountain, and then the face of God. It is after the soul has been freed from the world of sense that it enters the mysterious obscurity of holy ignorance ... to be lost in Him, who can neither be seen nor felt."

Molinos writes, showing the debt he owes as does the mediaeval hermetic tradition which had infiltrated the church, to the mysterious Greek philosopher in his quasi-alchemistic references to a three-step path (one might say degrees) of 'cleansing' or 'purgation', 'Illumination' and finally 'unity'.

"Because if thou wilt serve God, and arrive at the sublime Region of Internal Peace; thou must pass through that rugged Path of Temptation; put on that heavy Armor; fight in that fierce and cruel War, and in that burning Furnace, polish, purge, renew, and purifie thy self.

For which reason St. Ignatius Loyola said very well in his Exercises, that in the cleansing way, Corporal Penances were necessary, which in the illuminating way ought to be moderated, and much more in the unitive."

All of this was of course probably very novel for the church of 17th Century Europe: the introduction of what we might consider techniques of transcendental meditation, and it is a pity that Molinos tarnished these valuable techniques (as indeed to this day many Christians consider meditation of this kind to be dangerous and a way for permitting 'demonic' influences). It could be that Molinos having found the genuine peace of meditation, misinterpreted the reward of having a still mind and extrapolated that it is necessary to surrender the will as well, that is to abandon any objective frame of morality or reference and surrender the mind. Either that or like so many people who achieve notoriety, success and a throng of admirers, he wasn't devoted enough to resist the Earthy temptations such a position can present:

"You must know, that this Annihilation to make it perfect in the Soul, must be in a man's own Judgment, in his Will, in his Works, Inclinations, Desires, Thoughts, and in it Self: so that the Soul must find it self dead to its Will, Desire, Endeavour, Understanding and Thought; willing, as if it did not will; desiring, as if it did not desire; understanding, as if it did not understand; thinking, as if it did not think, without inclining to any thing, embracing equally Contempts and Honours, Benefits and Corrections. O what a happy Soul is that which is thus dead and annihilated! It lives no longer in it self, because God lives in it: And now it may most truly be said of it, that it is a renewed Phenix; because 'tis changed, spiritualized, transformed and deified."

We have a further 'alchemistic' reference, this time to the 'Phenix' which informs me, as well as references to a spiritual guide, that Molinos was actually a disciple or novice of some mentor figure who was guiding him through some ongoing transformative, alchemical process. A process which has existed since the earliest records of history and shrouded in mystery even until the present day where this process has now taken on almost industrial proportions in terms of its influence on many members of the public institutions, media and political realm, but is still a complete mystery to the vast majority.

Unfortunately, there is perhaps something in the character of Miguel de Molinos which allowed itself to justify his ceding repeatedly to temptation by blaming the devil and refusing to take personal responsibility. But there is much in his 'Guide' which suggests a background in Kabbalah as there are too many obvious Kabbalistic elements which show themselves partially submerged in his doctrine. We can also see how in recent times Molinos has been upheld as some kind of prophet by certain hermetic movements and Aleister Crowley wrote extensively in praise of him:

"In more remote times, the constituent originating assemblies of the O.T.O. included such men as … Molinos" Liber LII Manifesto of the O.T.O.

Crowley considered Miguel de Molinos to be one of his 'Gnostic Saints' as detailed in Liber XV and refers to the Spiritual Guide in the following terms:

"That you may gain some insight into the nature of the Great Work which lies beyond these elementary trifles, however, we should mention that an intelligent person may gather more than a hint of its nature from the following books, which are to be taken as serious and learned contributions to the study of Nature, though not necessarily to be implicitly relied upon."

Indeed, Crowley's reference to 'crossing the abyss' which was a personal spiritual boast for him may have been inspired by the writing of Molinos in his reference to mediation:

"By not speaking, not desiring, and not thinking, one arrives at the true and perfect Mystical Silence, wherein God speaks with the Soul, communicates himself to it, and in the Abyss of its own Depth, teaches it the most perfect and exalted Wisdom."

This abyss which Molinos refers to may be the darkness which one encounters when one starts to develop in transcendental meditation, of which I would say there are at least five stages which for reference I will briefly outline here:

Stage 0 I would say is when you first sit down to meditate. The mind is cluttered with thoughts and impulses initially, distractions appear in the mind once you try to meditate. You feel hungry, perhaps worry that you haven't turned off a tap somewhere in the house, or that you would be better off doing this at another time. If you persist with focussing on nothing you will reach stage 1.

Stage 1 is when you start to feel a little more relaxed, the mind has calmed a little and there are no immediate pressing thoughts trying to dissuade you from meditating like this. If you continue to meditate you will reach stage 2.

The next stage signals a tangible inner focus, whereas before you were aware of the outside world you now are becoming aware of the inner world. The world outside is now taking second place to an increasingly widening inner world which your mind appears to be filling. Thoughts will be significantly reduced and it is easy not to engage with them or wish to act on them. There is a tangible sense of a decrease in mental activity as you can almost start to count the neurons in the brain firing off with stray thoughts and impulsions which are becoming increasingly dampened down.

This is fittingly described by Molinos:

"By the way of Nothing thou must come to lose thy self in God (which is the last degree of perfection) and happy wilt thou be, if thou canst so lose thy self; then thou wilt get thy self again, and find thy self most certainly. In this same Shop of Nothing, Simplicity is made; interior and infused recollection is possessed, quiet is obtained, and the heart is cleansed from all manner of imperfections."

The third stage of transcendental meditation would be what I call, approaching the Abyss. What I term the abyss and perhaps more in common with Molinos and less so with Crowley, is the sense that the focus of the mind is now wholly engaged inward and a large empty darkness approaches the mind. A friend of mine I spoke to about meditation said this actually scared him and made him leave off meditation altogether.

Molinos notes:

"Know then that the streightest, most perfect and secure way of proficients, is the way of darkness: because in them the Lord placed his own Throne; And (Psalm 18.) He made darkness his secret place. By them the supernatural light which God infuses into the Soul, grow and increases. Amidst them wisdom and strong love are begotten, by darkness the soul is annihilated, and the species, which hinder the right view of the divine truth, are consumed. By this means God introduces the Soul by the inward way into the Prayer of Rest, and of perfect contemplation, which so few have the experience of. Finally; by darkness the Lord purgest the senses and sensibility, which hinder the mystical progress...See now if darkness be not to be esteemed and embraced."

I would hasten to add that here I assume that Molinos is speaking of the literal darkness of the mind in meditation and not in terms of a sort of Luciferian allegory for the forces of darkness.

This darkness seems to move closer to your mind and it is something tangible, not an absence perhaps but more a solid kind of emptiness. It moves closer and starts to fill the mind, like a rapidly incoming tide threatening to wash you, your mind and everything away into nothingness. Allow yourself to move into this darkness or it to move into you until it actually fills your whole mind, again Molinos has already been there and left a fitting description:

"O what infinite room is there in a Soul that is arrived at this divine Solitude! O what inward, what retired, what secret, what spacious, what vast distances are there within a happy Soul that is once come to be truly Solitary! There the Lord converses and communicates himself, inwardly with the Soul: there he fills it with himself, because it is empty; cloaths it with Light, and with his Love, because it is naked; lifts it up, because 'tis low; and unites it with himself, and transforms it, because it is alone."

Stage four is breaking through this darkness to the other side and what you thought was nothingness and negation and a total loss of the self turns out to be an infinite boundless space within yourself and total peace. Your mind has now left the physical world altogether and your mind is now operating wholly in, and exploring a higher realm of reality. Here you will feel interesting effects like a spinning around, as if your whole being is turning as if on a merry go round; this I believe is experiencing our electro-magnetic soul and its natural oscillation. You will also have a feeling of moving through this inner realm at great speed, as you explore this inner world which seems to be full of the whole universe and all past and present realities.

Some of these experience Molinos describes thus:

"The fourth step, which is Illumination, is an infused knowledge, whereby the Soul contemplates sweetly the divine truth, rising still from one clearness to another, from one light to another, from knowledge to knowledge, begin guided by the Spirit Divine. The fifth is a Savoury Pleasure of the divine sweetness, issuing forth from the plentiful and precious fountain of the Holy Ghost. The sixth is a sweet and Admirable tranquillity, arising from the conquest of Fightings within, and frequent Prayer; and this, very, very few have Experience of. Here the abundance of Joy, and Peace is so great, that the soul seems to be in a sweet sleep, solacing and reposing it self in the Divine breast of Love. Many other steps of Contemplation there are, as Extasies, Raptures, Melting, Delinquium's, Glee, Kisses, Embraces, Exultation, Union, Transformation, Expousing, and Matrimony, which I omit to explain, to give no occasion to Speculation…"

Aside from the inner peace and the exploration of what could be considered an antechamber to the Kingdom of Heaven one takes away many benefits from this kind of meditation into our daily lives in the physical realm. Such practise allows us to control the mind and emotions much better and remain calm and detached from events which would previously have had a negative impact on our mental well-being. We will also take this focus into our dreams which will become much more coherent and less chaotic as we will better be able to navigate and order the inner dreamscape.

Molinos refers to the ability to better deal with anxiety and worry, which might be termed 'invisible enemies':

"The strong Castle, that will make thee triumph over all thine enemies, visible and invisible, and over all their snares and tribulations, is within thine own Soul, because in it resides the Divine Aid and Sovereign Succour. Retreat within it and all will be quiet, secure, peaceable and calm. When thou seest thy self more sharply assaulted, retreat into that region of Peace, where thou'lt find the Fortress. When thou are more faint-hearted, betake thy self to this refuge of Prayer, the only Armor for overcoming the enemy, and mitigating tribulation: thou ought not to be at a distance from it in a Storm, to the end thou mayest, as another Noah, experience tranquillity, security."

It would seem to me that Molinos despite apparently fully engaging in a kind of pure Zen meditation and breaking through the threshold of darkness to the realm of mental bliss beyond, something seemed to have gone wrong and at a certain point reading through the Spiritual Guide we find a very different tone emerge, one which I myself cannot reconcile with my experience of such meditation and can only assume that something went wrong somewhere with Molinos, that either he was not able to master his will and became a prey to some negative force which was able to take control of his mind. We notice a corner being turned and suddenly, something appears to have gone wrong somewhere with Molinos' meditation because he starts to speak of pain and adverse physiological effects.

"With new efforts thoul't exercise thy self, but in another manner than hitherto, giving thy consent to receive the secret and divine operations, and to be polished, and purified by this Lord, which is the only means whereby thou will become clean and purged from thine ignorance and dissolutions. Know, however, that thou art to be plunged in a bitter sea of sorrows, and of internal and external pains, which torment will pierce into the most inward part of thy Soul and Body."

It is possible that Molinos was unduly influenced by the Alumbrado tradition of 'ecstatic' rites and believed that this was the way to experience the divine and he refers in his book to a certain "Illuminated Mother of Cantal" which is not traditional clerical terminology but more of the mystical and occult. Perhaps he was part of this tradition or at least sought out this experience, much to his cost I would say since whatever it was which possessed him and gave him 'pains' and 'torment' also seemed to influence his life and lead him to moral dissolution which was ultimately his undoing:

"Thou wilt think verily, that thou art possessed by an evil Spirit; because the signs of this interior exercise, and horrible tribulation, seem as bad as the invasions of infernal Furies and Devils. Then take care to believe thy Guide firmly, for thy true Happiness consists in thy obedience."

"The invisible enemies will pursue thee with scruples, lascivious suggestions, and unclean thoughts, with incentives to impatience, pride, rage, cursing and blaspheming the Name of God, his Sacraments, and holy Mysteries. Thou'lt find a great lukewarmness, loathing, and wearisomness for the things of God; and obscurity and darkness in thy understanding; a faintness, Confusion and narrowness of heart; such a coldness and feebleness of the will to resist, that a straw will appear to thee a beam. Thy desertion will be so great, that thou'lt think there is no more a God for thee, and that thou are rendered incapable of entertaining a good desire: so that thou'lt continue shut up betwixt two walls, in constant streights and anguish, without any hopes of ever getting out of so dreadful an oppression."

And the tenor of the book changes and now Molinos speaks of acquiring a spiritual guide, one who will apparently think on your behalf and in whose judgment, one should trust even above one's own:

"Thou shalt find thy self encompassed with troublesome scruples, griefs, anguish, distress, martyrdoms, distrusts, forsakings of the Creatures, and troubles so bitter, that thy afflictions shall seem past comfort, and thy torments unconquerable. O blessed Soul! how happy wilt thou be, if thou dost but believe thy Guide, and subject thy self to to him and obey him? Then wilt thou walk safe by the secret and interiour way of the dark night, altho thou may'st seem to thy self to live in Errour, and that thou art worse then ever; that thou seest nothing in thy Soul, but abomination and signs of condemnation."

And Molinos now, with a dim awareness of his true condition, namely that of being in the thrall of some kind of demonic control, yet this is still within his 'system' of Quietism and is a necessary part of some mystical process. I suspect something in his earlier Jesuit training and the endless contemplation of hell and his sins had evoked some spirit of the mind or of some other realm which perhaps has been fully loosened with the quietening of the controlling faculty of the mind and the will:

"Here thou wilt see thy self forlorn and subject to Passions of impatience, anger, rage, swearing, and disordered appetites, seeming to thy self the most miserable Creature, the greatest Sinner in the World, the most abhorred of God, deprived and stript of all Vertue, with a pain like that of Hell, seeing thy self afflicted and desolate, to think that thou hast altogether lost God; this will be thy cruel cutting and most bitter torment."

We also find a comment which may recall to experiences of Swedenborg and his being assaulted by the voices of demonic spirits:

"...because it would naturally be impossible, considering the force and violence wherewith sometimes they attack, to resist one quarter of an hour."

We find a similar account in the story of the Catholic Saint Teressa whom Molinos references and praises and calls 'the great Doctoress, and Mystical Mistress.' It also seems that she like Molinos was continually affected by 'troublesome thoughts':

"There is a necessity of suffering the trouble of a Troop of Thoughts, importune Imaginations, and the impetuosities of natural Notions, not only, of the Soul through the dryness and disunion it hath, but of the Body also, occasioned by the want of submission to the Spirit, which it ought to have."

She also wrote, or rather her confessor who recorded her words wrote:

"Devotion of Ecstasy, is where the consciousness of being in the body disappears. Sensory faculties cease to operate. Memory and imagination also become absorbed in God, as though intoxicated. Body and spirit dwell in the throes of exquisite pain, alternating between a fearful fiery glow, in complete unconscious helplessness, and periods of apparent strangulation."

It would be a good idea at this point to examine this Catholic saint, one of the few women to have been sanctified and furthermore declared a 'Doctor of the faith' by the Catholic church. Teresa Sanchez de Cepeda y Ahumada was born in Avila Spain in 1515. Her paternal grandfather was a Marrano, a Jew forced to convert to Christianity under pain of expulsion. In a fine example of the illusory nature of many of the Jews' conversions to Christianity, her grandfather apparently returned to the Jewish faith after 'conversion' and was investigated by the Inquisition but later managed to reintegrate himself into Christian life. Teresa's father was a wool merchant and one of the richest men in Avila and was knighted.

At 20 she entered the Carmelite Convent of the Incarnation which had been built on top of land which had been used as a Jewish burial ground. It was here that she started to experience 'spiritual ecstasy' combined with debilitating physical illness brought on by self-imposed physical mortification including excessive fasting which was to lead to continual ill-health throughout her life. Her fondness for self-flagellation was such that when she received Papal sanction for her principles; she created a new constitution for her convent which involved stricter rules and three lots of ceremonial flagellation every week.

During her illnesses she believed she had reached a 'perfect union with God' although many at the time suggested these experiences could be the result of diabolical rather than divine influence. She became convinced that Jesus Christ himself had physically presented himself to her although he was invisible to others and one vision in particular caused her further pain when an invisible seraph or angel repeatedly stabbed her in the heart with a golden lance:

"I saw in his hand a long spear of gold, and at the point there seemed to be a little fire. He appeared to me to be thrusting it at times into my heart, and to pierce my very entrails; when he drew it out, he seemed to draw them out also, and to leave me all on fire with a great love of God. The pain was so great, that it made me moan; and yet so surpassing was the sweetness of this excessive pain, that I could not wish to be rid of it ..."

Naturally this has nothing to do with God or anything divine and quite rightly the suspicions of some of her friends at the time seem well founded that there was a diabolical origin to these visions and torments. It was even reported that she experienced levitation and sometimes the other sisters at the convent had to physically hold her down.

Another female mystic later made 'Doctor of the Catholic church' was Saint Catherine of Siena. She was an early Christian mystic who emerged long before the Alumbrados and died a 100 years before the birth of proto-Alumbrado Maria de Santo Domingo. From her we can also find a development of the work of Pseudo-Dionysius and she may also have influenced the work of Molinos; in a letter to leader of the Dominican order, Raymond de Capua, who acted as her mentor and confessor, she wrote:

"Build a cell inside your mind, from which you can never flee."

However, this 'cell' that Catherine created was a theatre of nonsense and delusions where her mother was turned into the Virgin Mary, her father was Christ and her brothers became the apostles.

Like Saint Teresa she practised self-mortification and fasted to an extreme degree. Her confessor ordered her to eat properly but in the final year of her life she could no longer even eat or swallow water; whether this was psychosomatic and a kind of self-induced mania is unknown but is probably likely. Shortly before her death she suffered a stroke which paralysed her from the waist down and she died at the pitiably young age of 33 years old. Here we have to wonder why a woman could consider it useful to fast and abstain from food and even water to the point at which she eventually becomes crippled and incapable of even walking, then dies. There can be nothing inspired from God in any of this and I find the cases of these women, (some of whom have been canonised and are recognised as saints of the Catholic church) and those women who were persecuted and imprisoned as Alumbrados to be one and the same and to be inspired by a diabolical doctrine which is antagonistic to humanity and the message and ministry of Jesus Christ.

Catherine of Sienna was said to give away the clothing and food from her family without asking their permission and she pointedly refused to eat with her family claiming she preferred to eat in heaven with her 'real family'. In her own writings she also claimed that she was married to Jesus Christ as her mystic husband and that she had received a ring made of the 8 day old boy Christ's foreskin, which of course, was invisible to other people, like Saint Teresa whose physical Christ companion was also invisible to other people.

What we are dealing with here are, at best, psychotic delusions or at worst some kind of genuine contact between a human who has chosen to deprive himself of psychic protection in order to make contact with what he or she thinks is God, but something which perhaps does not have their best wishes at heart. Like those first seen at the beginning of this book with Barbara O'Brien but here we can trace them to a specific Alumbrado root which in turn has its root in the Jewish community and is likely an externalisation of the community practising the doctrines of the Kabbalah. It can be no coincidence that the Kabbalah in its final form also emerged from mediaeval Spain.

The result of this pathway seems to hint at a loss of personal volition but more pertinently, as Molinos records in a letter from "an illuminated Mother of Cantal wrote to a Sister, and great Servant of God" who is following some kind of Illuminati doctrine, provides some kind of demonic bridgehead which I would claim is the purpose of the Jesuit movement and these mystical movements arising from mediaeval Spain:

"To this purpose I remember, that a few days since, God communicated to me an Illumination, which made such an impression upon me, as if I had clearly seen him; and this it is, That I should never look upon my self, but walk with eyes shut, leaning on my Beloved, without striving to see nor know the way, by which he guides me, neither fix my thoughts on any thing, nor yet beg Favours of him, but as undone in my self, rest wholly and sincerely on him. Hitherto that Illuminated and Mystical Mistress, whose Words do Credit Authorize our Doctrine."

But what is that 'doctrine'? What has been specifically recorded about the Alumbrado's by history? The inquisition found the Alumbrados had some strange ideas which might conflict with what we today might imagine as a group of free-thinkers and pleasure seekers, but there seems to be something stranger and more complex at work. A strange kind of psychological journey which I hope this volume has at least partially tried to illuminate. It seems, at least from reports, that the sexual excesses of the Alumbrados and people like Miguel Molinos and the Kabbalists in general, could be, if Miguel is to be believed, a result of being wholly under the control of demonic impulsions. Naturally it might seem like a bit of an easy cop-out to say 'the devil told me to do it' as a way to evade responsibility, but the fact that we see the same trends occur again and again: the lack of conscious physical control of the body resulting in various kinds of hysteria and even attempts at levitation indicate that there is something more than a person's own will.

If one has a difficult time accepting the reality of discarnate spirits, one could say that subconscious psychological forces may have been unleashed as a result of the rigours of the various self-mortifications and repeated morbid Jesuit style visualisations of the horrors and terrors of hell, and that it is this which may lead to the wanton licentious excesses which the church authorities reported in connection with Alumbrado doctrines, doctrines which Molinos more or less explicitly alluded to being a follower of.

The book The Spanish Inquisition, 1478-1614: An Anthology of Sources, compiled and translated by Lu Ann Homza is an invaluable resource for first-hand recorded documentation about the Alumbrados. Naturally the information is that which was recorded by the church authorities and the Inquisition during the court processes against those Alumbrados suspected of heresy but there are many witness statements which are brought to bear and feature the words of the Alumbrados themselves.

All in all it paints a strange picture of those involved in the Alumbrados, with many apparent contradictions in the words of the defendants themselves and paints a tragic picture of people who, for whatever reason, whether an intention to subvert Spanish society and the church or from a genuine experiment in free-thinking, regardless the end result is the same: a picture of confused, disordered thinking, with some genuine wisdom which appears in sharp relief to the blurry mental background with a certain sense of emotional estrangement and likely mental impairment.

In 1525 the Inquisition published an edict on the numerated heresies of the Alumbrados which had been elicited from Alumbrado members themselves with the promise that "no punishment, public penance, or confiscation of goods would be imposed upon them". The most common response from the church authorities to each proposition or heresy was a familiar refrain: "This proposition is erroneous, false, heretical …." and sometimes with more apt descriptions, in the instance of proposition 46 "That the end of the world had to occur in twelve years." The church authorities were succinct: "This proposition is crazy."

And indeed, a lot of them are; it really is a poor reflection on your particular brand of mysticism if you manage to make the Catholic Church look sensible.

Some of the propositions are strange and hint at something almost anti-human; a list of directions one would follow in order not to take pleasure from life or possibly, propositions which had been arrived at as a result of a certain psychological transformation which may indicate some kind of schizoid illness. How else can one explain such items as proposition 31:

"That he held it as a mortal sin if he read some book to console his soul."

Or proposition 36: "That a man sinned mortally every time he loved a son, daughter, or other person, and did not love that person through God."

Or proposition 40: "Because a girl crossed the street, he said she had sinned, because in that action she had fulfilled her will."

Proposition number 1 is fairly unambiguous and quite a statement of intent: "There is no Hell, and if they say there is, it is to frighten us, just as they tell children, "Watch out for the bogeyman."

It is clear however that anyone believing such a thing in all its bald and unnuanced simplicity would feel no compulsion to moderate their behaviour and attempt to lead a good life nor any compunction about leading a bad one.

Such a statement really calls into question the whole of creation itself to some extent and that, if one is to believe there is a spiritual component to life and that another state of higher reality exists, then one is hardly likely to want to spend that in the company of the spirits of evil rogues looking to continue committing atrocities against their fellow spirits for all eternity. Clearly there must be some kind of spiritual filtering mechanism and a kind of like-with-like which is one of the most natural and readily comprehendible principles of reality, and such a mechanism would necessarily relegate those with irredeemably malicious or evil inclinations to be with their own kind where they can furnish and fashion their own mutually unpleasant spiritual reality.

Proposition 6 reported that one of the Alumbrados:

"…was sorry he had not sinned more; and knowing what God's mercy was, he wished he had sinned more in order to enjoy that mercy more. Because the greater the sinner, the more God loves him."

This Kabbalistic thinking should be very familiar to us by now after reading through this volume and indicated perhaps, the element of Kabbalistic Jewish 'Oral Tradition' working into Spanish society through the current of those who had only superficially converted to Christianity.

The picture which emerges of the Alumbrados is that they believed themselves infallible, since according to them: "God could not make a person more perfect or more humble than he already was," and also unrepentant of any wrong doings since "They call those people who lament their sins 'penance-addicts,' 'proprietors of themselves,' and 'weepers.'

They also believed that sex was a kind of holy sacrament: "married people were more united to God while making love than if they had been praying." And temptation should be welcomed:

"They did not have to renounce temptations and evil thoughts, but rather should embrace them and take them as a burden, and walk onward with this cross."

This particular Alumbrado trap is the snare which caught Miguel Molinos and cemented his reputation as a heretic and caused him to be sentenced to prison where he died. It is likely that without the stain of personal immorality which cast the whole of his life's work into disrepute, his Spiritual Exercises and the benefits of the kind of transcendental meditation could well have become part of the liturgy of the Catholic Church and have developed into a useful way to contact the divine principle for, in the words of Jesus: "…nor will they say, 'See here!' or 'See there!' For indeed, the kingdom of God is within you."

But pure nonsense cannot survive without the oxygen of truth and like all attempts at subversion or deceptive stratagems, it is necessary to accompany the lies with a bodyguard of truth and so this is why within the doctrines of the Alumbrados we find some very reasonable and evident truths such as Maria de Cazalla saying of the Catholic Church:

"I believe that the Child Jesus is lost in the sophisms and arguments that you pronounce."

Or of her "considering papal bulls, indulgences, and pardons to be a joke, and believing they benefited no one and achieved nothing, said, 'Look, I've bought Christianity and am carrying it around, for one is not a Christian unless you have these bulls; I'd rather throw the money into something else.'"

She was quite right of course, but even now we as a modern reader with a delicate taste for nuance might detect that the mockery goes a little too far and we can perhaps detect a veiled disdain not only for the Church but for Christianity itself. But there is something more, some of Maria de Cazalla's statements betray something more than scepticism or irreverence:

"María de Cazalla and others believed that there was no Mary Magdalene, nor a St. Anne who married three times, nor were there three Marys; they thought the whole thing was a joke. When she was told that the Church held such matters as true, she replied that it was a joke, and some stupid people had so ordered it...."

They seem to indicate a claim to some other information or knowledge since it is unlikely that most church goers of the time would question such things, but what if someone were part of a tradition which had its own information about such things, quite outside of the Catholic Church. Again, the connection to the Jewish community with its own extensive written historical records and oral traditions would fit this bill perfectly.

But if the accounts of Maria de Cazalla can't help but reveal a parallel knowledge-stream they also show again a certain inhumanity, one would also say, sociopathic or even borderline psychotic aspect of the Alumbrado tradition. What are we to make of such statements, which even the dreaded Inquisition rightly described as 'horrific':

"She heard from Bishop Cazalla that María de Cazalla said she conceived her children without carnal pleasure and did not love them as if they were her own, but rather as if they were her neighbors'.

And another similar reported statement from Maria de Cazalla:

"She reprehended a certain lady who deeply loved her own children, calling that lady a butcher of the flesh who had a piece of her heart in each child."

And after giving birth, instead of feelings of joy or such as might be normal this report similarly evokes a singular anti-human perspective:

"Likewise, when asked why people didn't come to see her after she had given birth, María de Cazalla said, 'May God remove that disgrace from me,' as if she considered childbirth disgraceful."

From this we can create a psychological profile strongly suggestive of Maria de Cazalla being in the population percentile suffering from a degree of psychopathy since an inability to feel emotions and even being repelled by them is a strong marker of such a disorder, also it was reported that "she felt no carnal pleasure in sex," a dissociative condition known as sexual anhedonia and if we factor in this dissociative element we might not be far from the mark if we consider that Maria de Cazalla may have been a schizophrenic.

It is possible however that she was not always like this, reports indicate that Cazalla was somehow 'changed' by conversing with other Alumbrados:

"Asked how she knew that María de Cazalla held the opinions of the Alumbrados, she said she knew because she saw María de Cazalla converse in secret with Isabel de la Cruz and Pedro Ruiz de Alcaraz. She saw them confer night and day, and saw her altered in all her habits and spiritual exercises, so much so that the needleworkers of Orche said María de Cazalla was crazy."

The 9th of Av 3830. A day of desolation. The cooling bodies, of those who were not already long dead of starvation, filling every street, sometimes piled as many as four or five high, were so numerous that the dying did not even have their own place to fall and tumbled into a grave made up of other people. For three days, without rest or seemingly any pause, the Romans had murdered. Peace would come only for lack of more victims. There were sobs of the fallen and those whimpering and forlorn whom the Romans could not even be bothered to kill; these sounds were accompanied by the gasps of pain of the dying and their final passing gave rise to a brief note of peace.

As the days passed the initial frenzy of the Roman's fury had passed until the massacres started to have all the gusto of a bored scribe or clerk. Their arms wearied from chopping down defenceless pilgrims: old men, the women and children, as by the end of the day, the scribe tires of holding his reed pen. Lazily but with implacable determination and resignation to a now tedious task the murders continued. All around was the sound of sudden screams which reached his ears and now the Romans hacked with a lack of discrimination so as to almost appear disinterested in their work.

None had been spared, the killing continued long after all had been assumed already killed. Those who had come to Jerusalem in celebration only months before had been only celebrating an early and bloody death.

The amount of blood issuing from the holy Temple was not to be believed, heaps of bodies seemed strewn like empty wine-skins while their blood carpeted the white marbles stones all the way down to the bottom of the sanctuary steps. The number of bodies grew the deeper into the Temple and the most bodies were found carelessly clustered around the altar and piety had neither protected them nor prevented the Legionary's arm.

The peak of chaos, lawless anarchy, disobedience and blasphemy and been reached and had manifested as Roman swords. With the mass death and the destruction of the city, the series of ritualised obscenities and dark satires which had been performed in the city in the name of its defence and that of the Jewish people, had come to a close and the curtain had come down on this fateful and awful chapter.

These are the stories they told but now none are alive who remember the day we lost our temple and lost our city: Great and Holy Jerusalem. How anyone lived to tell this tale cannot be known except perhaps the Romans didn't quite find everyone's hiding place, yet for those that hid and survived: to live to see such sights it might have been better to die.

There had been a million people crammed into the city, the children of Israel had come from every nation from among the cursed impious empire of the gentiles to their home in the world. All had come to the Great and Holy city of Jerusalem five months earlier to celebrate the Passover; by the 10th of Nissan there were a million Jews in the city. Some upon arriving had told of their presentiments, of fevered dreams and hearing voices in the darkness telling them not to come to Jerusalem for Jerusalem would be their tomb.

But they had come all the same telling themselves it was the voice of the accuser, the one who runs to and fro throughout the earth trying to catch those who will not obey Hashem. For as Isaiah, may his memory be a shield to us, said "Fear not, for I am with you; be not dismayed, for I am your God; I will strengthen you, I will help you, I will uphold you with my righteous right hand." Besides we had our great leader, appointed it seemed by God from the priestly line of Levites, the people of the first-tithe, the same line which gave our people Moses, Aaron Ezra and Malachi: Yohana ben Levi.

He who with the devil's own deceit had tricked the Romans at the gate of Gash Halav and asked Titus not to displease the Gods by despoiling the Sabbath. Titus agreed to defer their entering the city to the next day by which time the wily Yohana had escaped, a ruse worthy of Jacob himself. He returned to Jerusalem and gave us courage and hope that the Romans could be defeated and reminded us of the strength of our numerous great walls which the Romans would dash themselves against while we harassed them with a thousand furious projectiles and poured fire upon them. Even with wings, he said, they would never be able to fly over the walls of Jerusalem, seeing how hard pressed they had been in taking the little towns in Galilee, how much mightier was Jerusalem? He reminded us how we had defeated the great Thunderbolt legion not once but twice and taken their sacred standard as easily as taking a blind man's purse. The poor simple people ate up his poison like mana.

So they would not let their fears deter them and besides we were still celebrating our great victory four years earlier which had liberated Jerusalem from the control of the Gentiles when we destroyed the Twelfth Legion and captured their golden eagle. They are so foolish and credulous as children that such things mean a great deal to them and they were said to have spent thirty years trying to find the three gold eagles they had lost to the heathen of Germania who cooked the Romans they captured in pots and ate their flesh and did strange heathen magic with their bones.

But even so, on the road, the black smoke on the distant horizon and rumours of three or even four Roman legions again on the march. Still they were not to be deterred and it was not forgotten how Yahana had lied about the leader of the Jerusalem government, Hanan the High Priest and betrayed his trust. Yahana had wanted to negotiate with the Zealots and had sent John to be his ambassador but Yahana told the Zealots that Hanan meant to execute them and also claimed he had sent ambassadors to the Romans for help in taking the city back from the Zealots. The Zealots felt imperilled due to Yahana's trickery and in desperation sent messengers to the Edomites who arrived 20,000 strong demanding to be let into the city.

Hanan refused, distrusting their motives and not wanting to radically destabilise the stalemate they had reached, for he and his party and the common folk of Jerusalem wanted peace with Rome and wanted no part of this war. So at night Eleazar son of Simon, the leader of the Zealots had the Edomites surreptitiously let into the city where they, with mock outrage at being kept out and with calls for 'liberty' and accusing the rulers of being traitors, massacred the high-priest Hanan and the whole moderate government of Jerusalem and anyone else who was identified as being a 'moderate'. Thousands were dead when they had finished. Only afterwards did the Edomites learn how they had been tricked, and they left the city in repentance at the bloodshed they had been lured into performing.

It was clear now what kind of man Yahana was and though he had many supporters and 6,000 armed men at his command the populace knew that he would lead Jerusalem to its own destruction so they called on the bandit and brutal leader of a great force Shimon the Strong to depose him. Shimon arrived in Jerusalem with a mighty army of 15,000 men and was heralded by the people as a saviour of the city and of being the long-awaited Messiah, even though he was an Edomite and not even of Israel. During his rule Shimon had coins minted bearing his name and the messianic legend: Redemption of Zion.

Almost immediately he started executing people in the name of safeguarding public safety including the High Priest Matthias son of Boethus whom he murdered only after murdering his own three sons before his own eyes. Thousands more perished under Shimon's messianic rule.

Now Jerusalem had become fully ruled by bandits who daily committed murders against those they suspected of being in league with the Romans or of being in league with any of the other two factions which opposed them. Their leaders, among them the Messiah of Israel: Shimon the Strong, were the very worst of humanity; men who tortured, raped and did not spare women and children in their murderous excesses. In fact, the Messiah of Israel himself had led a force of raiding bandits that had murdered more than 700 women and children in the nearby town of En Gedd prior to their triumphant arrival in Jerusalem.

The common-people were nervous but they had to believe that God would protect them, for it was the Passover and they were his chosen people. If it wasn't the fear of

God that guarded them it was the fear of their Messiah. Then the clouds had come. A day time darkness had covered us from the sight of God and a terrible stillness came upon the air where even words spoken to our loved ones seemed to hang in the air and whither. It was a heavy spirit which had come, some avenging angel had come to punish God's children for their waywardness: perhaps for the murder of the high-priest and perhaps for the presence of the faithless band of assassins who now occupied the holy precincts of the Temple.

The Romans arrived and with Jerusalem filled with the million pilgrims, we were sealed in while the fury of the savage Gentile beast harangued our great walls. But how could they conquer? We had so many walls. Walls within walls. Our fortifications were built by the Romans themselves and the great Herod had brought in the Empire's finest craftsmen to make the city impregnable and we knew the secret ways out of the city and through the walls into the country beyond and could sneak out at night to get the hidden food supplies to feed to great city's many hungry mouths.

After two weeks they had breached the third wall near Jaffa's gate, then they took the second wall. Then Titus' legions themselves started building a wall and we wondered at it: some jested that the Romans were on our side and were helping us to defend the great city out of sheer admiration for its beauty. Jerusalem had won their hearts they said. Then with a sickness they realised the wall was a wall for us: to keep us trapped. We saw that we wouldn't be able to leave to go into the country for food.

Then fear came amongst the people as quick and unassailable as water; it ran through every street like a stream and trickled into every hovel and found its way seeping into the hearts of every man woman and child in the city. Almost immediately food became short. It was said that the Zealots in the Temple were destroying the grain supplies for the city in order to induce the people to fight all the harder.

People began to go hungry and with hunger they started to speak of surrendering to the Romans. God answered the fears and prayers of the Jewish people as the Romans sent the worthy Josephus to negotiate with Jerusalem. The people clamoured to reach Shimon the Strong, now ruling most of the city as King of Jerusalem, and begged him to surrender but he was outraged at the suggestion and threated to kill anyone who dared to speak of it and Shimon's men fired arrows at Josephus and wounded one of the Roman negotiators driving them and the last chance of peace away.

Then the hunger became intense when what little food the city had had, was exhausted. The three warring factions had been more intent on fighting each other than fighting the Romans and had also been destroying each group's food supply as a means of forcing them to come to terms. With no-one being able to enter the city for months starvation began in earnest with people reduced to eating shoe leather and whatever grasses and weeds could still be found. One in particular, to the everlasting shame of the children of Israel, Mary daughter of Eleazar had bought themselves survival at the abhorrent price of eating her own child.

Yahana had had some success in undermining the Roman's fortifications and siege engines by building tunnels beneath then setting fire to the tunnels so that they engines collapsed into the pit but by doing so he had also undermined the walls of the Antoine tower, the Romans had removed only four choice stones from the tower and at night, it fell. It was at this point the finally the three fighting factions united their efforts to repel the Romans but too late.

Nobody quite knows how the fire in the Temple precincts started. The Romans for their part had had no inclination of destroying the Temple, so it is said at least, since it was largely a Roman building and could be repurposed to any God they chose. Some blame the Zealots and a stray firebrand intended for the Romans accidently ignited a fire in the Temple. The Romans then seeing a fire had started thought to add to it and thereupon started to encourage the Temple's destruction as a means of demoralising the inhabitants and achieving a quicker victory also Titus may have known that the next day was Tisha B'Av: when the great Temple of Solomon was destroyed by the Babylonians and he wanted to ensure that this dread day would also see the fall of the second Temple and the fall of Jerusalem itself in blood and fire.

Those that were not killed immediately, possibly more though Roman boredom than benevolence, were in the stark minority. Any survivors who were found to be old or armed men were immediately killed. Any able-bodied men that were found were enslaved and became gladiators or were made to work on the extensive Roman building projects under terrible conditions back in Rome. Children were spared only to be sold as slaves.

The Romans now busied themselves in completely razing Jerusalem to the ground to make a corpse of the city as they had done to her people. Even the foundations and caves were brought up, perhaps reproachful that they had served to hide the Jews from their rage. What Jews remained now throughout the country and abroad were forbidden to ever return to what remained of the city under pain of death.

And the line of Jacob slept in the bosom of the earth. A crushed defeated people now without a Temple and no mother city and forced to pay Fiscus Judaicus or Jew tax in an effort to encourage the people to abandon their religion since it only applied to those who practised the religion of Judaism but not to ethnic Jews.

But the promise of Jacob lived on. Prior to the fall of the city Rabbi Yohanan ben Zakki, may the memory of his righteousness and holiness be a blessing for the life of the world to come, the first tana to be called Rabbi in the Mishnah, had arranged his escape from the city inside a coffin. He spoke with the then military commander Vespasian and Yohanan correctly predicted that Vespasian would soon become Emperor and that the Temple would shortly be destroyed. For this he was rewarded with his wish to create a Jewish Rabbinical academy at Yavneh. The school became a focal point for the reestablishment of the Sanhedrin after the destruction of Jerusalem and the absence of the Temple and the atonement sacrifices; from the council grew the future of Jewish identity: Rabbinical Judaism.

The years passed and Jerusalem was now home only to the tenth legion and Christians. But from their base in Yavneh the great council of the Sanhedrin planned. The years passed before the Jewish people found their strength again but when that time came, the world would tremble. Within two generations of the loss of a million Jews and the destruction of Jerusalem the Jewish Rabbinical Academy at Yavneh had managed to create a covert network of agents spreading all throughout the Roman Empire unknown and unsuspected by any except the Jews themselves who were now totally sworn to protect and fight for their people at any cost and they waited for their moment to strike.

In 3875 the Roman armies moved East to fight the Persians leaving only small garrisons behind them. This was the moment.

The Jews rose up as one man and slaughtered the Roman garrisons and massacred the inhabitants of cities of Libya, Cyprus, Egypt, Anatolia and as far East as Seleucia and Arbela in Babylon. By the end of the rebellion the lives of half a million Roman citizens had been taken in revenge for the crimes of the Romans. We burned their temples as they had burned ours and we pulled down their idolatrous statues of the demon Gods housed in their shrines. Their bath-houses, nests of un-righteousness we burned and slaughtered those we found fat, naked and debauched within.

They pursued some of the men to the city of Lod and besieged the city and foully executed those heroes of the line of Jacob wishing to bring justice to the Roman people. But our part remained undetected and we rejoiced over our victory and the terror we had riven into the heart of the Roman world at the invincible unconquerable Jew and we planned our next move.

And it was not long in coming. In the year 3890 Emperor Hadrian visited Judea and ordered the construction of a new Roman City for Roman citizens and Christians on the grave of Jerusalem and gave this new city a heathen name: Aelia Capitolina and it was to have a new temple dedicated to the heathen Ba'al Tzedek and Jews were only to be allowed to enter to commemorate the loss of their two temples on Tish B'Av. Hadrian's intention was to remind the Jews of the triumph of the Romans by giving them only a glimpse each year of what was once their great city.

In a series of deliberately targeted insults at the Jewish people Hadrian trod on a bees' nest he didn't even know had been growing under his feet for so long. He came to our land proudly with his sodomy slave: Antinous. He also ploughed up the foundations of our temple recalling with pain to us the words of the prophet Micah:

"Therefore, because of you, Zion will be plowed up like a field, and Jerusalem will become heaps of rubble, and the Temple Mount like a forest high place."

Two years later 3892 Emperor Hadrian made a law forbidding circumcision in the whole empire under pain of death and the bees nest became busy but none but those who knew it was there could see the furious activity underground, in the very caves and holes in the earth we met and we planned.

As time grew on the new city took shape and the insults continued, with pagan shrines and sanctuaries right on top of the ruins of our old holy places. A statue of the sodomite Emperor was put in the place of the Holy of Holies and a monstrous statue of a pig was erected before the northern gate. This was said to be a symbol of the Tenth Legion who were stationed here to keep the children of Israel out but the insult was intentional and not in the least incidental. But it was perfect. It gave us the excuse which we had been waiting for to put all our work into practice. And soon they would encounter our Messiah and his hand would be on the neck of our enemies.

The council of Pharisees of the Sanhedrin had been very busy and had found the star of Jacob at long last, or at least, they had made him. Long incubated in the Holy Law at Yavneh and trained in the ruthless guerrilla tactics what used to be called the Sicarii assassins, now rehabilitated from their old ways of banditry to be the key leaders of Jewish terror and political violence throughout the Roman world. This man was at once Messiah, redeemer, leader and trained killer; expert at all forms of torture with a particular personal preference for cutting off the hands and then cauterising the wound with fire to cause maximum pain and absolute delirium in his victims. Their screams and shrieks of agony always brought the hint of a smile to the edges of his lips.

The messiah was ready, it only needed the right provocation to unleash the full force of the hidden snap of the Jewish people, coiled like sleeping serpents for so long. The greater the forbearance the greater the rage once patience is exhausted, and the Rabbis at Yavneh knew that soon, the surprise was coming, and they smiled when they passed the Romans and saluted them in the Roman tongue, for they knew that a sword hung over their very necks which was about to fall and they could afford to be gracious to the dead.

And then one day the Romans, quite by accident despite their previous deliberate provocations, gifted us with the ultimate outrage. While they were making a foundation by the western wall they broke through to the subterranean tomb of Solomon and caused its collapse. It was as if Solomon himself had been struck by the Romans, their profanity and supreme arrogance not content with destroying the Jews but now reaching back in time to affront the kings and prophets themselves. Every Jew felt this and as one body we flushed red with pain and surprise yet in this act, provoking a king of peace, the fury of King David was roused and with just one word from Yavneh the thousands of waiting guerrillas holed up in their caves and subterranean hiding places, pounced upon the Romans the whole breadth of Judea. As one man, ambushes everywhere, the Romans literally at times killed in their garrison barracks half asleep and then when the cry of consternation and alarm was raised in the towns and cities the red hand of Israel slank back into their holes, like bears with a fresh carcass, to enjoy their kill.

Our greatest Tana, Rabbi Akiva, may his memory be a blessing and may Hashem avenge his blood, as president of the rabbinical academy of Yavneh, declared that the leader of the rebellion: Shimon Ben Kosevah was the Messiah and named him Shimon Ben Kochba, Shimon of the star and said that he had come down to Earth from heaven:

"..there shall come a Star out of Jacob, and a Sceptre shall rise out of Israel..." Not everyone agreed with Rabbi Akiva that Shimon was the Messiah of the children of Israel. It was said that the man was of Edomite ancestry and certainly not of the royal Davidic bloodline.

Nevertheless, the Romans reeled, with hundreds brutally murdered in the first day of the rebellion, and then, as they were nursing their wounds and mustering their forces the guerrillas struck again, this time choosing different garrisons and waylaying small detachments of Legionaries with surprise and ambush tactics. And it didn't stop until Jerusalem was cut off from reinforcements and the Messiah took the city slaughtering the 10th Legion like the pigs they were so proud of and throwing their unclean bodies into the burning valley of the wicked; those that did not fall that day fled and the city was reconquered by her children led by their Messiah.

Shimon had coins minted declaring himself 'Prince of Jerusalem' which celebrated year 1 of the liberation of the holy city along with a star representing Shimon as the Messiah and the Ark of Covenant found and placed back in the Temple.

Shimon had appealed to the Christians to join in the uprising, since the Christians had grown into quite a force all throughout the empire but particularly in Judea which they considered the home of their faith. But they could not be prevailed upon to fight for they said they were peaceful and that their Rabbi had told them that they must love their enemies and not resist evil but turn the other cheek. Shimon mocked them greatly for this but when he saw that they remained firm he grew angry. He found that not one of those called Christians would help them against the Romans therefore he went out and started to round them up from the villages he controlled and ordered them to renounce the False Messiah and blasphemer unless they wished to share his fate. They protested that they were Jews as well and were followers of the law of Moses and the Patriarchs and the prophets but he now had the rage inside him and bid them deny the false messiah who died on a tree because the time of the real messiah was upon them and all should unite under his banner. He would be the 'ruler of Israel' foretold by Isaiah, the False Messiah ruled over nothing. One Christian argued with Shimon and said that he ruled over Israel and would do so for eternity, since he was the redeemer and shepherd of the children of Israel, and that his throne is a heavenly, not an Earthly one.

Shimon laughed and ordered him to be put to death for blasphemy. He signalled two men to come and take him away. The Christian saw that he was dealing with an implacable man and resigned himself to his fate:

"The Lord Jesus will speak for me in heaven. Who will speak for you?"

At that, Shimon considered for a minute and shouted after the men leading away the Christian.

"Hold there men! I've changed my mind about this Christian," he looked long and hard at the Christian. Then spoke, "Torture him first, then kill him."

They took the man away who shouted out: "They are 'wise'—in doing evil! But how to do good they know not." And at that moment a cloud passed in front of the sun and also a cloud seemed to settle on the hearts of some of the men there as they thought about the words of Jeremiah and how Jerusalem now was in ruin without inhabitant as the prophet had foretold and the destroyer of nations, Rome, who will soon set out from his nation again and will meet Israel in war, and it was hard not to have a moment's doubt.

Almost as if to dispel the cloud Shimon shouted to those around him in bravado:

"And that goes for all those who follow the False Prophet and will not help Israel in her time of need. All those of the so-called party of Christians who will not fight will be tortured and killed. Let us see if that is enough to dissuade them from following their dead magician."

But strange to say it did not dissuade them. The piety and faith of the Christians was a strange almost unnatural thing to us in those times and we wondered sometimes whether they were either madmen and perhaps should be dealt with as such, with sympathy and medical treatment, but when we encountered them in the markets of Judea and Galilee there was no madness in them that could be discerned, but a strange and disconcerting serenity which was almost contagious and we had to draw back from them and harden our hearts for fear they would make us in league with their idolatry.

But they were now in terror and that Shimon had brought the same contempt for them as for the Romans and they fled for any cliff cave or subterranean hiding place which was not already occupied by Jewish guerrillas.

Our greatest Tana Rabbi Akiva was taken by the Romans for publicly teaching the holy Torah and never seen again until a couple of years later when the Romans presented his body for burial boasting of their cruelty saying that they were surprised how dedicated he had been to his silly Jewish religion for the sake of all the tortures he had borne including having the skin from his body torn with hot iron combs.

The Romans also murdered eight members of the Great Sanhedrin, the holiest Jewish council, torturing these great and holy men with unspeakable tortures which only a mind forged in hell would think to inflict on another human being. Rabbi Ishmael had the skin of hid head slowly removed from his head and Rabbi Hanania was burned at the stake, a Torah scroll was wrapped around him and stuffed with wet-wool so that his agonies endured for the whole day and into the night and all heard or heard the tale of his screams.

Shimon bar Yochai, the most fervent and devoted disciple of his teacher, while initially supportive of the rebellion against the Romans, with the death of his mentor now spoke ominously and although he didn't raise his voice or sow discord, since he saw this thing must now run its course for good or ill, he wondered if the Romans should finally crush the revolt what would be left of the children of Israel and how they would ever be able to rebuild themselves. He would disappear for long periods of time when he was said to dwell in caves and some even said in desperation to help improve the fortunes of Israel, he resorted to performing strange rites and imploring spirits which appeared to have strange and unholy names.

Hope however, still reigned abundant and at the report of the first Roman casualties the children of Israel in the distant lands had hearkened to the call which had gone out even before the rebellion had started, and now they surged back homeward, hopeful of finally retaking the land their great grandfathers had been exiled from and now they the children of those exiles were coming back in triumph to avenge them. The number of Jews in the countryside surged and the number of armed roving bands swelled in force and the sound of unusual and exotic dialects was heard all throughout the land as the great spreading tree of the cosmopolitan sons of Jacob now returned to be one people again.

But the ferocity of the children of Israel and the number of Roman cohorts including an entire detachment of the 9th Legion, which we massacred did not dissuade the Romans and even the total destruction of the twelfth legion by the triumphant children of Jacob.

No matter how many Romans were killed more came to replace them. From the start of the rebellion when there were two full Roman legions stationed in Judea until there were seven full legions by the end of the rebellion; a huge force of a hundred and twenty thousand Romans the like of which we had never seen. Some of these legionaries it was noted seemed to be more boys than men and the report went round that the Romans were running out of fighting age men because the Jews had killed the best part of them. This cheered us no end but all the same these Roman boy soldiers were just as well armed and well trained and they now seemed to have discovered a great many of our hiding places and our great networks of tunnels which communicated sometimes even between neighbouring villages and ensured our rebels were always well provisioned and ready to emerge from the very ground under the feet of the Romans to strike them dead. We had extensive tunnel networks ranging through the Judean hills and even into the northern Negev desert. There were also tunnels in Galilee and Samaria and even near Moab. Hundreds and hundreds of tunnels with our warriors waiting for the time to strike their ambush.

But then the Romans simply and brutally started destroying the villages, stone by stone until they were completely razed and the caves, grottos and cellars laid bare to their eyes and rendered useless to us. This is how they slowly started to beat us. And we felt the tide was turning against us at last.

Now Shimon bar Kosiba was not called Kokhba: the son of the star but they called him the Kozeba: the son of disappointment.

In all the Romans destroyed nearly a thousand of our villages and left homeless, the people, the women and children had no-where to go and were easily taken by the Romans to be sold into slavery. Many Jews, even those who had lately returned to Judea hopeful of reconquering their land were forced to flee back from where they had come, and they were lucky if they made it that far because the Romans were now indiscriminately killing or taking prisoner any Jews they found under the assumption that all Jews were in arms against the Romans, which was largely true, but how can women and children be considered 'enemy combatants'?

Marching on the camp of the 6th Legion at Tel Shalem to challenge the Romans with a giant show of force, Shimon had assembled some twenty thousand men to chase the Romans even from their main harrying point far outside of Judea's borders. After many successes and now fully believing that he was indeed the long-awaited Messiah and God had already decided to hand over the Romans to them and that God would direct the order of battle and give the victory. When the time came for the two armies to meet however God did not share his strategy with Shimon who despite his confidence, was not a match for the ruthless and well-trained Roman legion and its cohorts who behaved as if they were ten armies and all harassed Shimon and his force from all sides until he was forced to flee, fragmenting and disappearing into the shadows and contours of the surrounding countryside albeit with very heavy losses.

The Romans pursued and Shimon fled to the walled fortress refuge of Betar high in the Judean hills along with his men and civilians who had no-where else to go. This was to be the last stand. The siege began in the summer of 3895 but it was clear that we had finally only walled ourself into the refuge of a grave and as the fatal date, Tisha b'Av came nearer our hearts grew cold and we knew that doom would befall us yet again.

Bar Kokhba had become increasingly suspicious of anyone, even those closest to him and suspecting that his uncle Rabbi Elazar Hamuda'i was collaborating with the Romans, he murdered the holy man in cold blood. It was felt then that a curse had come over Shimon and all those who now stood with him, that the man was not the Messiah we had waited for all this time, but was simply a madman. There are many strange stories in circulation even now about Bar Kokhba, that he was so strong he could catch the Roman catapult stone and throw them back and stories about how the gentiles who took the land afterwards had no need to fertilise their vines because there was enough Jewish blood spilt to nourish them for seven years. All childish nonsense, but these are the stories we are told as children to keep our history alive, until we grow up and we discover what the truth was, and how it was hardly any less fantastic.

Besieged by two entire legions, the Romans took the city and massacred everyone, including all the children they found there, whom they rounded up, then in the space of an hour's unnatural horror, the Romans devoted themselves to lifting up the children and killing them by smashing out their brains on the stone pavements, it was not known why they killed them in this way, doubtfully they considered it a more humane method but possibly a more entertaining one.

The Romans took a twisted pleasure in finding new atrocities even as the war came to an end. A group of children who attended the Torah schools were told to assault the Romans with their writing styluses but the Romans, in order to mock their studious approach made a great procession of these children before wrapping them in the school's Torah scrolls until they resembled some strange kind of pagan idol or effigy, then they burned them alive.

As the dead lay in the ravaged, burned and butchered state the Romans had left them and no-one was permitted to return to bury the dead for 15 years after the fall of the fortress and it became a place of wild animals taking the flesh and gnawing the bones of our martyrs and some say the restless spirits of the dead haunted it and tried in vain to drive off the packs of mountain wolves from further desecrating their own corpses since the body must remain complete in order to be able to stand before the final judgement of God.

There were continued lamentations about the fate of the martyrs of Betar and much secret discussion on whether God would have pity on the wretched horde who would appear at the celestial throne missing limbs and with empty eye sockets where a crow had ungraciously picked them out. Those Jews that survived were hardly in a better state than the dead and were by the tens of thousands sold by the Romans in great sprawling slave markets, the average price being roughly the same as the price of a pack-horse, there being so many Jewish slaves on the market and the value being driven so low by abundance.

One day we will be the slave-masters, though the cleverness will be that those we intend to enslave will not even know that they are slaves, therefore they will not even be able to think of revolting for they will not even know that they are not free. Also, the nature of their slavery will be so disguised from them that they will act as our slaves thinking that everything they do is from their own free-will. That is the distinction of the superior Jewish mind over the coarse and profane Goyim one.

Now it wasn't enough for the Romans to destroy Jerusalem, now they had to destroy Judea and the Jews altogether. No Jews now were allowed to live in Judea and any found were either killed or enslaved. The Romans blasphemed the land with the name of its cursed former inhabitants and our great enemies: Palaestina and Jerusalem was rebuilt with a pagan name: Aelia Capitolina and started settling Roman citizens there.

Some said that Shimon had brought down this punishment on Israel and that we should have sought peace with the Gentiles, but I do not believe that. I believe what Shimon bar Yochai said when he said that at least we fought, but that now we must find a new way to fight. We cannot fight enemies like the Romans with their own crude methods.

The survivors fled from the death of Jerusalem and gathered to the divine presence through the lands scorched and ruined by the Romans to resemble an early hell for the people. Some even wondered whether it was the end of the Jewish people altogether and they would disappear from history at this point. At Yavneh the remnant gathered. Destitute, starving.

Shimon bar Yochai saw now as did all the survivors that it was impossible to ever beat the Westerners in open war in this generation or any of the coming generations. There would have to be another way but it would be a long-term project. They had nearly killed his people, burned his people's cities, towns and even eradicated the smallest village, stone by stone and it was clear the Romans intended to wipe them out forever, just as all the proud people had tried to do but as long as a remnant could be found, they would work his plan. A plan which would probably bear no fruit even in his lifetime or that of his children, but one day the Westerners would be brought low and his people would reign supreme on the ashes of their civilisation. It would be their cities which would burn, their towns raised, their holy shrines would be toppled. Their great temples would be made into latrines and places to keep livestock.

We would murder and torture their so-called holy men and make martyrs of their priests. We would devise tortures for these such to equal or even exceed the cruelty of the Romans to our own Rabbis. But we will not be the ones to bloody our hands in such filthy arts, by some agency we one day will be able to appoint the men of their own kind to do our bidding. We are working on the details even now but we will nurture and develop our system from one generation to the next and slowly and craftily release it into the Gentile world, always testing new methods but we shall use two main methods of control. We shall use the promise of gain to buy the loyalty of the Gentile against his own kind, then when we possess him; we shall use terror and fear to make him our slave until the only thing he fears shall be our invisible network which we already have partially constructed throughout the whole civilised world, a network which is even more extensive than the Roman Empire and which operates in regions and lands even the Romans know nothing about and would not dare to set foot.

They would not hack the bodies, nor rape the women and burn the holy places as the Romans had done to them. These were not fit tasks for God's chosen people. They would find others to do these things for them. They would devise a system, so serpentine and difficult to unfold and each step in the system removing one from his brother by more secrets and passwords which could not be communicated on pain of death that the group itself under its own power would be powerless, only those who knew the keys to this group and controlled its highest levels would be the masters.

They would recruit from the Westerners themselves to be the agents of their own downfall. It all became very clear in Shimon bar Yochai's mind, even in the midst of their utmost destruction and greatest loss, he knew that destiny had singled him out to conceive this plan which would stretch far far into the future, far beyond even the Roman's sight, perhaps even long after the Romans were gone, and would leave his people conquerors of the whole world. Their revenge would be terrible, more terrible if it were possible than the memory of the butchered men and women blood-staining the streets of the holiest city on Earth.

He shuddered at the thought of their total subjugation which though remote in time, was already an absolute certainty for him because he knew God would not stand this affront. As he reasoned he concluded that this had all transpired for this very reason, in order to make them the eventual masters over the Earth. The total loss of Judea and their final expulsion was a sacrifice in what had been one of many. History now made sense. The tragedy of the captivity, the loss of the two great Temples, the loss of Jerusalem and now Judea, but somehow his people would persist. They could never be destroyed, each time they were strengthened as if forged in the hottest fire to make them finally masters of all by the strength and sharpness of their metal. Each disaster had been a sacrifice and one day all of this pain would be soothed when they stood triumphant at the head of their own Empire and the Gentiles and Christians themselves were their slaves to do with what they chose.

The world they would create for them would be a hell on Earth.

But their religion would have to change. They would have to reintegrate some of the ancient half-forgotten forces of their forefathers, those they called demon worshippers and impious. Their rites practiced only by those called insane and shunned by righteous Jews. They would need their help.